COGNITIVE AND AFFECTIVE LEARNING STRATEGIES

THE EDUCATIONAL TECHNOLOGY SERIES

Edited by

Harold F. O'Neil, Jr.

U.S. Army Research Institute for
the Behavioral and Social Sciences
Alexandria, Virginia

Harold F. O'Neil, Jr. (Ed.) Learning Strategies

Harold F. O'Neil, Jr. (Ed.) Issues in Instructional Systems Development

Harold F. O'Neil, Jr. (Ed.) Procedures for Instructional Systems
Development

Harold F. O'Neil, Jr. and Charles D. Spielberger (Eds.) Cognitive and
Affective Learning Strategies

COGNITIVE AND AFFECTIVE LEARNING STRATEGIES

Edited by

HAROLD F. O'NEIL, JR.

U.S. Army Research Institute
for the Behavioral and Social Sciences
Alexandria, Virginia

CHARLES D. SPIELBERGER

Center for Research in Community Psychology and
Department of Psychology
University of South Florida
Tampa, Florida

ACADEMIC PRESS   New York   San Francisco   London   1979

A Subsidiary of Harcourt Brace Jovanovich, Publishers

ACADEMIC PRESS, INC.
111 Fifth Avenue, New York, New York 10003

United Kingdom Edition published by
ACADEMIC PRESS, INC. (LONDON) LTD.
24/28 Oval Road, London NW1   7DX

Library of Congress Cataloging in Publication Data
Main entry under title:

Cognitive and affective learning strategies.

   (The Educational technology series)
   Includes bibliographies and index.
   1. Learning, Psychology of––Addresses, essays,
lectures.   2. Cognition (Child psychology)––
Addresses, essays, lectures.   3. Affect (Psychology
––Addresses, essays, lectures.   I. O'Neil, Harold
F.,   Date II. Spielberger, Charles Donald,
Date III. Series: Educational technology series.
LB1060.C63   370.15'2   79–18162
ISBN 0–12–526680–4

PRINTED IN THE UNITED STATES OF AMERICA

79 80 81 82   9 8 7 6 5 4 3 2 1

Contents

6 Time Management as a Learning Strategy for Individualized Instruction 133

WILSON A. JUDD, BARBARA L. McCOMBS,
and JACQUELINE L. DOBROVOLNY

7 Teaching Task-Oriented Selective Reading: A Learning Strategy 177

JOSEPH W. RIGNEY, ALLEN MUNRO,
and DONALD E. CROOK

8 A Person-by-Situation View of Computer-Based Instruction 207

IRWIN G. SARASON

III ALTERNATIVE APPROACHES TO LEARNING STRATEGIES

9 Learning Strategies, Cognitive Processes, and Motor Learning 215

ROBERT N. SINGER and RICHARD F. GERSON

10   Decision Analysis as a Learning Strategy   249

ROY M. GULICK

**11   Developing Literacy and Learning Strategies in
       Organizational Settings   275**

THOMAS G. STICHT

**12   Applications of Cognitive Psychology
       to Education and Training   309**

M. C. WITTROCK

List of Contributors

Numbers in parentheses indicate the pages on which the authors' contributions begin.

THOMAS H. ANDERSON (77), Center for the Study of Reading, University of Illinois at Urbana–Champaign, Champaign, Illinois 61820

KAREN W. COLLINS (3), Psychology Department, Texas Christian University, Fort Worth, Texas 76129

DONALD E. CROOK (177), Behavioral Technology Laboratories, University of Southern California, Los Angeles, California 90007

WALTER E. CUBBERLY (45), Department of Educational Psychology, University of Texas at Austin, Austin, Texas 78712

DONALD F. DANSEREAU (3), Psychology Department, Texas Christian University, Fort Worth, Texas 76129

GEORGE M. DIEKHOFF (3), Department of Psychology, Midwestern State University, Wichita Falls, Texas 76308

JACQUELINE L. DOBROVOLNY (133), McDonnell Douglas Astronautics Company–St. Louis, Lowry Air Force Base, Denver, Colorado 80230

SELBY H. EVANS (3), Psychology Department, Texas Christian University, Fort Worth, Texas 76129

TUCKER FLETCHER (111), Department of Psychology, University of South Florida, Tampa, Florida 33620

JOHN GARLAND (3), Institute of Behavioral Research, Texas Christian University, Fort Worth, Texas 76129

RICHARD F. GERSON* (215), Movement Science and Physical Education Department, Florida State University, Tallahassee, Florida 32306

HECTOR, P. GONZALES (111), The Children's Psychiatric Center, Inc., 430 West 66 Street, Hialeah, Florida 33012

ROY M. GULICK (249), Decisions and Designs, Inc., 8400 Westpark Drive, McLean, Virginia 22101

CHARLES D. HOLLEY (3), Psychology Department, Texas Christian University, Fort Worth, Texas 76129

WILSON A. JUDD (133), McDonnell Douglas Astronautics Company–St. Louis, Lowry Air Force Base, Denver, Colorado 80230

GREGORY A. KIMBLE (99), Department of Psychology, Duke University, Durham, North Carolina 27706

BARBARA L. McCOMBS (133), McDonnell Douglas Astronautics Company–St. Louis, Lowry Air Force Base, Denver, Colorado 80230

BARBARA A. McDONALD (3), Stress Medicine Division, Naval Health Research Center, San Diego, California 92134

ALLEN MUNRO (177), Behavioral Technology Laboratories, University of Southern California, Los Angeles, California 90007

JOSEPH W. RIGNEY† (177), Behavioral Technology Laboratories, University of Southern California, Los Angeles, California 90007

IRWIN G. SARASON (207), Department of Psychology, University of Washington, Seattle, Washington 98195

ROBERT N. SINGER (215), Movement Science and Physical Education Department, Florida State University, Tallahassee, Florida 32306

CHARLES D. SPIELBERGER (111), Center for Research in Community Psychology and Department of Psychology, University of South Florida, Tampa, Florida 33620

THOMAS G. STICHT (275), National Institute of Education, Basic Skills Group, Washington, D.C. 90024

VICKI L. UNDERWOOD (45), Department of Educational Psychology, University of Texas at Austin, Austin, Texas 78712

CLAIRE E. WEINSTEIN (45), Department of Educational Psychology, University of Texas at Austin, Austin, Texas 78712

FRANK W. WICKER (45), Department of Educational Psychology, University of Texas at Austin, Austin, Texas 78712

M. C. WITTROCK (309), Graduate School of Education, University of California, Los Angeles, Los Angeles, California 90024

---

* Present address: Department of Psychology, Nova University, Fort Lauderdale, Florida 33314
† Deceased

Preface

Education and training are most effective when high-quality instruction is presented under conditions that are conducive to learning. Recent research findings suggest, however, that the learning strategies of many students are deficient. There is evidence, for example, that the aptitude and achievement scores of college-bound high school students have dropped over the past 10 years. Since the technological sophistication of our society has continued to accelerate, it seems likely that education and training problems will be encountered in the future with increasing frequency.

A promising approach to facilitating the effectiveness of education and training programs is to help students develop better learning strategies. This is analogous to improving the reading skills of elementary school children as a means for improving their performance in secondary and postsecondary education. By teaching learning strategies directly, it might also be possible to reduce the need and hence the cost of instructional support for individual courses. Helping students to improve their learning strategies should also result in less need for remedial loops and time-consuming practice, enhanced self-esteem for the learner, and fewer demands on the instructor's time.

Although there is at present only limited agreement with regard to fundamental concepts in the learning strategies literature, terms such as *basic skills, functional skills,* and *cognitive strategies* have been used to describe this domain. We prefer *learning strategies* because the term implies a broad general approach that includes affective and motor techniques as well as cognitive strategies. An example of a motor strategy would be the mental rehearsal or the actual practice of a motor skill. An example of an affective strategy would be the use of stress-reduction techniques to facilitate learning by helping the learner to concentrate on the task at hand. The availability of integrated systems for teaching cognitive, affective, and motor skills will enhance skill acquisition and retention, while contributing to the general effectiveness of educational and training programs.

In order to identify the state-of-the art of learning strategies, comprehensive reviews of the literature in the fields of cognitive psychology, artificial intelligence, behavior modification, motor learning, instructional development, and evaluation were undertaken. Building on the results of these reviews, which are published in Harold F. O'Neil, Jr. (Ed.), *Learning Strategies* (Academic Press, 1978), the present volume was designed to stimulate empirical research on the effectiveness of different types of learning strategies. In addition to descriptions of current research, the individual chapters present new ideas for future research in this field. Thus, this book provides a progress report on learning strategies that have already been developed and a means for sharing ideas concerning future research needs and directions. We believe the contents will be of interest to psychologists, educators, and advanced students in the fields mentioned previously.

The chapters in this volume are grouped according to their primary orientation, and each section concludes with a brief critique that examines thought-provoking key issues and directions for future research. Chapters 1-4 focus on cognitive approaches; Chapters 5-8 examine affective approaches. In the final section (Chapters 9-12), a variety of alternative learning strategies are described. It should be noted, however, that the grouping of chapters is not mutually exclusive, and that the influence of cognitive psychology is strongly evident throughout the book.

In developing this book, we are indebted to a number of people for their help and encouragement. In particular, we would like to acknowledge the invaluable intellectual stimulation and administrative support of Robert Young, Steven Andriole, and Craig Fields of the Defense Advanced Research Projects Agency; Robert Seidel, Harold Wagner, and Carol Hargan of the Human Resources Research Organization; and Joseph Zeidner of the U.S. Army Research Institute for the Behavioral and Social Sciences. It should be noted, however, that the views and conclusions that are expressed are those of the respective authors, and should not be interpreted as necessarily representing the official policies, either expressed or implied, of the Defense Advanced Research Projects Agency, the U.S. Army Research Institute for the Behavioral and Social Sciences, or the U.S. government.

Harold F. O'Neil, Jr.
Charles D. Spielberger

I

COGNITIVE APPROACHES
TO LEARNING STRATEGIES

1

Evaluation of a
Learning Strategy System[1]

DONALD F. DANSEREAU, BARBARA A. MCDONALD,
KAREN W. COLLINS, JOHN GARLAND,
CHARLES D. HOLLEY, GEORGE M. DIEKHOFF,
and SELBY H. EVANS

The research program reported in this chapter is based on two premises:

1. The cognitive activities students engage in when encountering academic or technical learning tasks are of crucial importance.
2. These activities can be modified through instruction and training to make them more effective and efficient.

The first point has been suggested by numerous experts in the field of educational research (e.g., Rothkopf, 1966), and the second point has been verified by experiments designed to evaluate various cognitive strategies (e.g., mnemonic techniques, Bower, 1972).

The prior work on modifying student strategies has either dealt in depth with a small part of the total set of tasks required of students (e.g., mnemonics training) or has focused on relatively superficial treatments of the total set of activities (e.g., typical study skills courses). The present program is designed to bridge the gap between these two approaches by providing in-depth training on a broad spectrum of strategies.

With regard to broad-level training, previously developed learning skills

[1] Preparation of this chapter was supported in part by the Defense Advanced Research Projects Agency under contract number MDA903-76-C-0218, and monitored by the Air Force Human Resources Laboratory, Technical Training Division. Views and conclusions contained in this chapter are those of the authors and should not be interpreted as necessarily representing the official policies, either expressed or implied, of the Defense Advanced Research Projects Agency or of the United States government.

A condensed version of this chapter has appeared in the *Journal of Educational Psychology*. Copyright 1979 by the American Psychological Association. Reprinted by permission.

3

programs have been shown to lead to improvement on general dependent measures such as college grade point averages (Briggs, Tosi, & Norley, 1971; Whitehill, 1972) and self-report study habit surveys (Bodden, Osterhouse, & Gelso, 1972; Brown, Webe, Zunker, & Haslam, 1971; Haslam & Brown, 1968; Van Zoost & Jackson, 1974). Although these programs seem to benefit students, they do suffer from some drawbacks that may restrict their effectiveness. First, the developers of these programs have not drawn very heavily on the psychological and educational research literature. Second, they have typically provided only superficial strategy training. Third, as mentioned previously, they have usually evaluated these programs with relatively global dependent measures (e.g., grade point average [GPA]). Consequently, there has been little evidence on which to base modifications.

The Survey–Question–Read–Recall–Review (SQ3R) approach proposed by Robinson (1946) provides the foundation for most of these programs. The five steps in the SQ3R technique require students to first **survey** the text chapter by reading headings, boldface print, etc. On the basis of the survey students are encouraged to **develop questions.** They then **read** the material with an eye toward answering these questions. Following the reading the students are encouraged to close the book and **recall** what has been read. Finally, they open the book and **review** the material. Generally, SQ3R training has been relatively nonspecific; very little information is provided on how to carry out the operations at a detailed level. It is assumed that the individual is able to arrive at these more specific procedures without guidance.

An assessment of students' knowledge and use of detailed learning-related strategies via a self-report inventory (Dansereau, Long, McDonald, & Actkinson, 1975) indicated that this assumption is probably unwarranted; students appear to have little knowledge of alternative learning procedures, especially at a detailed level. On the basis of a review of the literature related to academic learning (Dansereau, Actkinson, Long, & McDonald, 1974), it has been concluded that students would benefit from detailed training on a strategy system extrapolated from some of the findings in the educational and psychological research literature. The present research and development effort represents a second step toward this objective. It is an attempt to expand and modify a modestly successful small-scale program developed by Dansereau, Long, McDonald, Actkinson, Ellis, Collins, Williams, and Evans (1975).

The approach to this research has been strongly influenced by the fact that effective interaction with academic and technical materials requires that the student engage in a complex system of interrelated activities. To assist the student in this endeavor, a set of mutually supportive strategies has been developed. This set can be divided into *primary* strategies, which are used to operate on the material directly, and *support* strategies, which are used by the learner to maintain a suitable cognitive climate. Further subdivisions of these sets of strategies are presented in Figure 1.1. The primary set includes strategies for acquiring and storing the information (the *comprehension–retention* strategies) and strategies for subsequently outputting and using the stored information (the *retrieval–utilization* strategies). The substrategies that fall under these two categories are communicated to students by using the acronyms first-degree MURDER for comprehension–retention and second-degree MURDER for retrieval-utilization. The letters in each of the two MURDERs represent the names of the substrategies and the order of the letters represents the sequence that the student is instructed to follow in implementing the substrategies. Note: The M in both MURDERs stands for the mood-setting and maintenance strategies that fall in the support category (see Figure 1.1). To facilitate training and implementation, the comprehension–retention and retrieval-utilization strategies were designed to be mutually supportive by using analogous substrategies. Further details will be presented in the next section of this chapter.

The support strategies have been divided into three categories: goal setting and scheduling, concentration management, and monitoring and diagnosing. Concentration management has been subdivided further into mood setting and mood maintenance. All of these support strategies are designed to assist the student in developing and maintaining an internal state that is conducive to effective implementation of the primary strategies. Further information on the support strategies will be presented in a subsequent section.

PRIMARY STRATEGIES

The comprehension–retention and retrieval–utilization strategies will be discussed separately.

Comprehension–Retention Strategies

The goal has been to develop strategies that will assist the student in reorganizing, integrating, and elaborating incoming material. These strategies will be overviewed and then discussed separately in greater detail.

As mentioned earlier, the first-degree MURDER acronym has been used to communicate the set of comprehension–retention strategies to students. The steps in MURDER include setting the **mood** to study (will be discussed

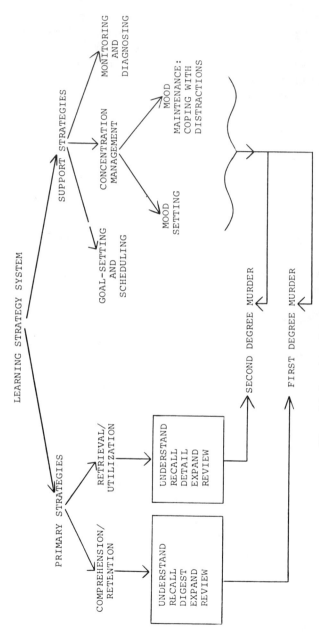

Figure 1.1 Overview of the learning strategy system.

under support strategies); reading for **understanding** (marking important and difficult ideas); **recalling** the material without referring to the text; correcting recall, amplifying and storing the material so as to **digest** it; **expanding** knowledge by self-inquiry; and finally, **reviewing** mistakes (learning from tests).

The four basic comprehension–retention steps (understand, recall, digest, and expand) are similar to the processes suggested by the SQ3R technique (Robinson, 1946) and some of its derivatives. These approaches all have two important aspects in common. First, the student is encouraged to process the same text material more than once (a multiple-pass approach). Second, a great deal of emphasis is placed on the active recall or recitation of what has been learned.

The potential effectiveness of multiple passes has been supported by experiments with advance organizers. Ausubel and his associates (see Lawton & Wanska, 1977, for a review of this literature) have found that providing a summary of the material before reading increases comprehension and retention performance. In our strategy and the SQ3R techniques the students create their own implicit advance organizers on the first reading and then use this information on a second pass through the material. Additional support for this approach arises from Norman, Genter, and Stevens's (1976) suggestions regarding the effectiveness of "web" learning. They contend that complicated material may be learned in successive passes. The first pass would presumably create a web, or network, of the important concepts, whereas subsequent processing of the material would allow the individual to fill in the details.

Generally, the "recall" phase of both our strategy and the SQ3R techniques forces the student to process the information actively by putting the text material into an alternate form (the student's own words or images, or an alternative symbol system). In addition, this process points out weaknesses in the student's understanding and retention that can be corrected on a second pass through the material. The importance of active recall in improving comprehension and retention has been directly supported by the experiments of Del Giorno, Jenkins, and Bausell (1974) and Dansereau *et al.* (1975), and indirectly supported by the work of Rothkopf (1966) and Craik and Lockhart (1972).

Although varying somewhat in surface structure, the main differences between the core of first-degree MURDER and the SQ3R approaches occur in the details of the steps. Typically training on SQ3R is nonspecific; the steps are described and the students are expected to translate these descriptions into operative substrategies. It appears, however, that a large number of students have a great deal of difficulty in making this translation. To alleviate this problem detailed instructions and practice exercises have been designed to communicate the substrategies. The nature of these sub-strategies will be briefly described below.

The "Understand" Strategy

While the students are doing their first reading they are encouraged to mark the portions of the text that they do not understand. During the "digest" phase they are instructed to home in on the marked portions that are still not understood (some understanding problems are naturally cleared up by further reading). The student is trained first to identify the nature and extent of the comprehension (understanding) problem (i.e., to determine whether it is a problematic word, sentence, or paragraph) and is then trained to attack the problem by breaking it down into its parts (e.g., prefix and suffix in the case of a word, or subject–predicate in the case of a sentence). If the students are still unsure of the meaning, they are encour-aged to look in other parts of the passage (the *surround*) in order to find related information (e.g., synonymns and redundant explanations). If there are still difficulties, the student is instructed to consult another source (e.g., a dictionary, teacher, or another textbook). The main thrust of this strategy is to put the student into the role of an active problem solver rather than a passive recipient of information.

The "Recall" Strategies

After an initial reading the student is instructed to recall the material read. This is considered to be the most important phase of the comprehen-sion–retention strategy, and consequently a number of substrategies that vary in the degree of transformation (translation of the text into an alter-native symbol system) required on the part of the student have been devel-oped: paraphrase–imagery, networking, and analysis of key ideas.

Paraphrase–Imagery. This technique is a simple combination of the paraphrase (the students intermittently rephrase the incoming material in their own words) and imagery (the students intermittently form mental pic-tures of the concepts underlying the incoming material) strategies developed in an earlier program (see Dansereau, 1978; Dansereau *et al.,* 1975). The student is trained on both techniques and is then instructed to vary the use of the techniques depending on the material being studied. In an earlier study it was found that both techniques led to improved perfor-mance on a delayed essay test in comparison to a no-treatment control group (Dansereau, 1978; Dansereau *et al.,* 1975).

Networking. Unlike the paraphrase–imagery technique, which requires the student to transform text material into natural language or pictures, the networking strategy requires material to be transformed into node–link maps or networks. Before giving more information on the technique per se we will present some general background information on the concept of node-link networks.

Quillian (1969) suggested that human memory may be organized as a network composed of ideas or concepts (nodes) and the named relationships between these concepts (links). For example, the relationships (links) between the concepts (nodes) *bird, parrot,* and *colorful* can be expressed as "A parrot is a **type** of bird," and "A parrot can be **described** as colorful." These node-link relationships can be represented spatially in the following network:

Since Quillian's early work a number of network models of memory have been proposed and tested (e.g., Anderson, 1972; Anderson & Bower, 1973; Rumelhart, Lindsay, & Norman, 1972). The results of these efforts indicate that at least some aspects of human memory can be functionally represented as networks. For this and a number of other reasons that will be discussed shortly, the node-link network was chosen as the basis for two of the recall techniques (the analysis of key concepts technique is also based on this conceptualization).

The networking strategy requires the student to identify important concepts or ideas (nodes) in the material and to represent their interrelationships (links) in the form of a network map. To assist students in this endeavor they are taught a set of named links that can be used to code the relationships between ideas. The networking process emphasizes the identification and representation of hierarchies (type–part), chains (lines of reasoning–temporal orderings–causal sequences), and clusters (characteristics–definitions–analogies). See Figure 1.2 for a schematic representation of these three types of structures and their associated links and Figure 1.3 for an example of a summary map of a nursing textbook chapter. Application of this technique results in the production of structured two-dimensional maps. These maps provide the student with a spatial organization of the information contained in the passage.

It is hypothesized that the transformation of prose into a network will assist the student in seeing the overall picture being presented by the author. In addition, coding the material in terms of named links should give the student the option of using these links to gain access to the material during retrieval. (This possibility will be discussed further in the section on retrieval–utilization.) Besides these direct benefits, an expanded network approach appears to have applicability to a number of other domains.

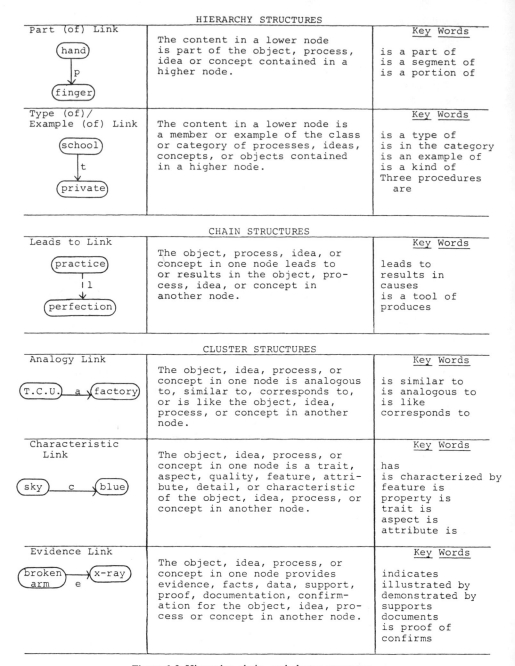

HIERARCHY STRUCTURES

Part (of) Link	The content in a lower node is part of the object, process, idea or concept contained in a higher node.	Key Words is a part of is a segment of is a portion of
Type (of)/ Example (of) Link	The content in a lower node is a member or example of the class or category of processes, ideas, concepts, or objects contained in a higher node.	Key Words is a type of is in the category is an example of is a kind of Three procedures are

CHAIN STRUCTURES

Leads to Link	The object, process, idea, or concept in one node leads to or results in the object, process, idea, or concept in another node.	Key Words leads to results in causes is a tool of produces

CLUSTER STRUCTURES

Analogy Link	The object, idea, process, or concept in one node is analogous to, similar to, corresponds to, or is like the object, idea, process, or concept in another node.	Key Words is similar to is analogous to is like corresponds to
Characteristic Link	The object, idea, process, or concept in one node is a trait, aspect, quality, feature, attribute, detail, or characteristic of the object, idea, process, or concept in another node.	Key Words has is characterized by feature is property is trait is aspect is attribute is
Evidence Link	The object, idea, process, or concept in one node provides evidence, facts, data, support, proof, documentation, confirmation for the object, idea, process or concept in another node.	Key Words indicates illustrated by demonstrated by supports documents is proof of confirms

Figure 1.2 Hierarchy, chain, and cluster structures.

10

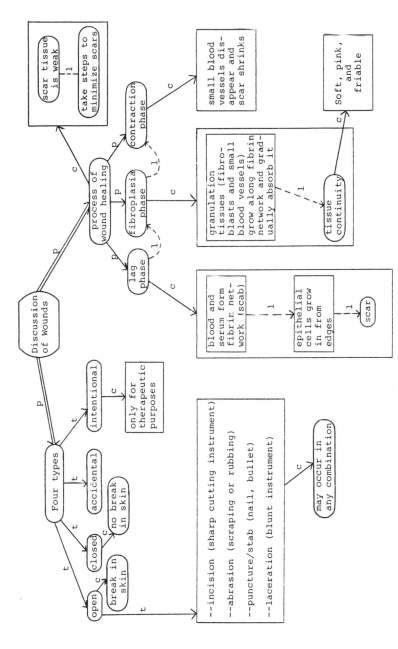

Figure 1.3 Example of a network of a chapter from a nursing textbook.

11

From the teacher's perspective networking can be used in the preparation of lectures as an alternative to outlining. Also, teacher-prepared networks can be presented as advance and post organizers. Additional benefits may be derived from using networks in teaching students who are employing networking as a learning strategy.

Networking can be used to facilitate individual and group problem solving by providing a mechanism for moving within the problem space. This approach has been used in the context of a graduate psychology seminar at Texas Christian University. Subjective reactions to the approach indicate that it has substantial promise as a problem-solving tool.

Conceptually, it seems reasonable to expect that ability to network (i.e., to discover and organize meaningful relationships among ideas, objects, and actions) should be related to general reading comprehension ability. If this expectation is borne out, networking may serve as an alternative assessment and diagnostic device. In fact, the noun phrases in a body of text can be replaced by nonmeaningful symbols. A student's ability to network this material would seem to reflect a type of comprehension skill that is separable from vocabulary level and prior knowledge.

Finally, the ease and/or accuracy with which a text can be networked may provide a more valid index of comprehensibility (readability) than is presently available.

Analysis of Key Concepts.   The final recall strategy is also derived from network models of memory (Diekhoff, 1977). In this structured alternative to networking the student identifies key ideas or concepts in a body of text, develops systematic definitions and elaborations of the concepts, and interrelates important pairs of these concepts. The student is aided in these activities by worksheets that specify categories of definition and comparison. These categories are isomorphic to the links described earlier (e.g., in defining operant conditioning one might say that it is a **type** of learning paradigm or a **part** of many behavior modification programs or that it **leads to** increases in the target behavior).

The major difference between analysis of key ideas and networking is that the key-ideas approach is structured and linear and provides for only local interrelationships between concepts, whereas the networking technique is relatively unstructured and spatial and provides for global interrelationships.

The "Digest" Strategy

The major portion of this strategy has already been discussed in the "understanding" strategy section. In addition, the student is given guidelines for identifying and storing important information. These guidelines were derived from interviews with effective learners and the literature on mnemonic techniques (e.g., Bower, 1972).

The "Expand" Strategy

After the students have gone back through the text material correcting understanding problems, amplifying the recalled material, and storing important information, they are encouraged to expand their knowledge via self-inquiry. In this regard, students are trained to ask and answer specific questions falling under three general categories:

1. Imagine you could talk to the author; what questions would you ask? What criticisms would you raise?
2. How can the material be applied?
3. How could you make the material more understandable and interesting to other students?

In the initial stages of training, students are required to put their answers on worksheets and are given experimenter-generated questions and answers as feedback. After this initial experience the students are encouraged to do these processes in their heads or to incorporate the material into their ongoing notes.

The "Review" Strategy

After getting feedback on the effectiveness of their studying (e.g., via a test), the students are encouraged to review their errors and determine the underlying causes. They are then instructed to modify their study methods to prevent future errors. A workbook is provided to guide these processes (see Dansereau, 1978, for further information).

Retrieval–Utilization Strategies

After students have comprehended and stored a body of information, their job is only partly completed. The student must be able to recall and use the information under appropriate circumstances (e.g., in taking tests or on the job).

Subjective reports from students and studies demonstrating "tip of the tongue" behavior (Brown & McNeil, 1966), and "feeling of knowing" (Hart, 1965) indicate that stored items are frequently available, but, at least temporarily, not accessible. When individuals encounter such a situation they may give up, randomly search, or attempt to execute a systematic retrieval strategy. It appears that students often opt for the first two alternatives rather than the third. This practice is unfortunate in that systematic attempts at retrieval often lead to success. Lindsay and Norman (1972) give a brief example of how the systematic approach works. In response to the query "What were you doing on Monday afternoon in the third week of September 2 years ago?," Lindsay and Norman's imaginary subject gradually homes in on the answer by breaking the query down into a rational sequence of subquestions that prove answerable by various mixtures of actual memories and logical reconstructions of what must have been ("Third week in September—that's just after summer—that would have been the fall term. . . . I think I had chemistry lab on Mondays. . . . I remember he started off with the atomic table. . . , etc.").

It is felt that students can benefit from instruction on how to undertake a systematic retrieval of this sort. The retrieval–utilization strategies will be overviewed and then discussed separately in greater detail.

As mentioned earlier, the second-degree MURDER acronym has been used to communicate the set of retrieval–utilization strategies to students. Although the letters, and in some cases the strategy names, are the same as those in first-degree MURDER, the reader should be aware that the detailed level strategies differ. The steps in second-degree MURDER include setting the **mood, understanding** the requirements of the task, **recalling** the main ideas relevant to the task requirements (using means–ends analysis and planning), **detailing** the main ideas with specific information, **expanding** the information into an outline, and **reviewing** the adequacy of the final response.

Although this strategy has been designed primarily for test taking and paper preparation, extension of the technique to other tasks should be relatively straightforward.

The primary aim of second-degree MURDER is to encourage the student to view recall and utilization as a multiple-pass process. Discussions with students indicate that when faced with an essay test question, for example, many of them begin writing their answers almost immediately. This approach forces students to recall, organize, and transform the ideas into prose simultaneously. As a result their answers are often jumbled and incomplete. The retrieval–utilization strategy is designed to help the students guard against this situation by forcing them to slow down and break the process into coherent steps.

The "Understand" Phase

If the task requirements are not understood, the subsequent actions a student takes will be irrelevant. To assist students in this phase, instructors encourage them to use their comprehension–retention strategies on the task instructions (e.g., test questions). For example, in preparing to answer a test question they would read the question, transform it into an alternative symbol system (i.e., a paraphrase or image, a network, or a set of defined key concepts, depending on their strategy preference), and then use the understanding problem-solving techniques (i.e., breakdown and surround) to clear up any understanding difficulties.

The "Recall" Phase

The goal of this phase is to arrive at the set of main ideas necessary to meet the task requirements. To meet this goal the student is instructed to relax and image the situation in which the target information was acquired. In addition, the student is made aware of the ties between retrieval strategies and the processes involved in problem solving (both require a search through a problem space). In particular, the student is instructed on means–ends analysis (setting and meeting subgoals) and planning (abstracting the problem to a more general level), two key components of the General Problem Solver created by Newell, Simon, and Shaw (1958). The idea is to examine the difference between your present state of knowledge and your goal state in order to set up reasonable subgoals. Acquisition of these subgoals presumably leads you closer and closer to your target state of knowledge. For example, if one were trying to remember who was the vice president of the United States in 1877, a reasonable first subgoal might be to determine who was the president during this time period. If this information were not immediately retrievable, the next step might be to set up the subgoal of trying to remember which major events took place during the latter 1870s. This process would continue until an achievable subgoal was reached. Then this information would be used to access the previous subgoal, and so on. In this way one would work back up the chain of subgoals to the target. In using the "planning" heuristic you would first generalize the retrieval task to a simpler one, solve the simple retrieval via means–ends analysis, and then use this solution as a plan to guide the more specific retrieval. For example, if you were trying to recall the location and function of a particular part of a cat's brain (e.g., the hypothalamus), you might first attempt to remember the location and function of the hypothalamus in mammals in general and then use these retrieval steps to guide the more specific inquiry.

Those students who have learned networking or the key concept technique can use the named links (relationships) as a language for exploring their memory systems. For example, is the information I am looking for embedded in a **leads to** chain? Is it **part** of a larger concept? Is it an example or **type** of a more general notion? This language provides a systematic way of moving from one point in the memory system to another. In some sense it serves the role of a general purpose mnemonic technique.

The "Detail" Phase

Once the main ideas are recalled the same techniques discussed in the previous section can be used to retrieve the details associated with these ideas.

The "Expand" Phase

In this stage the student organizes the information retrieved during the previous two stages. This may involve numbering the main ideas and the associated details to produce a coherent sequence from which to construct a response. If necessary a formal outline may be created. In organizing this material the student may discover gaps in the information that need to be filled in by further retrievals.

The "Respond" and "Review" Phase

This step requires the student to transform the recalled information into prose or a set of actions. Following this conversion the students are encouraged to examine their responses in light of the task requirements. Modifications are made if necessary.

SUPPORT STRATEGIES

As stated earlier, no matter how effective the primary strategies are, their impact on learning and utilization will be less than optimal if the internal psychological environment of the student is nonoptimal. Consequently, the support strategies are designed to assist the student in developing and maintaining a good internal state. These support strategies include goal setting and scheduling, concentration management, and monitoring and diagnosing the dynamics of the learning system. These three classes of strategies will be discussed separately.

Goal Setting and Scheduling

Goals and schedules can be viewed from a hierarchial perspective. For example, a student's daily goals (e.g., read Chapter 9 in the physics text) are embedded in a set of weekly goals (e.g., prepare for the physics midterm exam), which are in turn embedded in a set of semester goals (e.g., make an A in the physics course.) A companion example could be created for daily, weekly, and semester time schedules. Unfortunately, discussions with students indicate that very few of them create goals and schedules in accord with this hierarchical perspective. In fact, students apparently spend very little effort of any sort on systematic planning.

This lack of planning has a number of drawbacks:

1. Without concrete goals (especially short-term goals) the students will have a difficult time gauging the adequacy of their progress.
2. If the student has not analyzed required tasks into subgoals, there is a

strong possibility that the magnitude of the task will be misperceived. Some individuals view amorphous tasks optimistically and consequently do not budget sufficient time. Others view such tasks pessimistically and become very anxious about accomplishing them.

3. If goals and schedules are not written down, the students must keep this information in their heads. Certainly this state of affairs will act as a drain on the student's cognitive capacity.

4. Students who do not regularly schedule their study sessions cannot make use of the positive stimulus cue values associated with a consistent schedule.

To assist students in overcoming these problems a workbook for specifying concrete goals and time schedules has been developed. In using this workbook the students first are given guidance on specifying career goals. They then determine skill-oriented subgoals that are prerequisites for their chosen career goals. Following this they set concrete goals for the particular semester. Finally, in light of these goals they create a weekly activity schedule. The students are then instructed to monitor their progress in achieving their goals. If progress is not as predicted they are encouraged to alter their activity schedule or restructure their set of goals.

Concentration Management

The most common student complaints usually revolve around their inability to concentrate during a study or testing session. These concentration difficulties stem from two general sources: attitude (or mood) problems and problems in coping with distractions.

Strategies for Creating a Positive Learning Mood

Interviews and discussions with students indicate that many of them have conflicting attitudes about learning. At a distance they view learning as something that is necessary and desirable. However, when faced with an impending learning task they often experience a variety of negative emotions. Anxiety, anger, guilt, fear, and frustration are some of the labels they use in conjunction with these emotions. These feelings and the self-talk and images that accompany them serve to decrease a student's motivation to study and act as distractors during the learning process and during evaluation periods.

The strategy that has been developed to assist the student in overcoming attitude problems consists of a combination of elements from systematic desensitization (Jacobsen, 1938; Wolpe, 1969), rational behavior therapy (Ellis, 1963; Maultsby, 1971), and therapies based on positive self-talk (Meichenbaum & Goodman, 1971; Meichenbaum & Turk, 1975). The students are first given experiences and strategies designed to assist them in becoming aware of the negative and positive emotions, self-talk, and images they generate in facing a learning task. The vehicles for this first step are a short lecture, worksheets, and samples of attitudes and self-talk expressed by students in earlier studies. After this first step the student is asked to follow the negative feelings and thoughts to their logical conclusions (e.g., "Just what will happen if I fail this exam?"). Very often the individual has not thought beyond the fact that a particular outcome will be "awful" or that such and such an outcome is "critical" (Maultsby, 1971). Stopping at this stage can be very illusory and may cause emotions to be blown out of proportion. In addition, the accompanying self-talk and imagery may be extremely destructive when viewed in relationship to the student's long-term goals. To assist the students in matching their self-talk with their objectives, intructors ask them to evaluate the constructiveness of their internal dialogue and give them heuristics for making appropriate modifications (worksheets and experimenter-generated sample statements are used to assist the student in this task).

In preparing for an impending study session students report that they usually spend very little conscious effort in establishing a positive learning or test-taking state. It seems very likely that thoughts and feelings associated with their immediately previous situation will mix with negative cognitions about learning and will be carried over as distractors during task performance. To alleviate this situation the student is trained on a technique that forms the basis of systematic desensitization: imagination of the anxiety-evoking situation during relaxation. In effect, the student is instructed to relax and clear the mind by counting breaths; then the individual imagines a period of successfully coping with the distraction. The student is also encouraged to replace the negative talk and images with more constructive thoughts. This technique forms the mood-setting phase of the two MURDER processes described earlier.

Maintaining a Constructive Mood: Coping with Distractions

Interviews with students indicate that acts of will and fear-arousing self-talk are the most common methods of coping with distractions, frustration, and fatigue. Apparently these methods are at best only partially effective and tend to put the student under considerable tension. This tension probably contributes to subsequent negative feelings about future learning episodes.

We have been developing concentration-enhancing strategies to supplement or substitute for those typically used. Again, the first step involves awareness training: The students are given experiences and techniques to assist them in determining when, how, and why they get distracted, the duration of their distraction periods, and their typical reactions to distraction. They are then trained to cope with distractions by using the mood strategies of relaxation and positive self-talk and imagery to reestablish an appropriate learning state. (The training methods are analogous to those discussed in the previous section.)

Monitoring and Diagnosing

To be effective, students must be able to detect when their behavior is not sufficient to meet task demands so that they can make appropriate adjustments. We have not treated monitoring as a separate component, but have embedded monitoring principles in the concentration management component and the two MURDER strategies.

In the concentration management component the students are encouraged to skim the material to be studied and mark places in the text where they plan to check progress and take action. They read to the first action point and evaluate their learning state (i.e., concentration and level of understanding). If the state is not satisfactory, they attempt to correct the situation via relaxation, constructive self-talk, and imagery (i.e., the same techniques used in establishing the original learning state or mood).

In using the comprehension–retention MURDER strategy the students are encouraged to check their learning state after each recall. In this case, the students can evaluate the completeness of their recall as one measure of their progress. This additional information should assist the students in accurately judging the adequacy of their learning state for the task at hand.

RESEARCH FRAMEWORK

Our approach to the development and evaluation of the learning strategy system has been to evaluate the strategy system in its entirety, and then, based on this evaluation, to modify and evaluate the individual components. The modified components will then be recombined and the overall system will be subjected to further examination. The remainder of this chapter will include a description of an overall system evaluation and two presentations of studies designed to determine the effectiveness of critical components of the primary and support strategies.

The major intent of the overall system evaluation was to amass objective and subjective data as to which components were most valuable, compatible, etc. In this study, which will be reported in the next section, the emphasis was on gathering information for the purpose of system refinement rather than for formal evaluation.

ASSESSMENT OF THE STRATEGIES AND
TRAINING METHODS IN THE CONTEXT OF
A LEARNING STRATEGIES COURSE

Because of the complexities of academic learning, a mutually supportive set of interactive strategies is required to maximize learning potential. In order to examine and capitalize on these interactions, students must be taught large portions of the strategy system. Unfortunately the time and student motivation required for training precludes exploring this system in the context of typical short-term experiments. Therefore, to provide an overall evaluation, the component strategies were put together to form a one-semester (15-week) learning strategies course. This two-credit course was offered to Texas Christian University undergraduates during the 1977 spring semester on a pass–no credit basis.

Design

In order to evaluate the effectiveness of the strategy system, two interlocking experiments were created (see Figure 1.4). In one, the performances of differentially treated subgroups of the class were compared with each other and with a no-treatment control group (the comprehension–retention controls). The bases of these comparisons were scores on a series of tests over textbook material that had been studied 1 week earlier. These tests were given to the class members and the control group prior to the start of the course (the pretest), approximately halfway through the course (the midcourse test), and at the end of the course (the posttest).

In the second experiment, the performance of the class members on a set of self-report measures was compared with a separate no-treatment control group (the self-report controls) both before and after the course.

The decision to use no-treatment rather than placebo control groups was based on prior research with learning strategy training. Attempts at equating training time by having students practice their own or less effective, competing methods on the training material have led to suppression of mean performance in comparison with "untrained" students using their own techniques (e.g., Collins, 1978; Garland, 1977; Long, 1976). Subjective reports from participants in these placebo groups indicate that they do not view the training as meaningful and consequently become frustrated and bored with the task. These reactions apparently carry over to the assessment phase, leading to the reduction in mean performance. It should also be emphasized that the college-age students participating in these experiments have had 12 to 14 years of experience and practice with their own study methods (particularly with naturally occurring prose) and can therefore be considered no-treatment controls in name only.

Participants

Participants were Texas Christian University undergraduates, heterogeneous with respect to grade level and majors.

Three major groups of these students were employed in this experiment. The learning strategy class was composed of 38 students. They received 2 semester hours of college credit for successfully completing this pass–no credit course.

The comprehension–retention control group consisted of 28 students who were recruited from general psychology classes at Texas Christian University. After completing the experiment, they received credit for fulfilling an experimental participation requirement, a $6 fee, and learning strategy training materials.

Finally, the subjective report control group was composed of 21 students also recruited from general psychology. Upon completion of the experiment, they received learning strategy training materials, experimental credit, and a $4 fee.

Interviews with members of the control groups indicated that their prime motivation for participating was their interest in learning strategy training. Further, a comparison of the profiles of the three groups indicated that they were very similar in terms of the distributions of majors, grade levels, and sex.

Dependent Measures

The comprehension–retention measures and self-report measures will be described separately.

Comprehension-Retention Measures

Multiple-choice and short-answer tests were developed for three 3000 word passages: one extracted from a textbook on educational psychology (the pretest), one from a text on ecology (the midcourse test), and one from a text on geology (the posttest). The students were given 1 hour to study each of these passages and then 1 week later given 45 minutes to take the corresponding tests.

Self-Report Measures

These included a 37-item test anxiety scale (a slightly modified version of the one used by Sarason, 1956), the Brown–Holtzman Survey of Study Habits and Attitudes (W. Brown & Holtzman, 1966), a 46-item question-

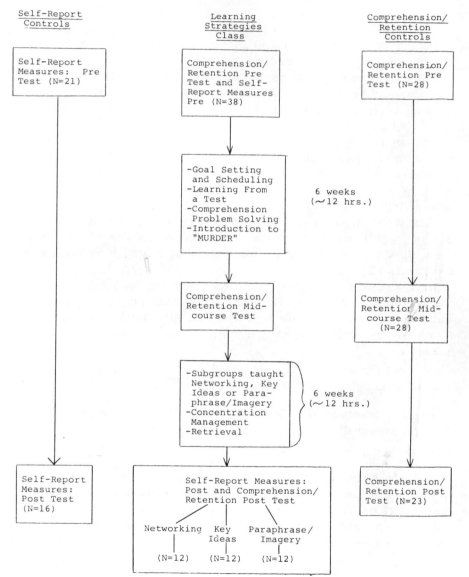

Figure 1.4 Training and assessment schedule for the learning strategies course.

naire designed to tap concentration difficulties and coping skills, and a 12-item learning attitude inventory designed to assess students' perceptions of their own academic abilities.

Procedure

For the comprehension–retention experiment the dependent measures were administered to the class members and the comprehension–retention controls before the course began (the pretest), approximately halfway through the course (the midcourse test), and after the course was completed (the posttest). For the final testing the 36 participating class members were subdivided into three groups depending on the comprehension–retention substrategy being employed: paraphrase–imagery ($N = 12$), networking ($N = 12$), or key ideas ($N = 12$).

For the self-report experiment the four measures were administered to the class members and the self-report controls before (pre-) and after (post-) the course.

Class members were given 2 hours of training each week for 12 weeks. The two control groups were not given any training during this time period.

The strategy components described earlier in this report formed the basis of the strategy class training. In general, the training on primary and support strategies was intermixed in order to illuminate the interactions between the components. Training methods included short lectures, practice exercises, and small group or pair discussions.

Specific training for the class members, following the pretest, consisted of 12 hours of training in goal setting and scheduling, learning from a test, comprehension problem solving, and introduction to MURDER. The class then took the midcourse comprehension–retention test ($N = 25$). Following this measure, class members received the final 12 hours of training. This final strategy training was taught to three subdivisions of the class: paraphrase–imagery, networking, and key ideas. Each subgroup received not only the specific recall–transformation strategy, but also training on concentration management and retrieval. Finally, class members participated in the posttesting session. Class members were instructed to apply the recall–transformation strategies they had learned to the material on the comprehension–retention posttest. The students also filled out the self-report measures at this time. (See Figure 1.4 for a graphic presentation of the procedures.)

Results and Discussion

The comprehension–retention and self-report results will be presented separately.

Comprehension–Retention

Each of the three comprehension–retention tests (pre-, midcourse, and post-) contained both multiple-choice and short-answer subtests. All tests were scored according to predetermined keys without knowledge of the student's group affiliation. The raw scores were then converted to percentages of the maximum possible on each test.

The overall treatment (strategy training) versus control differences will be presented first. The means and standard deviations of the total scores and changes in total scores for the comprehension–retention tests are presented in Table 1.1. (The sample sizes in this and subsequent tables vary depending on the number of students participating in each testing.) As can be seen in this table, there were *slight* (nonsignificant) differences in the pretest means. This situation also occurred with the other dependent measures. Consequently, all analyses were performed on changes from the pretest base lines. Since there has been controversy over the use of change (or difference) scores in the past, a brief justification for this approach will be presented. In a detailed analysis of this issue, Overall and Woodward (1975) concluded the following:

> Numerous writers have emphasized the unreliability of difference scores, which results from summation of measurement errors (Bereiter, 1963; Lord, 1963; Webster & Bereiter, 1963). While this may be a problem for certain types of correlational studies, it is not a cause for concern in the use of simple difference scores to measure treatment induced change in experimental research [p. 85].

This position is reasserted by Overall and Woodward in 1976 and supported by Huck and McLean (1975). Further, according to the criteria suggested by Huck and McLean, the analysis of difference scores is a more conservative procedure than analysis of covariance, given the conditions of the present study.

When two-tailed t tests were used, the differences between the class members and the control group approached significance with the change in total scores from pre- to midcourse t (51) = 1.85, $p < .067$), and from pre- to post- t (57) = 1.73, $p < .085$). It should be noted that both of these tests would be considered significant ($p < .05$) if one tailed criterion were employed. In both cases the learning strategy class members exhibited greater positive mean changes from the base-line pretest than did the controls. The negative change scores exhibited by the control group indicate that the midcourse test was more difficult than the posttest, which in turn was more difficult than the pretest (see Table 1.1). This ordering was supported by subjective ratings of comprehensibility elicited from the subjects at each testing.

TABLE 1.1

Means and Standard Deviations of the Total Scores (Expressed in Terms of Percentage Correct) and Changes in Total Scores for the Comprehension-Retention Tests

	Pretest	Midcourse	Posttest	Pre- to midcourse change for participants in both tests	Pre- to postcourse change for participants in both tests
Learning strategies class	$\bar{X} = 49.28$ $SD = 12.86$ $N = 36$	$\bar{X} = 49.73$ $SD = 14.49$ $N = 25$	$\bar{X} = 53.27$ $SD = 19.22$ $N = 36$	$\bar{X} = .79$ $SD = 10.70$ $N = 25$	$\bar{X} = 3.99$ $SD = 13.41$ $N = 36$
Comprehension-retention control group	$\bar{X} = 47.38$ $SD = 16.18$ $N = 28$	$\bar{X} = 42.29$ $SD = 19.96$ $N = 28$	$\bar{X} = 46.72$ $SD = 19.74$ $N = 23$	$\bar{X} = -5.09$ $SD = 11.83$ $N = 28$	$\bar{X} = -1.81$ $SD = 10.44$ $N = 23$

. The amounts (expressed in percentages) by which strategy class members outscored the control group on each of the comprehension–retention tests are presented in Table 1.2. (Only participants who took all three tests are included in the data display.)

These data suggest that the major impact of the strategy training occurred prior to the midcourse test. (The percentages by which the class members outscored the controls are at or near their peaks for each of the measures at the time of the midcourse test.) Although this is a tenable hypothesis, other factors exist that could have influenced these results. First, as has been stated earlier, the midcourse test was apparently more difficult than the posttest. It is possible that the strategy training has a greater impact on more difficult material, thus producing the results exhibited in Table 1.2. Second, during the training subsequent to the midcourse test and prior to the posttest, the class members were subdivided into three groups and each group was trained on a different recall–transformation technique: paraphrase–imagery, key ideas, and networking. If one or more of these techniques were not as effective (at the time of testing) as the more global strategy (i.e., MURDER with free recitation) taught prior to the midcourse test, then the data in Table 1.2 would not be unexpected. This possibility will be explored in the following paragraphs.

Between the midcourse and posttest the strategy class members were divided into three groups based on their stated preference for a particular comprehension–retention substrategy. Each group received approximately 4 hours of training on one of the following strategies: paraphrase–imagery, networking, or key ideas. At the time of postassessment students were instructed to use the substrategies they had received. Comparisons between these groups indicated that there were no significant differences between the "change" scores from the pre- to posttest or from midcourse to posttest (for each group, $N = 8$). The small sample size and the relatively large within-cell variance probably contributed to these findings. In any case, it should be noted that there were substantial differences in the percentage amounts by which these groups outscored the control group. Examination of Table 1.3 indicates that the networking group increased its advantage over the controls from midcourse to posttest while the key ideas group maintained approximately the same advantage and the paraphrase–imagery group decreased its advantage. Therefore, it is reasonable to speculate that the peak in class-control differences at the midcourse examination may be due to the lack of impact of the key ideas training and the apparent negative impact of the paraphrase–imagery training. The only group that seemed to benefit from the substrategy training was the networking group. Consequently, if all class members were taught networking, then one would expect that the class-control differences would have been greater on the

TABLE 1.2

The Percentage Amounts by Which the Strategy Class Members Outscored the Control Group on Each of the Comprehension-Retention Tests (Mean Differences between the Two Groups Expressed as Percentages of the Control Group's Mean Scores)[a]

Pretest			Midcourse test			Posttest		
Short answer	Multiple choice	Total	Short answer	Multiple choice	Total	Short answer	Multiple choice	Total
8.14	−.10	3.42	30.15	12.83	19.93	31.02	9.28	18.17

[a]Only participants who took all three tests are included in this data summary: class member N = 24; comprehension–retention control N = 23.

TABLE 1.3

The Percentage Amounts by Which the Strategy Subgroups Outscored the Control Group (N = 23) on Each of the Comprehension-Retention Tests (Mean Differences between the Strategy Subgroups and the Control Group Expressed as Percentages of the Control Group's Mean Scores)[a]

	Pretest			Midcourse test			Posttest		
	Short answer	Multiple choice	Total	Short answer	Multiple choice	Total	Short answer	Multiple choice	Total
Paraphrase–imagery (N = 8)	6.35	−1.14	2.06	19.48	14.11	16.35	7.47	9.24	8.57
Key ideas (N = 8)	15.61	3.58	8.87	44.81	14.81	27.01	46.40	14.92	27.84
Networking (N = 8)	2.65	−2.93	−.41	26.62	9.52	16.35	38.67	3.91	22.48

[a] Paraphrase–imagery, key ideas, and networking training occurred between the midcourse and posttests.

posttest than on the midcourse test. (It is also possible that the utilization of equally difficult midcourse and posttests would influence the results in a similar way.)

The reasons for the negative impact of the paraphrase–imagery training on posttest performance are not readily apparent, especially in light of prior work with versions of this technique (e.g., Dansereau *et al.*, 1975). There are two possible explanations. First, evaluators of paraphrasing and imaging have typically used shorter materials (generally passages of 1000 words or less; in this study the passages were approximately 3000 words in length). Because these techniques do not emphasize organization of the material, they may be relatively ineffective with longer passages. Second, students chose the type of training they would receive. The paraphrase–imagery technique was undoubtedly perceived as the easiest technique to learn and implement. Consequently, it may have attracted relatively un-motivated students. Their performance on the posttest may be more reflec-tive of motivational deficits than of strategy deficits.

Self-Report Measures

The self-report measures were scored according to predetermined keys and a total score was created for each individual on each test. The pre, post, and "change" (from pre- to postcourse administration) score means and standard deviations for the four self-report measures are presented in Table 1.4. The different sample sizes reflected in Table 1.4 are a conse-quence of the fact that uncompleted self-report inventories were not scored. Because there were initial mean differences between the two groups of participants, all statistical analyses were performed on the mean changes from pre- to postadministration.

The two-tailed t tests comparing the pre- to postcourse scores of class members with those of the controls reached significance on three of the measures: Survey of Study Habits and Attitudes, $t (39) = 2.57, p < .02$; The test anxiety scale, $t (45) = 3.57, p < .01$; the learning attitude inven-tory, $t (48) = 3.57, p < .01$. The t test approached significance on the concentration questionnaire, $t (44) = 1.55, p < .12$. In all cases the class members reported greater positive changes on academically related dimen-sions than did the self-report controls.

These results may, however, have been confounded by either or both of the following factors. First, because the class members were generally lower than the controls on the premeasures, the significant effects may have been due to "regression toward the mean." The power of this type of explana-tion is substantially diminished in the present case because previous ad-ministrations have shown that these four measures are typically very reliable. In addition, on the Survey of Study Habits and Attitudes, the class

TABLE 1.4
Means and Standard Deviations of the Pre-, Post-, and Change Scores for the Four Self-Report Measures

	Brown–Holtzman survey of study habits and attitudes			Modified test anxiety scale (lower score indicates lower anxiety)		
	Precourse	Postcourse	Change from pre- to post-	Precourse	Postcourse	Change from pre- to post-
Strategy class members	$\bar{X} = 24.7$ $SD = 10.3$ $N = 25$	$\bar{X} = 29.9$ $SD = 11.1$ $N = 25$	$\bar{X} = 5.2$ $SD = 6.3$ $N = 25$	$\bar{X} = 85.6$ $SD = 21.8$ $N = 33$	$\bar{X} = 71.2$ $SD = 22.3$ $N = 33$	$\bar{X} = -14.3$ $SD = 19.6$ $N = 33$
Self-report controls	$\bar{X} = 27.0$ $SD = 9.5$ $N = 16$	$\bar{X} = 26.7$ $SD = 9.3$ $N = 16$	$\bar{X} = -.3$ $SD = 6.9$ $N = 16$	$\bar{X} = 69.3$ $SD = 16.5$ $N = 14$	$\bar{X} = 69.8$ $SD = 20.6$ $N = 14$	$\bar{X} = .5$ $SD = 10.8$ $N = 14$

	Concentration questionnaire			Learning attitude inventory		
	Precourse	Postcourse	Change from pre- to post-	Precourse	Postcourse	Change from pre- to post-
Strategy class members	$\bar{X} = 174.0$ $SD = 37.7$ $N = 34$	$\bar{X} = 188.4$ $SD = 31.7$ $N = 34$	$\bar{X} = 14.3$ $SD = 27.5$ $N = 34$	$\bar{X} = -8.3$ $SD = 10.9$ $N = 34$	$\bar{X} = -3.2$ $SD = 11.8$ $N = 34$	$\bar{X} = 5.11$ $SD = 7.0$ $N = 34$
Self-report controls	$\bar{X} = 205.0$ $SD = 39.8$ $N = 12$	$\bar{X} = 204.8$ $SD = 31.1$ $N = 12$	$\bar{X} = -.2$ $SD = 26.9$ $N = 12$	$\bar{X} = -.4$ $SD = 10.9$ $N = 16$	$\bar{X} = -2.8$ $SD = 11.8$ $N = 16$	$\bar{X} = -2.4$ $SD = 6.2$ $N = 16$

members scored below controls on the pretest and above this group on the posttest. These results would not be expected if the only factor operating was regression toward the mean.

Another potential explanation for the results is that the class members may have been yeasaying on the postmeasures. The fact that the class members did not show significant changes on some of the items on these scales reduces the possibility that the group's responses to the postmeasures were artifactual.

Although the confounding factors cited above cannot be completely discounted, it seems very likely that the learning strategy training had a positive influence on the academic behavior and attitudes reflected in the four self-report measures.

Conclusions

The comprehension–retention and self-report results coupled with the positive feedback arising from the students' course evaluations indicate that the strategy system and training improved the students' learning behaviors and attitudes. In addition to making the formal assessments, participants in the strategy training program were also asked to rate informally the perceived value of each strategy component and to make suggestions for improvement. Although all components were rated positively, networking, concentration management, and the MURDER routine received the highest ratings. Eventually each of the components will be evaluated independently. At this time studies on networking and concentration have been completed. These two studies will be reported briefly in the next two sections.

EVALUATION OF NETWORKING AS AN AID TO COMPREHENSION, RETENTION, AND RETRIEVAL

The evaluation of the learning strategies course presented above indicated that networking appeared to be a promising comprehension–retention substrategy. However, it is very difficult to determine the direct impact of networking on the results. This is primarily due to the fact that networking was embedded in a larger training program. In order to achieve a purer assessment of networking, the following study was designed to evaluate this substrategy in isolation.

The expectation for the present study was that networking training would assist students in the assimilation and retention of the main ideas in a 3000-word prose passage in comparison with a control group using their normal techniques. In order to assess this hypothesis, four dependent tests were utilized: concept CLOZE and essay exams to measure comprehension–retention of main ideas, and short-answer and multiple-choice exams to measure comprehension–retention of details.

Method

Participants

Forty-four students were recruited from a general psychology class. Each student received experimental participation credit and a $5 fee. Twenty-one students received approximately 5½ hours of network training, while the 23 remaining students served as a no-treatment control group. A total of 6 students failed to complete the dependent measures and consequently were dropped from the experiment (4 in the treatment group and 2 in the no-treatment control group). Mean grade point averages for the networking ($N = 17$) and control ($N = 21$) groups were 2.81 and 2.88, respectively. The scores ranged from 1.93 to 3.90 for the former group and from 1.93 to 3.96 for the latter.

Procedure

The networking group participated in the following sequence of sessions:

Session 1. The students received a general introduction to the strategy, training on the links and structure names, practice on networking sentences, and an overview of networking as a general retrieval strategy.

Session 2. The students were introduced to the use of the hierarchical structure in developing a general-purpose organizing framework, and they were given practice on networking a series of 500–1000 word passages (experimenter-generated networks were provided as feedback during this exercise).

Session 3. The students were first given an additional practice passage exercise and then given the opportunity to practice networking on their regular general psychology textbooks.

Session 4. The students continued to practice on their own materials. They were also provided with a short review lecture on the networking procedure.

Session 5. The students completed a short prestudy questionnaire and spent 1 hour studying a 3000-word passage extracted from an introductory geology textbook (the content of this passage was unrelated to any of the practice materials used in prior sessions). The treatment group students were required to make maps of the material. These maps were collected for subsequent analysis.

Session 6. In this final session, which occurred 5 days after Session 5, the students were given 3 minutes to review the notes they had made during the previous session and then spent a total of 35 minutes taking multiple-choice (18 questions), CLOZE (7 questions; students were required to fill in important concepts that had been deleted from a paragraph summarizing the article), and short-answer (10 questions) exams over the geology passage. In addition, the students were required to summarize the passage in an essay (14 minutes).

The control group participated in two sessions identical to Sessions 5 and 6 just described. These students were instructed to use their normal methods in studying and testtaking.

Results and Discussion

All tests were scored without knowledge of group affiliation. The short-answer, multiple-choice, and CLOZE tests were scored in accord with predetermined keys. The essay test, which required the students to summarize the article, was scored for completeness and organization of the main ideas by a colleague not otherwise involved with the experiment (completeness and ideal organization were determined a priori). To assess reliability, the essay tests were independently scored by one of the authors. A Pearson product–moment correlation of .86 between the two sets of scores was judged to represent an adequate degree of interrater reliability. Raw scores were converted into percentages of the maximum possible on each test.

Examination of the notes taken during the study session (Session 5) by the networkers indicated that all of the participants correctly applied the mapping technique to the material.

The data from the four tests were subjected to a principal component factor analysis and the emergent factors were then rotated. The loadings of the two-factor Varimax solution are reported in Table 1.5. The pattern of loadings suggests that the multiple-choice and short-answer tests were highly related to Factor 1 and that the essay and CLOZE tests were highly related to Factor 2. This provides some validation for the a priori categorization of these tests presented in the introduction. To increase reliability and to facilitate subsequent communication, the multiple-choice and short-answer tests were summed to form one dependent measure (labeled ''details''), and the CLOZE and essay tests were summed to form another (labeled ''main ideas'').

TABLE 1.5
Factor Loadings for the Four Exams After Varimax Rotation.[a]

	Factor 1: "Details"	Factor 2: "Main Ideas"
Essay	.41	.64
CLOZE		.89
Short answer	.90	.20
Multiple choice	.83	—

[a] Loadings less than .17 are not reported.

The means and standard deviations for the networking and control groups on the dependent measures are presented in Table 1.6. A Hotelling T^2 test of the comparison between the two groups on the two dependent measures ("details" and "main ideas") was significant: $T^2 (2,35) = 2.62$, $p < .05$. Univariate tests were conducted in order to isolate the loci of between-group differences. The one-tailed t tests indicated that the networking group significantly outperformed the control group on the "main ideas" dependent measure: $t (36) = 1.91, p < .03$. The comparison on the dependent measure to assess details was not significant: $t(36) = .06$, $p < .91$.

This pattern of results suggests that networking assists students in acquiring and organizing the main ideas but does not necessarily help in the acquisition of details. The major differences between the groups occurred on the essay and summary CLOZE tests, both of which assessed retention of the main ideas. No differences occurred on the multiple-choice and short-answer tests, which were designed to assess detailed knowledge of the passage material. Since these measures have been shown to be sensitive to treatment effects in prior research (Dansereau, 1978), this lack of significance further suggests that the differences on the "main ideas" dimension are not caused by placebo factors.

In order to determine whether the networking treatment differentially impacted on students differing in academic achievement, the networking and control groups were divided into subgroups of students with high and low grade point averages (see Table 1.7). A series of 2 × 2 factorial analyses of variance (networking–control × high–low grade point average) were run on the two dependent measures ("main ideas" and "details") in order to assess the presence of interactions (treatment main effects were not of interest at this point since they had been evaluated in prior analyses). The results of these two-way analyses indicated that there was a significant interaction on the "details" measure— $F (1,34) = 4.25, p < .05$—and that all other interactions were nonsignificant. Examination of Table 1.7 indicates that on this measure networking students with low GPAs substan-

TABLE 1.6

Means and Standard Deviations for the Treatment and Control Groups on the Dependent Measures[a]

| | | Measure | |
Group		"Main Ideas"	"Details"
Networking (N = 17)	$\bar{X}$	63.21	40.08
	SD	20.71	10.17
Control (N = 21)	$\bar{X}$	47.15	39.83
	SD	28.07	14.99

[a] Scores are reported in percentages.

TABLE 1.7

Means and Standard Deviations for the Treatment and Control Subgroups on the Two Dependent Measures[a] and Grade Point Average

| | | Measure | | |
Group		"Main Ideas"	"Details"	GPA
Networking				
Low GPA				
subgroup (N = 9)	$\bar{X}$	62.53	43.17	2.34
	SD	20.34	11.84	.23
High GPA				
subgroup (N = 8)	$\bar{X}$	63.97	36.61	3.28
	SD	21.09	6.26	.35
Control				
Low GPA				
subgroup (N = 11)	$\bar{X}$	40.46	34.94	2.45
	SD	27.93	13.56	.31
High GPA				
subgroup (N = 10)	$\bar{X}$	54.51	45.21	3.31
	SD	26.32	14.65	.34

[a] Scores are reported in percentages.

tially outperformed the control students with low GPAs, whereas the reverse held for students with high GPAs. Although nonsignificant, a different pattern of interaction occurred on the "main ideas" measure. On this measure the two networking groups were equal and both were superior to the control group(s). As expected, the high GPA control group substantially outperformed the low GPA control group.

One possible explanation of the results is that the high GPA networking students already had effective learning strategies prior to training. Consequently, they were probably less motivated to learn the new technique and may have found it more interfering because of its competition with their typical approaches. Low GPA networkers, on the other hand, not already having effective learning strategies, were more likely to be motivated to learn the technique and perhaps found it less interfering with their normal methods. Further research will be conducted to shed light on this potential achievement × treatment interaction.

Approximately 17 out of 21 of the control subjects produced notes during the study session. Examination of these sets of notes indicated that all sets were congruent with the organization of the text and consisted primarily of verbatim reproductions of main ideas. This is in marked contrast to the notes of the networking subjects. The notes of this group were organized in two dimensions and bore little relationship to the linear organization provided by the text. Consequently the better performance of the networking group on the "main ideas" factor supports and expands prior research on reorganization and encoding variability (see Shimmerlik, 1978).

EVALUATION OF ALTERNATIVE CONCENTRATION MANAGEMENT TECHNIQUES

Many students have stated that concentration difficulties strongly affect their ability to comprehend, retain, and retrieve academic materials. Although the concentration management component was not formally assessed in the learning strategies course, informal, subjective evaluations elicited from the participants indicated that this component was well received.

Further, observations by the instructors and suggestions from the participants provided a number of directions for modifications. Consequently, the present study was designed to examine two alternative concentration management strategies, singly and in combination, that would potentially ameliorate the negative effects of nonconstructive affect on comprehension, retention, and retrieval.

One strategy, self-initiated relaxation (SIR), required the student to learn and use a combination of relaxation techniques (i.e., progressive relaxation [Jacobsen, 1938], and breath-counting [Naranjo & Ornstein, 1971]) to set and maintain constructive study and test-taking states (moods). The second strategy, self-coaching (SC), was an extension of the positive self-talk techniques created by Meichenbaum and Goodman (1971). Using the analogy of an athletic coach as a framework, students were taught to coach (talk) themselves into constructive study and test-taking states and to maintain these states by monitoring and counteracting distractions. Finally, a third strategy was created that combined self-initiated relaxation with self-coaching (SIR + SC). In this strategy the self-coach had available self-talk and relaxation strategies to create and maintain constructive internal states.

Method

Participants

Eighty-two students were recruited from general psychology classes. Each student received experimental participation credit and a $3 fee. A total of nine students were dropped from the experiment because of invalid data. This led to the following distribution of students in the four groups: (a) self-initiated relaxation ($N = 17$); (b) self-coaching ($N = 19$); (c) self-initiated relaxation plus self-coaching ($N = 17$); (d) no-treatment control ($N = 20$). The mean cumulative grade point averages (GPAs) computed prior to the experiment for the four groups are presented in Table 1.8. A one-way analysis of variance indicated that there were no significant differences between groups on GPA: $F(3,69) = 41$, $p = .75$.

Procedure

The three treatment groups were given 2½ hours of training. This training included rationale, instructor-guided exercises, examples portraying effective use of the strategy, and practice implementing the technique. Following training, all four groups studied a 3000-word passage extracted from an undergraduate geology textbook (labeled "geology") under non-distracting conditions for 60 minutes. In addition, they studied a 1200-word passage on the biological effect of pressure (labeled "pressure") under intermittent auditory distraction (a tape recording of conversations; average "on" time 30 seconds, average "off" time 1 minute) for 20 minutes. Five days after studying, all participants were tested over both passages. The geology test consisted of three subtests: short-answer,

TABLE 1.8
Means and Standard Deviations for the Four Groups on Grade Point Average

| | GPA | |
Group	$\bar{X}$	SD
Self-initiated relaxation (SIR)	2.88	.67
Self-coaching (SC)	2.93	.74
Self-initiated relaxation + self coaching (SIR + SC)	3.11	.60
No-treatment control	2.93	.54

multiple-choice, and CLOZE; the pressure test consisted of short-answer questions.

Results

All four comprehension–retention tests were scored according to predetermined keys without knowledge of group affiliation. Because of initial between-group mean differences in grade point average (GPA), which, although nonsignificant, could potentially influence scores on the dependent measures (see Table 1.8), four analyses of covariance were conducted. The adjusting variable (covariate) used in these analyses was GPA; the independent variable was group affiliation, and the dependent variables were the scores on each of the four comprehension–retention tests. The analyses of covariance indicated that mean differences between the groups were significant with the geology multiple-choice test—F (3,68) = 3.71, $p < .025$—and the CLOZE test—F (3,68) = 3.14, $p < .05$—and that group differences approached significance with the pressure short-answer test—F (3,68) = 2.11, $p = .108$. There were no significant differences on the geology short-answer test—F (3,68) = .29, $p = .83$. The means for the four groups on the three geology tests and the pressure short-answer test are presented in Table 1.9.

Tukey's post hoc comparison procedure (Kirk, 1968) was used to analyze further the mean differences on the geology multiple-choice and CLOZE tests. On the multiple-choice test, the performance of the self-initiated relaxation plus self-coaching (SIR + SC) group was significantly better than that of the self-initiated relaxation (SIR) group. No other differences reached significance using the Tukey post hoc procedure. (Note: Examination of the data employing Duncan's Multiple Range Test [Kirk, 1968] indicated that the performance of the SIR + SC group was also significantly better than that of the control group.) On the CLOZE test, the SIR + SC group significantly outperformed the control group. All other differences were nonsignificant.

The concentration questionnaire administered to all groups during the last session contained 28 scaled items designed to tap attitudes and behaviors related to concentration during normal studying and test taking. A total score was created for each participant on this questionnaire by summing the scores of the responses to each question. (Certain item responses were reflected to maintain a consistent scoring direction.) High scores indicated positive attitudes and constructive behaviors.

An analysis of covariance (again using GPA as the covariate) performed on this data was significant: F (3,68) = 2.79, $p < .05$. A Tukey's post hoc procedure indicated that the SC group had a significantly higher mean

TABLE 1.9
Unadjusted and Adjusted Means for the Four Groups on the Geology and Pressure-Dependent Measures

| | Geology | | | | Pressure[a] | | | |
| | Multiple choice (max. = 35) | | CLOZE (max. = 10) | | Short answer (max. = 52) | | Short answer (max. = 25) | |
Group	Mean unadjusted	Mean adjusted for covariate	Mean unadjusted	Mean adjusted for covariate	Mean unadjusted	Mean adjusted for covariate	Mean unadjusted	Mean adjusted for covariate
SIR (N = 17)	21.82	22.07	5.88	5.95	16.38	16.85	5.74	5.92
SC (N = 19)	23.79	23.89	6.63	6.66	18.25	18.45	6.42	6.50
SIR + SC (N = 17)	27.23	26.76	7.65	7.51	19.65	18.74	8.32	7.96
No-treatment control (N = 20)	23.70	23.79	5.60	5.63	17.18	17.36	4.95	5.02

[a] Studied under auditory distraction.

score than the control group; all other mean differences were nonsignificant. Means for the four groups on the concentration questionnaire are presented in Table 1.10.

Discussion

The results indicate that the self-initiated relaxation plus self-coaching strategy was successful in facilitating performance on the comprehension–retention tests under both distracting and nondistracting conditions. Subjective reports elicited from students participating in the treatment groups indicated that the training and strategies were perceived as valuable. Many of the participants stated that they would continue to use the strategies in their normal studying.

GENERAL CONCLUSIONS AND FUTURE DIRECTIONS

A learning strategy system composed of primary and support strategies was developed. In addition, a set of training procedures was created to facilitate the communication of this system to college-age students. This system was assessed in the context of a 15-week (2½ hours per week) learning strategies course. The objective and subjective results of this assessment indicated that the strategies and training had a positive impact on the behaviors and attitudes of the participating students. Informal evaluations and observations were made to determine directions for modifications and to specify which components were most potent. As a consequence of these analyses, two studies were conducted to provide further information on the networking strategy and alternative concentration management techniques. Both studies provided positive support for the effectiveness of the particular substrategies.

After additional component assessment studies have been conducted, the

TABLE 1.10

Unadjusted and Adjusted Means for the Four Groups on the Concentration Questionnaire

Group	Concentration questionnaire	
	Mean unadjusted	Mean adjusted for covariate
SIR ($N = 17$)	151.02	151.32
SC ($N = 19$)	163.58	163.71
SIR + SC ($N = 17$)	156.01	155.44
No-treatment control ($N = 20$)	145.56	145.68

strategies will be modified further and resynthesized. The resulting strategy system will then be assessed in the context of an intensive, 15-hour workshop.

REFERENCES

Anderson, J. R. A simulation model of free recall. In G. H. Bower (Ed.), *The psychology of learning and motivation* (Vol. 5). New York: Academic Press, 1972.

Anderson, J. R., & Bower, G. H. *Human associative memory*. Washington, D.C.: Winston, 1973.

Bereiter, C. Some persisting dilemmas in measurement of change. In C. W. Harris (Ed.), *Problems in measuring change*. Madison: University of Wisconsin Press, 1963.

Bodden, J. L., Osterhouse, R., & Gelso, C. The value of a study skills inventory for feedback and criterion purposes in an educational skills course. *Journal of Educational Research,* 1972, *65* (7), 309–311.

Bower, G. H. Mental imagery and associative learning. In L. Gregg (Ed.), *Cognition of learning and memory*. New York: Wiley, 1972.

Briggs, R. D., Tosi, D. J., & Norley, R. M. Study habit modification and its effect on academic performances: A behavioral approach. *Journal of Educational Research,* 1971, *64* (8), 347–350.

Brown, R., & McNeil, D. The "tip of the tongue" phenomenon. *Journal of Verbal Learning and Verbal Behavior,* 1966, *5,* 325–337.

Brown, W. F., & Holtzman, W. H. *Survey of study habits and attitudes* (Form C). New York: The Psychological Corporation, 1966.

Brown, W. F., Webe, N. O., Zunker, V. G., & Haslam, W. L. Effectiveness of student to student counseling dropouts. *Journal of Educational Psychology,* 1971, *62,* 258–289.

Collins, K. W. *Control of affective responses during academic tasks.* Unpublished master's thesis, Texas Christian University, 1978.

Craik, F. I. M., & Lockhart, R. S. Levels of processing: A framework for memory research. *Journal of Verbal Learning and Verbal Behavior,* 1972, *11,* 671–684.

Dansereau, D. F. The development of a learning strategies curriculum. In H. F. O'Neil, Jr. (Ed.), *Learning strategies*. New York: Academic Press, 1978.

Dansereau, D. F., Actkinson, T. R., Long, G. L., & McDonald, B. *Learning strategies: A review and synthesis of the current literature* (AFHRL-TR-74-70, Contract F41609-74-C-0013). Lowry Air Force Base, Colorado, 1974. (AD-A007722)

Dansereau, D. F., Long, G. L., McDonald, B., & Actkinson, T. R. *Learning strategy inventory development and assessment* (AFHRL-TR-75-40, Contract F41609-74-C-0013). Brooks Air Force Base, Texas, 1975.

Dansereau, D. F., Long, G. L., McDonald, B., Actkinson, T. R., Ellis, A. M., Collins, K. W., Williams, S., & Evans, S. H. *Effective learning strategy training program; Development and assessment* (AFHRL-TR-75-41, Contract F41609-74-C-0013). Lowry Air Force Base, Colorado, 1975. (AD-A014722)

Del Giorno, W., Jenkins, J. R., & Bausell, R. B. Effects of recitation in the acquisition of prose. *Journal of Educational Research,* 1974, *67,* 293–294.

Diekhoff, G. M. *The node acquisition and integration technique: A node–link based teaching/ learning strategy.* Paper presented at the annual meeting of the American Educational Research Association, New York, April 6, 1977.

Ellis, A. *Reason and emotion in psychotherapy*. New York: Lyle Stuart, 1963.

Garland, J. C. *The development and assessment of an imagery based learning strategy program to improve the retention of prose material.* Unpublished master's thesis, Texas Christian University, 1977.

Hart, J. T. Memory and the feeling of knowing experience. *Journal of Educational Psychology,* 1965, *56,* (1), 22–30.

Haslam, W. L., & Brown, W. F. Effectiveness of study skills instruction for high school sophomores. *Journal of Educational Psychology,* 1968, *59,* 223–226.

Huck, S. W., & McLean, R. A. Using a repeated measures ANOVA to analyze the data from a pretest–posttest design: A potentially confusing task. *Psychological Bulletin,* 1975, *82,* 511–518.

Jacobsen, E. *Progressive relaxation.* Chicago: University of Chicago Press, 1938.

Kirk, R. G. *Experimental design: Procedures for the behavioral sciences.* Belmont, Calif.: Brooks/Cole, 1968.

Lawton, J. T., & Wanska, S. K. Advance organizers as a teaching strategy: A reply to Barnes and Clawson. *Review of Educational Research,* 1977, *47* (2), 233–244.

Lindsay, P. H. & Norman, D. A. *Human information processing: An introduction to psychology.* New York: Academic Press, 1972.

Long, G. L. *The development and assessment of a cognitive process based learning strategy training program for enhancing prose comprehension and retention.* Unpublished doctoral dissertation, Texas Christian University, 1976.

Lord, F. M. Elementary models for measuring change. In C. W. Harris (Ed.), *Problems in measuring change.* Madison: University of Wisconsin Press, 1963.

Maultsby, M. *Handbook of rational self-counseling.* Madison, Wisc.: Association for Rational Thinking, 1971.

Meichenbaum, D. H., & Goodman, J. Training impulsive children to talk to themselves: A means of self-control. *Journal of Abnormal Psychology,* 1971, *77,* 115–126.

Meichenbaum, D. H., & Turk, D. *The cognitive–behavioral management of anxiety, anger, and pain.* Paper presented at the Seventh Baniff International Conference on Behavioral Modification, Baniff, Canada, 1975.

Naranjo, C., & Ornstein, R. *On the psychology of meditation.* New York: Viking/Esalin, 1971.

Newell, A., Simon, H. A., & Shaw, J. D. Elements of a theory of human problem solving. *Psychological Review,* 1958, *65,* 151–166.

Norman, D. A., Genter, D. R., & Stevens, A. L. Comments on learning: Schemata and memory representation. In D. Klahr (Ed.), *Cognition and instruction.* Hillsdale, N.J.: Erlbaum Associates, 1976.

Overall, J. E., & Woodward, J. A. Unreliability of difference scores: A paradox for measurement of change. *Psychological Bulletin,* 1975, *82,* 85–86.

Overall, J. E., & Woodward, J. A. Reassertion of the paradoxical power of tests of significance based on unreliable difference scores. *Psychological Bulletin,* 1976, *83,* 776–777.

Quillian, M. R. The teachable language comprehender. *Communications of the Association for Computing Machinery,* 1969, *12,* 459–476.

Robinson, F. P. *Effective study.* New York: Harper and Brothers, 1946.

Rothkopf, E. Z. Learning from written instructive material: An exploration of the control of inspection behavior in test-like events. *American Educational Research Journal,* 1966, *3* (4), 241–249.

Rumelhart, D. E., Lindsay, P. H., & Norman, D. A. A process model for long-term memory. In E. Tulving & W. Donaldson (Eds.), *Organization of memory.* New York: Academic Press, 1972.

Sarason, I. G. Effect of anxiety, motivational instructions and failure on serial learning. *Journal of Experimental Psychology,* 1956, *51,* 253-260.

Shimmerlik, S. M. Organization theory and memory for prose: A review of the literature. *Review of Educational Research,* 1978, *48* (1), 103-120.

Van Zoost, F. L., & Jackson, B. T. Effects of self-monitoring and self-administered reinforcement on study behaviors. *Journal of Educational Research,* 1974, *67* (5), 216-218.

Whitehill, R. P. The development of effective learning skills programs. *Journal of Educational Research,* 1972, *65* (6), 281, 285.

Webster, H., & Bereiter, C. The reliability of changes measured by mental test scores. In C. W. Harris (Ed.), *Problems in measuring change.* Madison: University of Wisconsin Press, 1963.

Wolpe, J. *The practice of behavioral therapy.* New York: Pergamon, 1969.

Cognitive Learning Strategies:[1]
Verbal and Imaginal Elaboration

CLAIRE E. WEINSTEIN, VICKI L. UNDERWOOD,
FRANK W. WICKER, and WALTER E. CUBBERLY

In the past, instructional innovations and improvements have been primarily limited to the domains of curriculum development and delivery systems. However, recent findings reported in the literature by cognitive and instructional psychologists suggest that the role played by the individual student's information processing capabilities may be a critical factor for improving learning and retention skills. This change in conceptualization requires the reinstatement of the individual learner in our models of the learning act and the focusing of attention on the information processing capabilities that an individual brings to any learning or performance situation. Above all, many educators espouse the humanistic goal of teaching students to think for themselves in order that they may function in an independent and creative manner in work contexts. And yet many educational practices and technologies place learners in an essentially passive role in which they are expected to learn simply because they are told to do so—that is, to absorb information or skills automatically as a result of being exposed to the right teaching methods or curriculum.

A fundamental paradigm shift is taking place for both cognitive psychology and educational practice. Learning psychologists and educational psychologists have tended to view learning as the relatively automatic

[1] The research reported in this chapter was supported in part by Contract No. DAHC19–76–C–0026 with the Defense Advanced Research Projects Agency and monitored by the Army Research Institute for the Behavioral and Social Sciences. Views and conclusions contained in this chapter are those of the authors and should not be interpreted as necessarily representing the official policies, either expressed or implied, of the Defense Advanced Research Projects Agency, the Army Research Institute, or of the United States government.

COGNITIVE AND AFFECTIVE
LEARNING STRATEGIES

45

product of appropriate environmental or experimental circumstances that condition a new, or learned, response. Research and training efforts in both fields are moving away from a passive model of learning based on rather simple models of classical or instrumental conditioning. They are moving, via what Dember (1974) calls the "cognitive revolution" in psychology, toward a model of the learner as an active, self-determining individual who processes information in complex, often idiosyncratic ways that rarely can be predicted entirely in advance, represented in simple formulas, or wholly captured in conventional laboratory learning experiments. From this viewpoint, the learner actively employs complex learning or cognitive strategies that must be well in hand before confronting a new learning task. Learners are seen as active interpreters, processors and synthesizers of a continual barrage of information from the outside environment and from their own thinking processes. Thus, it becomes possible to focus analysis and research on the learner's ability to develop and use effective cognitive skills as well as on the impact of this usage for the training process. To date, however, educational research has contributed very little to our understanding of, or ability to foster, these essential cognitive, or learning, strategies.

Learning acts require the presence of several internal states in the learner, including information storage and retrieval capabilities, intellectual skills, and cognitive strategies (Gagné & Briggs, 1974). A learner must already possess certain information necessary for understanding new content. In addition, the learner needs a variety of intellectual skills in his repertoire such as problem-solving skills, concept acquisition skills, and discrimination learning skills. Cognitive learning strategies are needed to select and govern the learner's behavior in attending to the instructional situation, in managing the information storage and retrieval, and in developing the problem solution.

One way that learners can process to-be-learned information is through the use of cognitive elaboration. The use of this strategy requires a learner to create a symbolic construction that, when combined with the new information, makes this information more meaningful (Rohwer, 1970). For example, when learning from text, the learner could relate the material to previous knowledge either directly or by analogy. Alternatively, elaboration could involve creating logical relationships among components of the material or the drawing of inferences, or implications. One explanation for the success of each of these procedures is that they make the new information more meaningful by forming a relationship between the new, unfamiliar material and the old, already learned information.

Studies by Atkinson and Raugh (1975), Borkowski and Kamfonick (1972), Borkowski, Levers, and Gruenenfelder (1976), Butterfield, Wambold, and Belmont (1973), Danner and Taylor (1973), MacMillan (1970),

Rohwer and Ammon (1971), Ross (1971), Ross, Ross, and Downing (1973), Senter and Hoffman (1976), Smith and Marshall (1976), Tversky and Teiffer (1976), and Yuille and Catchpole (1973, 1974) suggest that learners can be trained in the use of elaboration skills. Although this research has established the utility of mediational skills and the possibility of enriching an individual's repertoire through exposure or practice in their use, the studies of training effects have been limited in terms of the amount of practice time provided and the number of strategies taught, as well as the narrow definitions of the tasks and stimulus materials used. Highly similar content materials and tasks were employed for training as well as testing sessions. Thus, even when positive transfer of effects have been demonstrated, the data allow only limited generalizations of these findings by both the learners and the experimenters. This restricts the utility of these results in guiding the design of effective techniques to facilitate the development of mediational skills in deficient learners.

In addition, even in those studies in which the experimenters attempted to teach more than one type of strategy, the learners in any particular training group received instruction in the use of only one method. It is doubtful that any skilled learner relies on only one strategy to cope with the variety of learning tasks one must perform. An optimal training program for teaching learners to use generalizable cognitive skills would seem to require incorporating not only varied learning tasks and materials but also a variety of cognitive strategies. In this way it is hoped that they will not only learn the particular strategies taught to them but also learn to generate their own strategies.

In a preliminary study designed to investigate these issues, Weinstein (1978) used a number of different cognitive strategies, learning tasks, and stimulus materials to train ninth graders in the use of generalizable elaboration skills. The cognitive strategies, drawn from the research literature in cognition and instruction, included various forms of verbal and imaginal elaboration. The learning activities included traditional laboratory tasks, such as paired-associate learning, and everyday school tasks, such as reading comprehension. The learning materials were selected from appropriate curriculum materials in a variety of academic disciplines.

Seventy-five ninth-grade students were randomly assigned to one of three groups: training–experimental, control, or posttest only. Students in the experimental group participated in a series of five 1-hour elaboration skill training sessions, administered at approximtely 1-week intervals. Students were exposed to a set of 19 learning tasks. They were required to create a series of elaborators, or mediational aids, for each of these tasks. Experimenter-provided directions for the early tasks emphasized the properties of an effective elaborator. The later training sessions provided opportunities for additional practice in using these skills with little or no experimenter-provided instructions. Students in the control group were exposed to the same stimulus materials but their task was simply to learn the information without any type of strategy prompts or directions. A posttest-only group was not exposed to the stimulus materials but did participate in the posttesting sessions. The immediate posttest was administered 1 week after the conclusion of the training and the delayed posttest was administered approximately 1 month later. Both immediate and delayed posttests consisted of reading comprehension, free recall, paired-associate, and serial recall tasks.

The results of the data analyses for the immediate posttest revealed significant differences among group means on the free recall task and Trial 2 of the paired-associate learning task. In each instance the experimental group's performance surpassed the performance of the control and posttest only, which did not differ significantly from each other. On the delayed posttest a significant difference was obtained for the reading comprehension task and Trial 1 of the serial learning task. Again these differences favored the experimental group. It seemed that students could learn to utilize these elaboration strategies in a variety of task situations, but further research was still required to determine the optimal conditions of their learning and use.

Our current research and development effort is part of the Cognitive Learning Strategies Project located at the University of Texas at Austin. The project personnel are involved in a series of studies designed to further both our understanding of the covert processes underlying the use of cognitive strategies and the procedures required to enhance an individual's strategy repertoire.

The purpose of this chapter is to describe the progress we made during the initial phases of this project. During these initial stages a series of interrelated exploratory experimental and demonstration studies was conducted. Several of these studies will be discussed.

EXPLORATORY STUDIES

The first step in the development of a cognitive learning strategies training program was to determine exactly what strategies are used by effective learners. Semi-structured interviews were conducted with 72 junior- and senior-level students enrolled in a teacher education course at the University of Texas at Austin. A total of 15 learning tasks were created for this study. The students were randomly assigned to three groups, each of which received a different subset of the learning tasks to perform. Each student was given 5 tasks using the following materials: two different paired-associate lists, two different free recall lists, and one reading. As students studied the materials, they were to write down the methods, processes, or mental tricks they used to learn the information contained, as well as any other methods they thought might be helpful. The interviewer then discussed in detail the specific methods identified by each student.

Eight different learning methods were identified:

1. Using study skills, practicing, or production—for example, rereading, rewriting, note taking, underlining, and reviewing
2. Using physical word similarities and differences—for example, noting similarities in spelling and counting syllables
3. Selecting a part of the words or reading—for example, using abbreviations or acronyms and abstracting main ideas
4. Creating mental images
5. Using meaningful elaboration—relating material to previous knowledge or experience and analyzing logical relationships
6. Finding meaningful similarities and differences
7. Creating a phrase or sentence and paraphrasing
8. Categorizing

From these data, the Learning Activities Questionnaire was developed to gather information about the use of learning strategies by people in different settings and at different educational levels. There are seven different learning activities that serve as stimulus materials for the questionnaire. These tasks had elicited the greatest range of different learning methods in the interview study. These activities include three paired-associate learning tasks, two free recall tasks, and two reading comprehension tasks.

The questionnaire has three sections. In Part I, the learners are asked to study each of the learning activities and then respond to a series of open-ended questions about the methods they might use to remember the material. In Part II, the learners are asked to review the learning activities, but this time they simply use check marks to indicate which examples from a set of provided methods (drawn from the eight categories just described) they would use to remember the materials. Part III asks the learners to indicate any other methods they might use to learn or remember materials in textbooks, novels, newspapers, magazines, or work-related materials.

The Learning Activities Questionnaire has been pilot-tested with several groups of students. Revisions were made to increase readability and to make the questionnaire more manageable. In addition, subsequent administrations indicated that the information obtained from Parts II and III was redundant with that obtained from the open-ended questions in Part I. However, for every group of learners to whom the questionnaire has been administered, the number of strategies checked in Part II has greatly exceeded the number of strategies reported on the open-ended questions in Part I for each learning activity. In Part I the learners are asked to create a list of strategies, whereas in Part II they are asked to select the strategies they would use from a provided list. Though the differences between the results obtained with these two approaches may be due to the differing task demands, debriefing sessions with a number of the participants indicated that social desirability was a potent factor. In addition, many individuals, when completing Part II, checked any strategy they thought would be useful for learning rather than the ones they would actually use. These findings cast additional doubt on the validity of using checklists in this type of research. For these reasons, Parts II and III of the questionnaire have since been deleted.

Data have been gathered on the types of strategies used by graduate students, community college students, and three groups of Army recruits possessing either a high school diploma, a general education diploma, or no diploma. Because of overlapping classifications, the results were synthesized into five different categories of strategies instead of the eight original categories used to code the data from the interview study. These were

1. Rote strategies—strategies that emphasized repetition
2. Physical strategies—any strategy that involved using the physical properties of the material to be learned, such as spelling patterns
3. Imaginal elaboration—any strategy involving the formation of a mental picture in order to learn the material
4. Verbal elaboration—actively working with the material by asking and answering questions about it, determining implications of the content, relating it to information already known, etc.
5. Grouping—rearranging the material to be learned into smaller subsets according to some perceived characteristic that is commonly shared

The patterns found in the data are fairly consistent. Both college student groups reported using a variety of strategies. The graduate students reported a greater number of verbal and imaginal elaboration strategies than the community college students, but both groups also reported using a number of less effective rote strategies. The noncollege groups reported using fewer types of strategies than any of the college groups, and many of the recruits in these groups reported using no strategies or only rote strategies.

For example, in Part I of the questionnaire the learners must describe the methods or strategies they would use to learn the material for paired-associate, free recall, and reading comprehension tasks. On the free recall task there were significant differences between the groups on the number of reported strategies in the various categories. Whereas 83% of the graduate students reported using verbal elaboration strategies to help them learn this material, only 41% of the community college students reported using one or more verbal elaboration strategies. In the high school group 27% of the recruits reported using this method, compared with 34% of the general-education-diploma group and 24% of the no-high-school group. A similar pattern was obtained when we examined the results for the paired-associate learning tasks.

For the reading comprehension tasks, rote strategies were further subdivided into the categories of passive versus active. An example of a passive rote strategy would be simply repeating the material, but paraphrasing would be an active rote strategy. The other categories—use of physical characteristics, imaginal elaboration, and verbal elaboration—are the same as defined previously. The results for reading comprehension were somewhat different from those for the free recall and paired-associate tasks. The graduate student group reported the highest usage of the learning strategies, including passive and active rote strategies. The community college group reported using fewer strategies overall than the graduate students, but included similar usage of verbal and imaginal elaboration strategies and a lower usage of physical characteristics and both types of rote strategies. The high school and general-education-diploma groups, when compared with the community college group, reported a similar number of active rote strategies, but lower usage of the other strategies. The no-degree group reported high usage of passive rote strategies and a lower number of other strategies.

The data obtained from the Learning Activities Questionnaire indicate that there are significant differences between groups of learners in the kinds of strategies they employ to learn. Our next tasks were to investigate the cognitive processes underlying these strategies and to develop training programs to teach them to less skilled learners.

EXPERIMENTAL STUDIES INVESTIGATING INSTRUCTIONAL VARIABLES, TYPES OF TRAINING, AND PERFORMANCE ASSESSMENT MEASURES

In order to identify the conditions necessary for effective and efficient training of different groups in the use of cognitive learning strategies, a series of experiments was designed to investigate several relevant instructional variables. These variables included length of training, type of training, use of feedback, sequencing of tasks, and performance assessment measures. Several of these studies will be discussed.

Training versus Instruction: How Much Is Enough?

The first study that we conducted in our investigation of instructional variables examined the relative effectiveness of training students in the use of the method of loci, a cognitive mnemonic strategy, versus simply instructing students in its use. The method of loci was selected because it is a well-documented memory aid with a fairly standardized set of instructions. Thus we could anticipate that the instructions would be effective in improving performance. The question of interest was whether additional training in the use of this method would significantly improve performance above the level achieved by instructions only. Using the method of loci involves the selection of a series of imaginary loci, or places. These places can be around the home or neighborhood, or they can be along a commonly taken route. After memorizing these locations, the student can learn and remember lists of words by associating one word with each of the memory locations. This second part of the process is achieved by creating a clear, novel mental image or picture of the object or idea represented by each word. The image must include the location used to store the word. In this way, as the learner mentally moves through the locations, he or she is able to recall the mental images and remember the words stored there.

Additionally, for this study, it was postulated that an elaborated version of this method involving the development of a story line including the loci would further assist recall, in spite of the additional memory burden this strategy might impose. This story line was expected to aid recall by having each location follow in a logical order related to the theme of the story created individually by each student. In summary, the purpose of the present study was to determine the relative effectiveness of training versus standard instructions in both elaborated and nonelaborated versions of the method of loci.

Method

Participants.   The 100 students who participated in this study were drawn from several sections of an introductory educational psychology course at the University of Texas at Austin. Participation in research was part of the course requirement.

Materials.   From the norms developed by Paivio, Yuille, and Madigan (1968), 120 words were divided into six lists of 20 words, with each list containing half high-concrete words (ratings in the range of 5.75–6.96 on a seven-point scale) and half low-concrete words (ratings in the range of

1.73–3.88 on a seven-point scale). In addition, the different word lists were matched for meaningfulness (values ranged from 5.0 to 6.0, representing the average number of associates given by an individual in a 1-minute period).

Design and Procedure.   The students were randomly divided into five groups of 20 students per group. All training and testing sessions were conducted in groups of four to seven individuals, and lasted for a period of 1 hour. In most of the previous studies involving the method of loci, the students were given instructions in the use of the technique, an opportunity to select their locations, a practice word list, and then a test to determine their level of mastery. For the standard instruction group, this procedure was used. After receiving these instructions, the students were asked to select a series of 20 memory locations, or loci, that they could use to remember a list of words. These loci had to be campus locations such as buildings, statues, offices, flagpoles, or other objects or places that they were familiar with on the university grounds. They were also reminded to make each location unique and distinct so that it would be easier for them to recall how to travel mentally from one location to the next in a logical and consistent order. Ten minutes were allowed for the students to create and memorize their series of locations.

After learning their loci the students practiced using the method with a list of 20 words. The words were presented at a 5-second rate on a Da-Lite screen using a Kodak slide projector with an automatic timing device. After studying the word list the students were given 3 minutes in which to recall the 20 words in the order of presentation.

Upon completion of the practice list the students were administered the posttest. The posttest consisted of using their series of loci to recall two additional lists of 20 words. The procedure used was the same as that used with the practice list. The words were presented at a 5-second rate and there was a 3-minute recall period. The test session for all four experimental groups followed the same procedure.

Students in the elaborated instruction group followed the same procedure but received additional instructions directing them to use the elaboration strategy of developing a story line while practicing the method of loci.

The training group received a separate 1-hour practice session prior to the test session. During this additional session they received the standard instructions for the method of loci, an opportunity to select locations on a route between their home and the campus, and three 20-word practice lists. Corrective feedback concerning use of the method was provided for each student after each practice list. The experimenter would discuss the locations selected by the students as well as the quality of the images they were creating. One week later these students returned for the test session.

The elaborated training group went through the same procedure as the training group, but during the training session they received additional instructions directing them to use the elaboration strategy of developing a story line while practicing the method of loci. Finally, students in the control group did not receive any mnemonic instructions or practice but did take the posttest. They were instructed to use whatever strategy they thought would work best during the serial recall task.

Results and Discussion

A three-way analysis of variance (groups × concreteness × lists) of the data resulted in a significant main effect of groups: $F(4,95) = 9.48$, $p < .001$. Newman–Keuls post hoc analysis indicated that the training, elaborated training, and elaborated instruction groups did not differ significantly, nor did the instruction and control groups, but the three former groups were significantly different from the two latter groups. Thus, training was shown to be more effective than standard instructions for using the method of loci. The finding that the instruction group did not perform significantly better than the control group is inconsistent with previous studies using the same procedures (Crovitz, 1969; Montague, 1972; Norman, 1976; Ross & Lawrence, 1968).

The addition of a story line did not affect the performance of the elaborated training group as compared to the training group but did increase the performance of the elaborated instruction group over that of the group receiving instructions only. In a 2 × 2 analysis of variance (training × elaboration) on the total scores over both lists, the interaction was significant: $F(1,96) = 5.43$, $p < .05$. It appears that either training (including practice), or elaborated instruction (through the use of a story line) will significantly improve performance with the method of loci when compared to instruction only. However, these effects may not be additive—the performance of students in the elaborated training group was not significantly different from those in either the training or elaborated instruction groups.

As expected, the main effect of concreteness—$F(1,95) = 27.21$, $p < .001$—reflected the superior recall of high- as compared to low-concrete words, and scores on List 2 were higher than those on List 1: $F(1,95) = 8.91$, $p < .01$. None of the two-way interactions were significant.

However, the three-way interaction of groups, concreteness, and lists was significant: $F(4,95) = 4.90$, $p < .01$. This interaction effect seems to be primarily due to the differential effects of practice on the instruction and control groups' performance with high- and low-concrete words (Figure 2.1). The control group evidenced the greatest increase from List 1

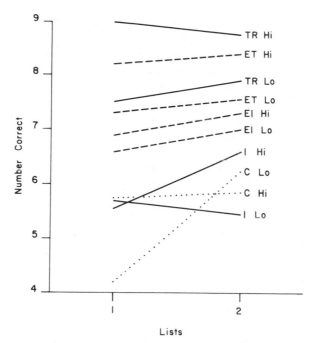

Figure 2.1 Interaction of groups, concreteness, and lists in the method of loci study for training and instruction alone (——), story elaboration (– – –), and control (· · ·). (TR = training, ET = elaborated training, I = instruction, EI = elaborated instruction, C = control; Hi and Lo refer to concreteness ratings of words).

to List 2 on the numbers of low-concrete words recalled, followed by the instruction group's increase in recall of high-concrete words.

In conclusion, there is some evidence that training, with practice, or elaboration through the addition of a story line can significantly improve the effectiveness of the method of loci. Further research is needed to determine the optimal techniques for training students to use this type of strategy.

Training versus Instruction: Cognitive Learning Strategies

Since the amount of training and practice students receive while learning the method of loci appears to be an important variable, a follow-up study was conducted to see whether training was important for other, more general, cognitive learning strategies. The three general strategies selected were mental imagery, meaningful elaboration, and grouping.

The cluster of strategies involving mental imagery calls for the learner to form a mental picture of the person, events, or information to be learned. Elaboration involves enhancing the meaningfulness of to-be-learned material by relating it to the learner's current cognitive structure. For example, a student or trainee reading through a passage might ask and answer such questions as, "What is the purpose of this material?" or "How does this relate to my experience, beliefs, and attitudes?" or "What are the logical relationships in the material?" or other similar questions designed to involve the learner in actively relating to the new information. Grouping, as used in this research, is actually a combination of strategies whereby the learner first categorizes the information according to meaningful relationships by putting similar materials together and then uses mental imagery or verbal elaboration to learn the elements of each category.

The purpose of this study was to investigate the relative effectiveness of an elaborated, long form of instruction versus a short form of instruction for teaching these three strategies.

Method

Participants.   The 36 participants who volunteered for this study were college students enrolled in freshmen English classes at the University of Texas at Austin. Two intact classes of 18 students each were used. One class was randomly chosen to be the instruction group, and the other the training group. Previous scores provided by the instructor indicated that these two groups were equivalent on various performance and departmental reading measures.

Materials.   A sample passage was used to familiarize the students with the cognitive strategies to be learned. The sample passage was taken from George Kneller's *Foundations of Education* (1971). In this portion of Kneller's work he challenges a number of fundamental issues in current American educational practice. This passage was selected to tap the students' interest in education and to foster their interest in the training program. The results from a pilot test had indicated that it was effective in achieving these goals.

In order to provide for additional practice and for testing purposes, several short reading passages were taken from the Science Research Associates (SRA) Lab IVa Rate Builder (1959) corresponding to ninth- and fourteenth-grade reading levels. The ninth-grade reading level passages were each about 225 words long, dealt with fairly concrete topics, were relatively unsophisticated in content, and consisted of commonly used words. The fourteenth-grade reading level passages were each about 400 words long, dealt with more abstract topics, were relatively sophisticated in content, and used a higher vocabulary level than the ninth-grade readings. For this study then, the ninth-grade-level readings were considered relatively easy, and the fourteenth-grade-level readings relatively difficult.

Two passages were selected for the training portion of this study. The first passage presented was an easy one dealing with the physical requirements for space travel. The second passage, a difficult reading, dealt with IQ.

The testing materials consisted of two passages, one ninth-grade-level reading dealing with child prodigies and one fourteenth-grade-level reading concerning the conflict between good and evil. The tests on these two readings were composed of 10 open-ended questions and 10 multiple-choice questions.

The multiple-choice questions were modifications of questions included with the SRA (1959) readings. Previous use of the SRA series questions in this type of research with college students often resulted in a ceiling effect. In an attempt to avoid a ceiling effect in this study and to achieve a sufficiently wide range of scores, the original multiple-choice items had been rewritten by the experimenters and then pilot-tested with a group of students similar to those participating in this study. The open-ended questions were created by the experimenters and were also pilot-tested. Both multiple-choice and open-ended questions were used in testing the effectiveness of the training variables in order to see whether there were any differences between the two groups in terms of recall (open-ended questions) versus recognition (multiple-choice questions).

Design and Procedure.   The training group participated in two 50-minute sessions. In the first session this group received the elaborated, long form of the instructions. This consisted of a description and explanation of the strategies, numerous examples of their use, instructions to practice the strategies, and provisions for the experimenter to provide feedback to the students concerning their level of mastery. The three strategies—mental imagery, meaningful elaboration, and grouping—were introduced and demonstrated one at a time using the sample passage from Kneller (1971). After the introduction of each new strategy, the students were instructed to practice this strategy on a portion of the sample passage. The students gave examples of their application of the strategy and received feedback from the experimenter as to the appropriateness of their examples. During the last part of the first session the students were given two practice readings, one easy (ninth-grade level) and one difficult (fourteenth-grade level). These materials were used to practice applying the strategies, as well as to receive additional feedback from the experimenter.

During the second session, the students were given a review of the strategy descriptions. Immediately following this they were given 3 minutes in which to study an easy reading. After this study interval they were administered posttests composed of 10 open-ended and 10 multiple-choice questions. Six minutes were allotted for the open-ended test and 3 minutes for the multiple-choice test. This procedure was then repeated with a difficult reading except that 7 minutes were allowed for the reading portion, 6 minutes for the open-ended test, and 4 minutes for the multiple-choice test.

The instruction group participated in only one session, which was the same as the second session for the training group. They received an explanation of the three strategies and examples of their use but did not practice the strategies or receive feedback from the experimenter. They were tested on the same easy and difficult readings as the training group and were provided with the same time limits. Because of the limited number of students available for this study and previous data indicating the effectiveness of the instructional materials, no control group was used.

Results and Discussion

A three-way analysis of variance (groups × reading difficulty × type of question) indicated that training in the use of cognitive learning strategies produced significantly better performance than did instruction only, $F(1,34) = 4.31$, $p < .05$. As expected, scores were higher on easy as compared with difficult readings—$F(1,34) = 70.16$, $p < .01$—and also higher on multiple-choice as compared with open-ended questions—$F(1,34) = 12.39$, $p < .01$.

The interaction of reading difficulty and type of question was significant—$F(1,34) = 12.20$, $p < .01$—indicating that the difference between multiple-choice and open-ended test scores was greater on the easy than on the difficult reading. The three-way interaction was also significant: $F(1,34) = 7.70$, $p < .01$. The training group scored slightly higher than the instruction group on both tests over the difficult reading and the multiple-choice test over the easy reading. However, on the open-ended test over the easy reading, the training group scored significantly higher than the instruction group (Figure 2.2). This suggests that training in the use of cognitive strategies is more helpful than simple instructions for **recall** of information from relatively easy text, but not more helpful for recognition of that same material.

The low scores of both groups on the tests over the difficult reading may reflect the presence of a floor effect. It was expected that the passage at the fourteenth-grade reading level (equivalent to the sophomore year of college) would be relatively difficult for these freshmen. For this reason, more time was allotted for reading the difficult passage and for answering the questions over it. However, these time limits may not have been sufficient for the students to use the strategies effectively with the more difficult reading materials.

An alternate hypothesis is that the amount of training provided may not have been sufficient for the strategies to be learned well enough to be used

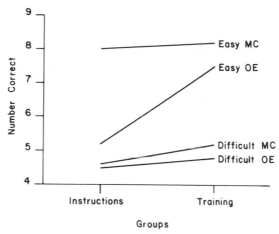

Figure 2.2 Interaction of groups, reading difficulty, and type of questions in the Training versus Instruction: Cognitive Learning Strategies study (MC = multiple-choice, OE = open-
ended).

by the students on difficult tasks. This is supported by the results for the
tests over the easy reading. On the simpler, multiple-choice questions the
scores of the training and instruction groups were very similar. However,
on the open-ended questions (requiring recall rather than recognition of the
material), the training group scored significantly above the instruction
group. Perhaps even more training and practice are needed for freshmen to
use these strategies with the fourteenth-grade-level reading materials.
Previous research by Weinstein (1978) indicated that reading comprehension scores of ninth graders trained to use cognitive learning strategies continued to increase after additional practice over time. Further research will
be necessary to determine whether additional training will produce performance improvements with difficult materials.

Thus, there has been some support from both the study on the method
of loci and the present investigation for the hypothesis that training, including practice and feedback, in the use of cognitive strategies does
significantly enhance the effectiveness of their use. Furthermore, there
were some indications from the results of the latter experiment that extensive training may be necessary to foster the optimal use of these strategies,
particularly when difficult material is to be learned.

TRAINING AND MATERIALS VARIABLES

At the same time that the foregoing studies were being conducted, a
similar series of experiments investigating other types of instructional

variables was in progress. The objective of this series of experiments was to determine the types of training and the sequences of materials presentation that would lead to the most efficient program of training in the use of cognitive learning strategies. The first study of this group tested the generalizability of training in the use of cognitive strategies across different types of learning tasks.

Type of Training Task

Method

Participants. The 75 students who participated in this study were drawn from several sections of an introductory educational psychology course at the University of Texas at Austin. Participation in research was part of their course requirement.

Materials. Four paired-associate lists of 10 noun pairs each were constructed using the norms provided by Paivio *et al.* (1968). List 1 was composed of high-concrete words (range: 4.75–7.00) of average meaningfulness (range: 4.00–6.50). List 2 included average-concrete words (range: 3.00–4.75) of high meaningfulness (range: 6.50 and above). List 3 consisted of low-concrete words (range: 1.00–3.00) of average meaningfulness (range: 4.00–6.50). List 4 was chosen randomly.

The reading selections were taken from the SRA (1959) materials corresponding to grade levels 8, 10, 12, and 14. The training materials included an eighth-grade reading about cars of the future, a tenth-grade reading concerning the balance of nature, a twelfth-grade reading about influenza epidemics, and a fourteenth-level reading that dealt with conceptions of time. The testing materials included a twelfth-grade reading about impulsive buying in supermarkets, a fourteenth-level reading concerning the nature of the human psyche, and the multiple-choice tests provided with each of these two readings in the SRA (1959) materials.

Design and Procedure. Students were assigned to one of three treatment conditions depending on the type of tasks they practiced: paired associates, readings, or a combination of paired associates and readings. Students were trained and tested in groups ranging in size from five to nine individuals. Each group was randomly assigned to one of the three treatment conditions. Students in the paired-associate group ($N = 25$) were trained in the use of cognitive strategies for paired-associate lists only. For the readings group ($N = 25$), short written passages were used to demonstrate and practice the strategies. For the combination group ($N = 25$), the strategies were demonstrated and practiced on both the paired-associate tasks and the written passages. All students were given the same posttest, which included a paired-associate task, a free recall task, and multiple-choice questions over two written passages.

The students were trained in the use of three different cognitive strategies—mental imagery, elaboration, and grouping—each of which was described to them as an aid in organizing, remembering, and adding meaning to the study materials.

These strategies were explained and demonstrated one at a time using a sample paired-associate list in the case of the paired-associate group, a sample reading in the case of the readings group, or both in the case of the combination group. Following the explanation of each strategy, the experimenter asked the students to use the strategy with the sample material and then asked the group for two or three examples of the aids they created. The experimenter provided feedback by commenting on the examples provided by the students, either by saying why it was a good example, or by elaborating on it to make a more appropriate example of the strategy under discussion. For the paired-associate group and the readings group, the strategies were discussed only once. For the combination group, however, each strategy was discussed twice, once in conjunction with paired-associate tasks and then in conjunction with written passages. After all three strategies had been presented, the students worked on the four practice tasks.

For the paired-associate group, the practice lists were presented in the same order as they were discussed in the materials section of this study. The students were allotted 8 minutes to practice using the three cognitive strategies to learn the word pairs in each list. The students in the readings group were given 10 minutes to practice using the strategies to learn the information contained in each of the four practice readings. More time was allotted for the reading tasks than the paired-associate tasks because data from a pilot study suggested that the reading tasks took longer to complete.

The combination group was also given four practice tasks. These were the second and fourth tasks from each of the other two groups. Students in this condition were first given a paired-associate task (List 2) and then the tenth-grade-level reading, followed by another paired-associate task (List 4) and the fourteenth-grade-level reading. They were given 8 minutes to practice the strategies on each paired-associate list and 10 minutes to practice the strategies on each reading.

At the beginning of the first practice task, students in each of the groups were instructed to try to use all three strategies—imagery, meaningful elaboration, and grouping—in learning the material. These instructions were repeated at the beginning of every practice task thereafter. In addition, the students were asked to write down the aids that they developed for the first two practice tasks. This procedure created an opportunity for the experimenter to provide feedback as to the appropriateness of each student's use of the strategies. The students were then asked to practice the use of the strategies mentally (i.e., without writing down their aids) on the last two practice tasks.

The testing phase began immediately after training was concluded. The four tasks used for testing were a paired-associate task, a free recall task, and two reading comprehension tasks.

For the paired-associate test, 40 nouns from the Paivio *et al.* (1968) norms were selected and paired at random, yielding 20 word pairs. The word pairs were presented one at a time on a Da-Lite screen using a Kodak slide projector with an automatic timing device. The study–test method was used with a 10-second exposure of each pair for the study portion and an 8-second exposure of the stimulus word for the test portion.

For the free recall test, 20 nouns were selected at random from the Paivio *et al.* (1968) norms. The words were presented one at a time by a slide projector, at a presentation rate of 6 seconds per word. After all 20 words were presented, the students were given 2 minutes to write down as many of the words as they could recall, regardless of order.

For the reading comprehension test, two reading selections were taken from the SRA (1959) materials. The first was a twelfth-grade-level reading and the second was a fourteenth-grade-level reading. The two readings each had 10 multiple-choice questions associated with them, and these were utilized as the test materials.

The students were each given a printed copy of the first reading selection and allowed 5 minutes to study the passage using the strategies they had learned. Then the readings were collected, and a sheet of 10 multiple-choice questions was given to each student. Students were given 2 minutes to answer the questions. The second reading, which was slightly longer than the first, was handed out and the students were given 6 minutes to study this passage. The reading was then collected and the sheet of questions for this reading was handed out. The students were given 3½ minutes to answer the questions. The times allowed for the study and test portions were established during pilot testing with a similar group of students. The entire session lasted approximately 2 hours, with the testing phase requiring 35 minutes of that time.

Results and Discussion

Analysis of variance of the test scores revealed no significant differences among the three treatment conditions on any of the tests. Although these results could indicate either no effects for any of the treatments or that students can readily generalize their improved skills, any conclusions must remain tentative because of the group performance patterns. On the first (easier) passage, group means indicated nearly perfect scores for all three of the treatment groups; on the more difficult reading nearly identical low mean scores were found (see Table 2.1). It is possible that the tests used, which were drawn without alteration from the SRA (1959) materials, may have been inappropriate in their level of difficulty for the students in this study. That is, there may have been a ceiling effect for the test over the easier reading and a floor effect for the test over the difficult reading. Consequently, for the studies that followed this one temporally (including the Training versus Instructions: Cognitive Learning Strategies study previously discussed), the experimenters designed and pilot-tested items specifically constructed for this project rather than relying on the standard questions.

In another study conducted following this one, the variables of difficulty and order of difficulty of training and testing materials were investigated to help determine the optimal parameters for a cognitive learning strategies training program.

Order of Training Materials

Method

Participants. A total of 50 students enrolled in several sections of an introductory course in educational psychology at the University of Texas at Austin participated in this research study as part of their course requirement.

TABLE 2.1

Means and Standard Deviations for the Three Experimental Groups in the Type of Training Task Study

Test	Maximum score	Group	N	Mean	SD
PAL	20	Paired-associate group	25	13.44	4.43
		Readings group	25	12.80	3.69
		Combination group	25	13.88	3.32
Free recall	20	Paired-associate group	25	11.20	3.55
		Reading group	25	11.20	2.48
		Combination group	25	12.40	2.57
Reading 1	10	Paired-associate group	25	9.60	.71
		Readings group	25	9.48	1.01
		Combination group	25	9.64	.64
Reading 2	10	Paired-associate group	25	5.36	1.50
		Readings group	25	5.36	1.75
		Combination group	25	5.28	1.40

Materials.   The practice and testing materials consisted of short passages taken from the SRA (1959) materials corresponding to ninth- and fourteenth-grade levels. Of the reading selections chosen at each of these grade levels, two were selected as practice passages and one was chosen as a test passage. The ninth-grade readings were designated as simple passages (S), and the fourteenth-level readings were designated as difficult passages (D).

The themes of the selected readings were varied to avoid special emphasis in any single content area. The first simple practice passage discussed tornadoes; the second pertained to the etymology of the word *satellite*. The first difficult practice reading concerned attitudes toward death in American culture; the second was concerned with the conflict of good and evil in world literature. The simple testing passage dealt with unusual plants that eat animals, and the difficult testing passage discussed the nature of the human psyche.

Accompanying the simple and the difficult test readings were two tests for each reading. These tests were composed of both open-ended questions and multiple-choice questions written by the experimenters and pilot-tested with students similar to those participating in this study. All four of the tests had 10 questions each.

All instructions were included in printed student packets. These packets included explanations of the cognitive learning strategies and examples of their use.

Design and Procedure.   The 50 students were randomly assigned to one of two treatment groups, which differed only in the order of presentation of the practice readings. The first group ($N = 23$) received the two simple passages followed by the two difficult passages (SSDD). The second group ($N = 27$) received the two difficult passages followed by the two simple passages (DDSS). The presentation order of passages within the same difficulty level was identical for both groups. Training and testing were conducted in groups of four to seven students.

All students were trained to use imagery, elaboration, and grouping with the sample passage by Kneller (1971). The practice readings were then presented one at a time. The students were instructed to practice applying all three of the learning strategies to each passage to learn the materials contained in it, and to write down examples of the aids they created. Six minutes were allowed for the students to read each simple passage and apply the strategies; 10 minutes were allowed for each difficult passage. During this time, the experimenter provided individual feedback and guidance to the students.

Following practice on the four readings, all students were tested on their ability to use the strategies to learn the material contained in the two test readings. The simple test reading was presented first to all students, with 3 minutes allotted for reading. Following this study interval, the appropriate open-ended test was given, with 6 minutes allowed to complete the test. The multiple-choice test followed. This test had a 3-minute time limit. The students were then given the difficult test reading and allowed 7 minutes to study this passage. Six minutes were allowed for the open-ended test and 4 minutes were allowed for the multiple-choice test over this passage.

A control group ($N = 25$), which had been obtained as part of another study, received neither training in the strategies nor an opportunity to practice learning materials of the type studied by the training groups. However, these students were examined over the same testing materials.

Results and Discussion

A 3 × 2 × 2 analysis of variance (groups × reading difficulty × question type) was used to analyze the data. The main effect of groups was not significant, but the main effects of reading difficulty and question type were significant: $F(1,72) = 15.06$, $p < .001$ for reading difficulty; $F(1,72) = 23.41$, $p < .001$ for question type. Thus, scores were higher on simple than on difficult readings, and were also higher on multiple-choice than on open-ended questions.

The interaction of groups and reading difficulty was significant— $F(2,72) = 4.25$, $p < .05$—indicating that the group that received two simple passages followed by two difficult passages (SSDD) and the group that received two difficult passages followed by two simple passages (DDSS) performed above the control group on the simple reading, but on the difficult reading, the SSDD and control groups performed above the DDSS group. The interaction of reading difficulty and question type was significant—$F(1,72) = 90.11$, $p < .0001$—indicating that open-ended test scores were higher on the simple reading, but multiple-choice test scores were higher on the difficult reading. The interaction of groups and question type was not significant.

The interaction of groups, reading difficulty, and question type was significant: $F(2,72) = 3.88$, $p < .05$. The form of the interaction was similar for all groups; however, the extent of the interaction differed (see Figure 2.3). For the SSDD group, multiple-choice and open-ended test scores were not different on the simple reading, but on the difficult reading open-ended test scores were below multiple-choice test scores. For the control group, open-ended test scores were above multiple-choice test scores on the simple reading but were below them on the difficult reading. The form of the interaction for the DDSS group was similar to that of the control group, except that the open-ended test scores on the difficult reading were farther below the multiple-choice test scores.

In general, the multiple-choice test scores did not differ greatly across groups or readings, but the open-ended test scores did, such that the scores of the DDSS group were below those of the SSDD and control groups. Open-ended tests are more reflective of recall processes than are multiple-

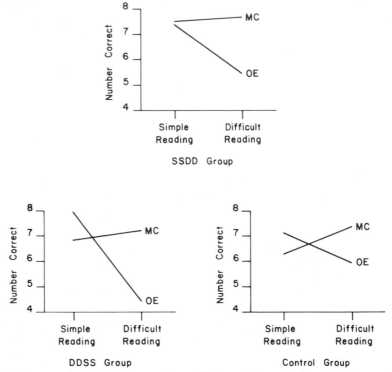

Figure 2.3 Interaction of groups, reading difficulty, and question type (MC = multiple-choice, OE = open-ended).

choice tests, and in educational contexts, recall is usually more highly valued than recognition. Therefore, the results of this study suggest that in developing a training program for the teaching of cognitive learning strategies, the level of student performance may be decreased if presentation of training materials begins with difficult materials and progresses to simple materials. Though this may seem like a common-sense notion, it is important to note that until recently such variables have rarely been investigated by researchers in the field.

SUMMARY

The results of our studies investigating variables affecting training in the use of cognitive strategies indicate that simply instructing students to use the strategies is not as effective as training that includes supervised practice. The amount of practice necessary appears to be dependent upon the difficulty level of the materials with which the strategies will be used, as well as on the types of assessment instruments. More training and practice may be necessary for more difficult materials and/or tests that require recall rather than recognition of the materials. Presenting more difficult training tasks first seems to have a detrimental effect on recall, but not recognition, of the to-be-learned material, particularly when this material is also rather difficult for the learner.

THE REVISED FORM OF THE TRAINING PROGRAM: A FIELD TEST

The data obtained from these investigations were analyzed and integrated with the data obtained from a number of other studies to produce a new form of the training program. This version of the cognitive learning strategies program is divided into several components. Although these will be discussed here as separate sections, there is some overlapping of program components during actual presentation, particularly with respect to the motivational component. Part I of the program is designed to motivate the learners to apply their best efforts to mastering the strategies. Our previous fieldwork, in both academic and military settings, provided evidence to indicate that many individuals do not immediately understand the relevance of these techniques for the material they are required to learn. Furthermore, many expressed or evidenced a large amount of anxiety about attempting to use new, unfamiliar strategies to help them learn material that they needed to know for a test or job performance evaluation. The purpose of this section of the program is to demonstrate the relevance of the techniques to the individual's own learning needs and the benefits that can derive from using them to facilitate acquisition and retention of information.

Part II provides an overview of the training sequence and explanations of how it relates to helping individuals learn information required for course work or employment purposes. This section of the program also discusses how these learning strategies can be used for the individual's everyday learning needs. Finally, there is a brief discussion of the role these techniques can play in increasing learning effectiveness in a number of situations, thereby making students less reliant on prepared curricula and course structure. The importance of acquiring effective learning strategies that can be adapted to one's own needs and abilities is discussed.

The next section of the program provides some highly salient examples of the use of learning strategies in common situations. The purpose of this part of the program is to provide some early successful experiences with learning strategies. The "one-is-a-bun" mnemonic[2] is introduced and built upon using content materials that are highly relevant to the particular group of learners. This is followed by a review of the techniques and discussion of why they are helpful for learning.

Part IV is the main section of the program. The cognitive learning strategies of imagery, meaningful elaboration, and grouping are presented in the context of numerous examples of learning tasks. This section begins with simple paired-associate tasks and continues through a series of reading passages. The content areas represent a variety of topics; their selection is dependent upon the characteristics of the learner population.

The last section is a final review of the entire program and all its components. This is followed by a series of posttests that are used to evaluate each learner's performance. The posttests include reading comprehension, paired-associate, and free recall tasks.

As part of the contract with the Defense Advanced Research Projects Agency, which contributes to the support of the Cognitive Learning Strategies Project, a field test of the training program was conducted with Army enlisted personnel. A number of difficulties were encountered in attempting to adapt and implement the program in a field setting. Several of these problems are discussed in the following report of the field test.

Method

Participants. A total of 108 junior enlisted personnel representing 11 different companies stationed at a large Army base located in the Southwest were assigned to participate in this research in lieu of their regular duty assignments. Their selection was made by company commanders, the only restrictions being that participants must be males who had earned high school diplomas.

Participants were divided into three groups of 36 men: training, control, and posttest only. Because of misunderstandings about the necessity of attendance at all research sessions (five for the training and control groups,

---

[2] The one-is-a-bun mnemonic is a memory system that involves both verbal and imaginal elaboration. First, numbers are associated with rhyming words (one–bun, two–shoe, three–tree, etc.). These words then become image-evoking cues for learning an ordered list of words. The learner associates the items on the to-be-learned list with the rhyming words by forming a compound image. For example, the number *one* is associated with the word *bun.* If the first word to be learned is *clock,* the learner would try to create an image interrelating a clock and a bun. To recall the list of words, the learner counts off the numbers, in order, and retrieves the corresponding compound image.

two for the posttest-only group), a number of trainees were reassigned to other duties, both on and off the base, which precluded their continuation in the research. A total of 45 participants had to be dropped from the study prior to the first posttest. An additional 7 participants failed to appear for the second posttest. The sample sizes for the first and second posttests were, respectively, training, 18, 15; control, 18, 17; and posttest only, 27, 24.

Materials. Selection of training and testing materials for this trainee population proved to be problematic because no information was available concerning the trainees' reading level. In addition, no pretesting of materials was permitted. Criteria for selection were that the materials be of potential interest to this group and that the difficulty level of most readings be at, or close to, the eighth-grade level. Thus, the training readings included two SRA (1959) eighth-grade-level passages, one discussing gladiator fights and one presenting an historical perspective on money; a passage distinguishing the arteries from the veins that was taken from an English textbook (Tressler & Christ, 1960); two passages from an encyclopedia (Compton, 1974a, 1974b), one describing the shrew as the smallest mammal and the other discussing the uses of limes; and one more difficult SRA eleventh-grade-level passage that presented a brief biography of a Canadian aviator.

In order to demonstrate the use of the cognitive strategies with military training materials, another passage from a technical manual of instructions for noncommissioned officers (Employment of Army Aviation Units in a High Threat Environment, 1976) was also included. This technical manual was supplied by Army personnel. The reading level was unknown, but the vocabulary and sentence structure appeared to be more difficult when compared with the other materials included in the training.

Each set of posttest materials included a free recall list (20 words), a paired-associate list (21 word pairs), and two readings followed by open-ended questions for each reading (the first posttest also included multiple-choice questions for the readings). The free recall and paired-associate lists were constructed using the Paivio *et al.* norms (1968) and included words of average concreteness (range = 3.00–5.50) and moderately high meaningfulness (range = 4.75–6.75). These lists had been used successfully in a previous study with ninth-grade students (Weinstein, 1978).

The readings for the first posttest included a newspaper article about bobcats (Harris, 1977) and another passage from the Army technical training manual describing low-flying aircraft and helicopter defense tactics. The second posttest readings included a passage from an eighth-grade government textbook (Carter, 1972) and a ninth-grade-level reading about child prodigies from the SRA (1959) materials. The multiple-choice and open-ended questions for the readings were written by the experimenters. There were 10 questions for each test.

Training Design and Procedure. Training was conducted in three 1½-hour sessions separated by 3-day intervals. The first posttest was administered 3 days after the conclusion of the training, and the second posttest was administered 9 days later.

Training Group. The first session for the training group began with an introduction to the purpose of the research, emphasizing the personal advantages of developing skills that facilitate learning and remembering new material, whether it be Army technical material or girl friends' phone numbers. This was followed by an overview of the training sequence including brief explanations of terms and concepts to be used in the training sessions. Familiar examples of elaboration strategies were discussed, such as "the alphabet song" and the rhyme beginning "Thirty days hath September," to demonstrate that the trainees had probably already used some types of elaboration strategies. These examples provided the basis for a discussion of learning as an active process in which people can manage a large portion of their own learning rather than having to rely exclusively on prepared training systems, and in which they can be taught more effective methods of learning, whether the to-be-learned material relates to the acquisition of new job skills or to everyday learning needs, such as remembering the name of a new officer who has recently been transferred into a unit.

After these discussions, the one-is-a-bun mnemonic was introduced and built upon in great detail, demonstrating the use of imagery and verbal elaboration to learn some highly relevant content materials, such as a list of the best-selling brands of beer in Texas. This example was designed to provide an initial successful experience in using a memory strategy and to instill in the trainees the confidence that these techniques can be learned relatively quickly, that they make sense, and that they do work. This example was followed by a brief review of the one-is-a-bun technique and a discussion of how it helped in learning the list—that is, the mediating functions of imagery and verbal elaboration for relating new information to previous knowledge and experience.

The main section of the training program was then begun. Each of the cognitive learning strategies—imagery, elaboration, and grouping—was explained and demonstrated using simple everyday learning, or memory tasks. These included a paired-associate task in which names of businesses were paired with street names, a serial recall shopping list, and a free recall grocery list.

Tasks were presented one at a time, with the experimenter providing examples of how to use the strategies. Trainees were then asked to give examples of their own use of the strategies. The experimenter provided additional examples when the trainees were slow in responding, until they understood the task and could generate their own examples.

The second day of training began with a brief review of the strategies, followed by practice in applying them to three reading comprehension tasks. The readings, which included only eighth-and ninth-grade reading level material, were distributed one at a time. While the trainees worked on each reading, writing down their strategies as they worked, the experimenters circulated among them, providing supportive and corrective feedback. After all trainees had completed a task, several examples of trainee-generated strategies were discussed, and then the next reading passage was distributed.

The third training session was similar to the second session in that it began with a review of the strategies followed by practice in using them on four reading comprehension tasks. However, it differed in that the reading tasks were progressively more difficult: two from Compton's Encyclopaedia, one eleventh-grade-level SRA reading, and a passage from the technical training manual. In this session, less feedback was provided on the use of the strategies and more emphasis was placed on comprehension and recall. After the trainees finished applying the strategies to each reading, the experimenter asked several questions similar to those which might occur on a reading comprehension test. This procedure was followed for all four reading passages.

Control Group. The control group also met for three sessions, in which they were exposed to the same materials as the training group. However, they received no instructions in the use of cognitive learning strategies. Instead, they were told to learn the materials in whatever way seemed best to them. During the third session they received the same questions used with the training group.

Posttest-only Group. The trainees in this group did not meet at all prior to testing. They did, however, complete all of the posttests.

The testing sessions were the same for all three groups, except that the training group was reminded to use the cognitive strategies. The sequence of tasks was the same for the first and second testing sessions, although the specific content differed. All words used in the free recall and paired-associate tests were displayed on a Da-Lite screen using a Kodak slide projector with an automatic timing device.

The free recall test was administered with an 8-second presentation rate and a 2½-minute recall period. The paired-associate test was presented next, using a modified study–test method with an 8-second presentation rate for both study and test phases.

The reading comprehension tests were administered as the final phases of posttesting. Two passages were distributed one at a time. For each passage, the trainees were told the length of time allotted for reading and that they would be tested over the material contained in the passage. In both sessions, the trainees were allotted 8 minutes to study the first passage and 16 minutes to study the second passage. Additional time was allotted for the second reading in each posttest session, as these were longer than the first readings. Ten minutes were given for the completion of each posttest.

Results and Discussion

One-way analyses of variance on each of the dependent measures indicated that there were no significant differences among the three groups on either the first or second posttests. (See Tables 2.2 and 2.3 for a summary of the performance data from the posttesting sessions.) This was the first attempt to adapt the cognitive learning strategies program for Army recruits, and it is clear that a number of modifications in both the program and the dependent measures are needed for this population.

It is unfortunate that the dependent measures could not be pilot-tested with Army recruits prior to this study. It is apparent from the results obtained (see Tables 2.2 and 2.3) that a number of these measures were not appropriate for these men. For example, the scores on the paired-associate and free recall tasks were extremely low. The group means for the Army personnel were lower than those reported by Weinstein (1978) using the same task materials with ninth graders. Future field tests in similar settings must be predicated upon the availability of posttest tasks appropriate for Army recruits.

TABLE 2.2
Means and Standard Deviations for the First Posttesting Session of the Field Test

Task	Maximum score	Group	N	Mean	SD
Reading 1 (newspaper article)	10	Experimental	18	5.89	2.55
		Control	18	5.62	2.86
		Posttest only	27	5.29	2.36
Reading 2 (Army technical training manual	10	Experimental	18	3.49	2.10
		Control	18	4.06	2.60
		Posttest only	27	3.22	2.22
Free recall	20	Experimental	18	8.06	3.39
		Control	18	8.22	2.60
		Posttest only	27	7.96	2.01
PAL	21	Experimental	18	3.28	3.80
		Control	18	3.28	3.60
		Posttest only	27	2.07	2.59

TABLE 2.3
Means and Standard Deviations for the Second Posttesting Session of the Field Test

Task	Maximum score	Group	N	Mean	SD
Reading 1	10	Experimental	15	4.34	2.77
(SRA ninth-		Control	17	5.15	2.87
grade level)		Posttest only	24	4.90	2.43
Reading 2	10	Experimental	15	4.27	2.77
(eight-grade		Control	17	5.84	2.98
government text)		Posttest only	24	4.61	2.88
Free recall	20	Experimental	15	8.87	2.90
		Control	17	7.82	3.07
		Posttest only	24	7.33	3.29
PAL	21	Experimental	15	4.40	3.29
		Control	17	2.82	2.60
		Posttest only	24	3.21	3.37

During the debriefing sessions many of the participants provided anecdotal evidence supporting the usefulness of the program, and several modifications were suggested. A number of the men wanted more emphasis on imaginal learning strategies and more time devoted to the individual learning and testing tasks. Further research is needed to determine the optimal procedures for learning strategy training programs with Army populations.

FUTURE DIRECTIONS

The research and development effort described in this chapter will continue as part of the Cognitive Learning Strategies Project at the University of Texas at Austin. The goals of this project are to refine our understanding of the covert processes involved in utilizing cognitive strategies for learning and retention and to design, develop, and field-test training programs to modify learners' information processing strategies. In addition to continuing our investigations of verbal and imaginal elaboration, we will incorporate additional self-management skills such as the use of study skills specifically designed to provide learners with a means for organizing new material in a way that is compatible with their own learning processes or styles so as to facilitate the use of cognitive learning strategies. As we increase our understanding of self-management skills that contribute to effective and efficient learning, we will be able to provide heuristic means for the individual learner to use in identifying, monitoring, modifying, and implementing a plan for achieving instructional goals.

ACKNOWLEDGMENTS

We would like to thank the following staff members of the Cognitive Learning Strategies Project for their assistance in conducting the research upon which this chapter is based: Magdalena M. Rood, Lynn K. Roney, Thomas P. Washington, David C. Duty, Chuck Roper, Hobart M. Hukill, Dean Johnston, and Ann Schulte.

REFERENCES

Atkinson, R. C., & Raugh, M. R. An application of the mnemonic keyword method to the acquisition of a Russian vocabulary. *Journal of Experimental Psychology: Human Learning and Memory,* 1975, *104,* 126–133.

Borkowski, J. G., & Kamfonik, A. Verbal mediation in moderately retarded childen: Effects of successive mediational experiences. *American Journal of Mental Deficiency,* 1972, *77,* 157–162.

Borkowski, J. G., Levers, S., & Gruenenfelder, T. M. Transfer of mediational strategies in children: The role of activity and awareness during strategy acquisition. *Child Development,* 1976, *47,* 779–786.

Butterfield, E. C., Wambold, C., & Belmont, J. M. On the theory and practice of improving short-term memory. *American Journal of Mental Deficiency,* 1973, *77,* 654–669.

Carter, R. *Of, by and for the people.* Winchester, Ill.: Benefic Press, 1972.

Compton, F. E. *Compton's encyclopaedia and fact index* (Vol. 14). Chicago: Encyclopaedia Britannica, 1974. (a)

Compton, F. E. *Compton's encyclopaedia and fact index* (Vol. 22). Chicago: Encyclopaedia Britannica, 1974. (b)

Crovitz, H. F. Memory loci in artificial memory. *Psychonomic Science,* 1969, *16,* 82–83.

Danner, F. W., & Taylor, A. M. Integrated pictures and relational imagery training in children's learning. *Journal of Experimental Child Psychology,* 1973, *16,* 47–54.

Dember, W. N. Motivation and the cognitive revolution. *American Psychologist,* 1974, *29,* 161–168.

Employment of Army aviation units in a high threat environment (Field Manual 90–1). Washington, D.C.: Department of the Army, September 30, 1976.

Gagné, R. M., & Briggs, L. J. *Principles of instructional design.* New York: Holt, Rinehart and Winston, 1974.

Harris, M. Bobcat threatened by demand for pelts. *Daily Texan,* August 2, 1977, p. 5.

Kneller, G. S. The challenge of experimentation. In G. S. Kneller (Ed.), *Foundations of education.* New York: John Wiley, 1971.

MacMillan, D. L. Facilitative effect of verbal mediation on paired-associate learning by EMR children. *American Journal of Mental Deficiency,* 1970, *74,* 611–615.

Montague, W. E. Elaborative strategies in verbal learning and memory. In G. H. Bower (Ed.), *The psychology of learning and motivation: Advances in research and theory* (Vol. 6). New York: Academic Press, 1972.

Norman, D. A. *Memory and attention.* New York: John Wiley, 1976.

Paivio, A., Yuille, J. C., & Madigan, S. Concreteness, imagery, and meaningfulness values for 925 nouns. *Journal of Experimental Psychology,* 1968, *79,* 509–514.

Rohwer, W. D. Images and pictures in children's learning. *Psychological Bulletin,* 1970, *73,* 393–403.

Rohwer, W. D., & Ammon, M. S. Elaboration training and paired-associate learning efficiency in children. *Journal of Educational Psychology,* 1971, *62,* 373–386.

Ross, D. M. Retention and transfer of mediation set in paired-associate learning of educable retarded children. *Journal of Educational Psychology,* 1971, *62,* 323–327.

Ross, D. M., Ross, S. A., & Downing, M. L. Intentional training vs. observational learning of mediational strategies in EMR children. *American Journal of Mental Deficiency,* 1973, *78,* 292–299.

Ross, J., & Lawrence, K. A. Some observations on memory artifice. *Psychonomic Science,* 1968, *13,* 107–108.

Science Research Associates lab IVa rate builder. Chicago: Science Research Associates, Inc., 1959.

Senter, R. J., & Hoffman, R. R. Bizarreness as a nonessential variable in mnemonic imagery: A confirmation. *Bulletin of the Psychonomic Society,* 1976, *7,* 163–164.

Smith, R. A., & Marshall, P. H. Independent storage and decodability of natural language mediators. *Perceptual and Motor Skills,* 1976, *42,* 294.

Tressler, J. C., & Christ, H. I. *Junior English in action.* Boston: D. C. Heath, 1960.

Tversky, B., & Teiffer, E. Development of strategies for recall and recognition. *Developmental Psychology,* 1976, *12,* 406–410.

Weinstein, C. E. Elaboration skills as a learning strategy. In H. F. O'Neil, Jr. (Ed.), *Learning strategies.* New York: Academic Press, 1978.

Yuille, J. C., & Catchpole, M. J. Associative learning and imagery training in children. *Journal of Experimental Child Psychology,* 1973, *16,* 403–412.

Yuille, J. C., & Catchpole, M. J. The effects of delay and imagery training on the recall and recognition of object pairs. *Journal of Experimental Child Psychology,* 1974, *17,* 474–481.

3

Study Skills and
Learning Strategies[1]

THOMAS H. ANDERSON

In this chapter, the process of studying text material is viewed as a criteria-related, self-directed form of reading text. It is a form of reading unlike reading a novel for entertainment or reading the newspaper to pass time on a commuter train. Rather, it is a form of reading in which specific information must be gained by engaging a text or reference book in order to perform well on some future event, such as taking an exam, giving a speech, or writing a paper.

The other important feature of studying, as it will be discussed in this chapter, is that it is student-directed. The student is the prime agent in deciding when and how the study sessions should proceed. In contrast, other types of studying, such as teacher-directed, computer-managed, or programmed instruction, provide the student with decisions about what to do next.

To help describe the process of studying, the concept of metacomprehension is used frequently in this chapter. According to Flavell (1978), a broad definition of metacomprehension is "knowledge or cognition that takes as its object or regulates any aspect of any cognitive endeavor." For the needs of this chapter, however, some of the more specific characteristics of metacomprehension (e.g., cognitive monitoring and compre-

[1] Financial support for this research came primarily from Defense Advanced Research Projects Agency under Contract No. N00123-77-C-0622 and the National Institute of Education under Contract No. US-NIE-C-400-76-0116. Views and conclusions contained in this chapter are those of the author and should not be interpreted as necessarily representing the official policies, either expressed or implied, of the funding agencies or of the United States government.

hension failure) are crucial. These are key concepts of student-directed studying, since students must reliably monitor their own acquisition, maintenance, and production of knowledge. The notion of metacomprehension is woven into each of the three major sections in this chapter, which discuss the prereading, during-reading, and postreading activities involved in the process of studying.

STAGE 1: PREREADING ACTIVITIES

The first stage of prereading activities begins when the students have resolved some of the motivational aspects of studying (e.g., Do I have time to study? Am I too upset to study? Are there easier ways to learn this material?) and are convinced that they must use the textbook in order to learn. Once the decision has been made to engage text, the student must clarify the criteria associated with the study session. The two following sections discuss some of the processes that students can apply to aid them in clarifying criteria.

Clarifying the Criteria and Objectives of Studying

Though studying can occur for many diverse reasons, most often students engage in textbook studying to prepare for an examination. Also, textbook studying is seldom isolated from other instructional components of an educational system, such as lectures, computer-assisted instruction, laboratory work, and discourse with classmates and teachers. In the prereading stage, the prime task of the student is to apply knowledge gained from these other instructional sources in order to help specify as clearly as possible the nature of the forthcoming examination. In other words, the students need to determine what topics will be tested, as well as the expected levels of understanding of each topic.

The most readily available sources of information to help students decide on the nature of the forthcoming examination are lecture notes, course guides and objectives, and copies of previously administered exams. The student's job is to organize these materials so that they will be maximally useful at later stages in the study session.

One suggested organizational technique is to develop a study guide upon which subject matter entries can be made as they are encountered. We have found it useful to have one sheet set aside for all potential test items that will require students to name, describe, define, or give examples and applications. For example, when an instructional objective states that the student will be able to identify copperheads or describe the battle of Shiloh Church, or when a test item requires the student to list two important safety precautions when using an arc welder, then the student would write copperheads, Shiloh Church, and arc welder safety on the study guide.

On a second page labeled "Comparisons," the student lists those topics that require a "compare and contrast" level of understanding. Items from lists of objectives and tests, such as "Discuss the effectiveness of Davis and Lincoln as military leaders," or "What was the major difference between the constitution of the United States and the Confederate states?" would be entered in the study guide as "Davis versus Lincoln" and "U.S. versus C.S. constitutions."

On a third study guide page would be written those items that have a temporal, procedural, or causal relationship. Items such as "Why did the people in the South mourn Lincoln's assassination?" "Why should all arc-welding hardfacing be done in a flat position?" or "Before checking to see that the voltage is zero, what should be done?" would be entered as "Lincoln's assassination $\longrightarrow$ South mourning"; "flat position $\longrightarrow$ hardfacing"; and " $\longrightarrow$ voltage is zero."

Finally, a fourth study guide page would contain those items that would not fit conveniently onto the first three. Those items that require complex tasks such as analyzing, evaluating, and critiquing would be included on this fourth page. Our preliminary work with this technique indicates that a student can translate 40 items from a multiple-choice test onto these worksheets in about 15 minutes. We believe that this is not an unreasonable amount of time to spend on this task.

In summary, this prereading activity requires that the students translate items from tests, lists of objectives, and lecture notes into topic entries and write them on the proper study guide page. Constructing these worksheets is a technique that aids in organizing the pertinent information related to the study criteria. Another valuable source for gathering information is the textbook. The next section describes how that procedure works.

Surveying

It is easy when reading some of the most influential how-to-study literature (Pauk, 1974; Robinson, 1970) to be lulled into thinking that surveying is a straightforward, rather noninvolved process. Many authors suggest that students read the title, read the subtitles, look at the pictures, read the summary, etc. while quickly turning from page to page throughout the chapter. Seldom are these suggestions described in enough detail to inform the student on what information is supposed to be found in the title, the pictures, or the summaries.

In an effort to gain more insight into surveying and to begin formulating a first-order model of this process, we gave 12 skilled readers a chapter each to study in preparation for a later event, such as taking a test or attending a lecture. We contacted all the studiers in advance and asked them to set aside approximately a 1-hour block of time in an effort to make the task demands as realistic as possible. To start the study session, they were told that they should **study** either in preparation for a test to follow or to attend a lecture. Then the text was given to them and their initial behaviors were observed. Specifically, we wanted to know whether or not they would attempt any type of survey activity, and second, we wanted to know more about the cognitive processes involved in the surveying activity. The following model was generated from this source of observational and self-report data.

We discovered that virtually every one of these subjects attempted some form of survey. The shortest survey was only 10 seconds, and the longest was in the range of 15 minutes. During these relatively short periods of interaction with the text, a number of very complex behaviors and procedures took place. We tried to capture the gist of most of our observations and student reports in the three questions that students seemed to be attempting to answer as they surveyed. These questions are

1. How much do I already know about this topic and text?
2. How interested am I in this topic and text?
3. How difficult or time-consuming will it be for me to learn what I need to know from the text?

The evidence that students were seeking in order to help answer the questions came from a number of sources, and our categorization of these sources leads us to the next descriptive part of the model.

The first level of information that students attended to was the salient, information-rich, nonsentence parts of the text chapter. These parts include the title, subtitles, marked words, highlighted sections, pictures, charts, graphs, maps, and reference lists. Most textbooks make it easy to locate such information quickly with only a glance at each page. A brief pass through a chapter in which the student inspected only these types of information typically took 2 minutes or less. The second level of information that these students attended to was information-rich portions that are in predictable places in the text and can be located rapidly. This kind of information includes introductory and summary paragraphs, the first and last paragraphs in the subsections, and the first sentence of any paragraph. To engage in this second level of information gathering required 10–15 minutes in a typical chapter. In a third level of activity during the survey, students engaged in selective reading of larger parts of the text. For example, they may have read most of a subsection, or perhaps several consecutive paragraphs.

The process of using these three levels of information to help answer the three "How . . . I" questions above is a very dynamic and complex one. Seldom did a student survey using information only at one level. For example, almost no one read only the title and subtitles and inspected the charts, figures, graphs, etc. Instead, the students moved very rapidly among the several levels of information. The movement among the levels, however, did not seem to be random, and the following model accounts for some of that behavior.

1. The students initially engage Level 1 in order to answer the three questions.
2. They will move from Level 1 to Levels 2 and 3 if they cannot reliably answer the three "How . . . I" questions by using Level 1, or if the material is particularly interesting to them.
3. The students will move from Level 3 to Levels 1 and 2 if they are able to answer the questions reliably, or if the text becomes less interesting.
4. If the text is not formatted to facilitate using Levels 1 and 2 (i.e., if the text has only paragraphs with no headings or format markings of any kind), then the surveying process breaks down and the students try some other strategy, such as starting at the beginning of the passage and carefully reading each paragraph.

In addition, our observations have led us to believe that answers to the three "How . . . I" questions can be used to make predictions about how well the study session will proceed. The study session will **stop** after surveying (*a*) when the subject already knows the content, and/or (*b*) when the subject is very uninterested in the topic, and/or (*c*) when the time required to learn the text greatly exceeds the time available for study. Also, the study session will probably be of **limited duration** when interest in the topic and text is, at best, low and difficulty of the topic is high. The study session will probably **proceed** smoothly under the following conditions: (*a*) when at least some, but not all, of the text material is already known; (*b*) when the topic is somewhat interesting; and (*c*) when the time estimate to learn the required material is low to medium.

In many respects the process of surveying is much more complex than that of reading and studying the text itself, as described in the next section, Stage II. Skilled students use rich (but terse) information from the text and from their own knowledge of the world to make decisions about their own level of understanding and attitudes toward the text and topic. Skilled readers can do this in a very short period of time, usually on the order of a few minutes.

STAGE II: DURING–READING ACTIVITIES

After clarifying the nature of the studying outcomes and constructing a study guide, reading extended text can begin. Frequently, there is a distinct break in the flow of studying behavior between Stages I and II. That is, students stop looking rapidly through the chapter as in surveying and start at the beginning to read each section. Sometimes, however, students never move out of Stage I; this happens when the studying criteria are explicit enough to enable a student to locate rapidly and read the relevant sections of text while surveying. Occasionally, for example, the charts and graphs will contain all of the necessary information; this is often the case with technical manuals. When the situation arises in which students must engage larger chunks of text and must proceed to Stage II, a metacomprehension model of studying is proposed to help account for the diversity of activities that occurs.

In this model the student engages in a sequence of instructional episodes. Most episodes include the following components: (*a*) information gathering; (*b*) student responding; (*c*) response judging and feedback; and (*d*) making decisions concerning what to do next. An example of a short episode would be a frame in a programmed instruction text. In a programmed text a short chunk of information is presented, a question is asked, and the student provides an answer that can be compared with a "preferred answer" printed elsewhere in the text. Feedback and directions about what to do next are provided. Thus, a programmed text frame would be a prototypic example of a short instructional episode where only a limited amount of metacomprehension is required.

As previously mentioned, the focus of this chapter is to consider studying as a self-directed form of instruction. To study effectively the student must know when and how to use each component of the model, and to do this well requires that the student be a good metacomprehender. Some forms of instruction, such as teacher-directed or computer-managed instruction, use other techniques to substitute for metacomprehension. For example, students engaged in traditional computer-managed instruction do not often have to ask the question, "Do I know if I understand this material?" During each episode the computer informs the students whether or not they understand the material. The next sections describe the way in which the four components apply to studying, and discuss some relevant research.

Information Gathering

An instructional episode begins when the student starts reading to extract meaning from sentences and paragraphs in a more or less sequential order. When students have an organized study aid, such as the study guide described earlier, it can be used to help generate text-specific search markers—that is, reference points where reading should start and stop. In other words, students can be more selective in what information they choose to process.

The skill of selecting important text sections to read carefully is a very important one when considering the sheer information load of a text chapter. For example, the number of so-called idea units in a typical chapter of text is minimally 50 per page. To calculate this we used a conservative technique, similar to one for calculating pausal units (Brown & Smiley, 1977), in which we defined an idea unit as that verbiage bounded by punctuation marks, conjunctions, and/or infinitive phrases. Commas that were used to set off members of a list or a city–state combination were not considered. Using these data, a 30-page chapter would have, **at a minimum,** about 1500 pausal units or ideas.

To determine how students collect information from extended text, Reynolds, Standiford, and Anderson (1978) had college students read a text at a computer terminal in an inserted question research paradigm. Using the terminals allowed measurement of reading times on short segments of material. They found that the question groups performed better, relative to controls, on posttest items that repeated inserted questions, as well as on new posttest items from the same categories as the inserted questions. Analyses of time data showed that there was no overall difference in reading times between the two groups—those who had inserted questions and those who did not—but subjects who received inserted questions spent more time on the parts of the text that contained information of the type needed to answer the questions. In other words, students modified their information gathering processes in accordance with the task, as defined by the inserted questions.

In another experiment, Baker (in preparation) presented passages containing designed confusions—that is, contradictions of information involving main points of the passage or involving passage details—to subjects at a computer terminal. After reading the passage, subjects were given a series of on-line questions to assess their awareness of the confusions. They were first asked to decide which of two alternatives was most consistent with each passage where the alternatives were paraphrases of either the contradictory target or its corresponding nonconfusing control statement. Depending on which answer subjects gave, they were automatically branched by the computer to further questions probing their interpretations of the passage.

Results showed that subjects spent more time reading paragraphs with contradictions than those without contradictions if the contradictions involved a main point. However, when the contradictions involved passage details, subjects spent less time reading the paragraphs in which the contradictions appeared than those without contradictions. Thus, subjects were sensitive to the contradictions and therefore altered their reading behaviors in an unexpected but defensible way. For example, it appears that the subjects did in fact notice the contradictions on detail items but decided to gloss over them rather than take additional time to resolve them.

This section on information gathering is not meant to be an exhaustive review but rather an attempt at illustrating some of the variables that affect this process. Thus, it is rather clear that the nature of the task demands, as well as the interaction of clarity of presentation and importance of information, influences information gathering strategies.

Student Responding

This second component in an instructional episode requires that the student stop gathering information and engage in a response-demand event. In general, two types of mechanisms can interrupt the information gathering process: (a) a response-demand event initiated by either the student or the teacher (human or computer), and (b) the Automatic Monitoring Mechanism (AMM), which provides students with "noises" concerning their studying comprehension, called "clicks" of comprehension and "clunks" of comprehension failure.

A major, well-researched form of response-demand event is the use of adjunct questions. The so-called direct effect of adjunct questions occurs when students receiving adjunct questions perform better on criterion questions that are identical to those used in the adjunct form than students in a read-only condition. There is also an indirect effect of adjunct questions: a superior performance by students receiving adjunct questions on new criterion questions that were not used in the adjunct form compared with the performance of students in the read-only condition.

Anderson and Biddle (1975) reviewed literature on adjunct questions and concluded that the use of adjunct questions generally has a facilitative effect on learning from prose. When the questions are placed after the text read by the students, they have a significant facilitative effect on the repeated items and on the new items, showing direct and indirect effects. When adjunct questions appear before the text the students are to read, they have a positive direct effect but a negative indirect effect. In addition, the closer the questions are physically located to the information to which they refer, the higher the performance when those questions are repeated later. Moreover, when questions are grouped together after even lengthy prose, such as the end of a chapter in a textbook, they can have a pronounced direct effect. When students are required to provide an overt answer to the adjunct questions, there are more consistent positive direct and indirect effects than when they are required to make only a covert response. When the adjunct questions are higher-level questions—that is, when they require the student to go beyond the surface meaning of the text in order to answer the question—they have direct and indirect effects. The point is rather clear that adjunct questions can play a strong facilitative role in studying and learning text material.

In a related line of research in which students are required to engage in a response-demand event, results from recent investigations on student-generated questions by Frase and Schwartz (1975), Schmelzer (1975), and Duell (1977) are encouraging. These researchers present four studies showing that when students (high school and older) formulated questions during study by either writing them down or verbalizing the questions to a friend, they scored significantly better on a posttest than students who studied using various other controlled techniques.

André and Anderson (1978) report another study using student-generated questions in which some of the controls and techniques used by the previous authors were relaxed. Duell (1977) required students to generate multiple-choice items rather than constructed-response-type items. Frase and Schwartz (1975) used text material that was so factually dense that virtually all of the students' questions were about specific facts. André and Anderson (1978), on the other hand, taught students to generate open-ended questions concerning the main idea of each paragraph as they read it.

In a first experimental study, a randomly selected group of students was trained to use the question-generating technique. Another group of students served as a control; these students were given the same series of training passages to practice on as those given to the experimental group. However, this control group was not told specifically how to study the materials. On a second day, all students were given a new passage to read and study, followed by a criterion test that measured students' knowledge of important outcomes. Results from this study showed that there was a significant interaction between students' verbal ability and the effects of the strategy they employed. Specifically, the higher-verbal-ability students showed no significant gain by using the student-questioning technique over whatever other techniques they employed. The difference was seen in the students with less verbal ability; they showed a significant gain by using the questioning technique.

In a second study, the same two treatments as used above were employed with the addition of a third. This additional group was not trained to use the questioning technique, as was the experimental group, but the un-trained students were asked to try the technique on the criterion materials. Results from this study show that both groups using the questioning technique scored higher than their control group although they were not significantly different from each other. Results also reveal a treatment-by-ability-level interaction, indicating that the lower-verbal-ability students benefited more from the treatment than did the higher-verbal-ability students.

Another finding from these studies shows that when students constructed a good question about a main point, the probability that later they could correctly answer a question on the criterion test concerning the main point was twice as great as when they were not able to construct a question. This finding is viewed as evidence that the quality of students' questions can serve as a comprehension monitoring index for the student at an important time in the study process when the student can take action to learn the material better. That is, if the student cannot easily generate a good question, then it may be necessary to reread the text section or consult another source. In addition, this technique provides the student with a record of questions that can be studied in preparation for a later test.

Of course, many students engage in the more familiar types of response-demand events such a notetaking, underlining, and outlining. There is a long history of research on the effects of these kinds of activities and, in general, they are not very facilitative (see Anderson, 1978). However, these activities are shown to be facilitative if they generate an extensive alternate form of the text that can be used for future reference because the original source (a) will not be available later; (b) is very lengthy; and/or (c) is not appropriately organized with reference to some criterion. A landmark study by Barton (1930) illustrates this point. He taught 96 high school students from two schools the fundamentals of outlining. The prime objective of the instruction was to teach the students to find main, subordinate, coordinate, and irrelevant points in each paragraph. Students applied the outline strategy to subject matter contents of geography, American history, and ancient history. Test performance of the students who used the outline strategy for a semester was significantly higher than test performance from a matched group who had a similar instructional program excluding the outline training. This is the most impressive study in the literature and demonstrates, with few reservations, the beneficial effect of a student-generated study aid.

In summary, there is evidence that when students stop reading and respond to questions, generate questions, or construct extended outlines or paraphrases, learning from prose is facilitated. However, pausing briefly to underline or to jot down brief notes typically is not a highly effective response-demand event.

Another mechanism that can interrupt students while they are reading text is the so-called Automatic Monitoring Mechanism. It is called "automatic" because it seems to operate at a subawareness level and the student is aware of its operation only after it has made its noises (i.e., clicks and clunks). In an initial investigation of the Automatic Monitoring Mechanism, we observed and questioned graduate students as they engaged in study. Though we were aware that this technique would intrude on and possibly disrupt the study process, it seemed to be a good method for indexing many of the otherwise covert processes. To date we have collected interview data from eight students. Our most heavily constricted technique required each student to read aloud, to predict the content of each paragraph prior to reading it in depth, to summarize the paragraphs after reading them, and to relate all other thoughts concerning the study session. Our most lenient technique required each student to study normally and to place a question mark beside any section of text that was confusing and/or slowed down or stopped the reading process. After studying the text, all students were given a test over the material and the nature of the question marks and/or notes was discussed in a posttest interview.

The following observations and conclusions are some of the results of those interviews.

1. The first technique discussed above—a heavily constricted technique—was so highly interactive that it seemed to become a learning strategy in itself; that is, the students seemed to learn more from the exchange with the experimenter than from the text itself.

2. During the poststudy interview, students could discuss in detail the nature of the question marks that they entered on the text while studying. Consequently, we were not required to interrupt the study process by requesting reports from students.

3. Students have a rather well-established study strategy that is not easily modified by telling them about various task demands or types of studying materials.

4. Students can impose temporary meaning on novel words or phrases encountered in a text with the intention of clarifying the meaning later, if

important, or ignoring it if unimportant. In general, students employ extremely sophisticated strategies concerning the semantic importance of text that they encounter. For example, words used in footnotes or words not essential to understanding the gist of a sentence were usually considered unimportant, and their meanings were seldom verified in a dictionary or glossary.

5. Students had trouble remembering to write the question marks when they were confused. They reported that having to remember placing the question marks interfered with studying.

6. Students exhibited many emotional behaviors (i.e., smiles, frowns, muscle tension, perspiration) and a general emotional fatigue after the study session.

In conclusion, we saw these study sessions as a series of very sophisticated cognitive and emotional processes that are difficult to monitor and are generally below the student's level of awareness. Occasionally these processes reached an awareness level in the form of the previously mentioned click of comprehension or clunk of comprehension failure. Clicks were often accompanied by feelings of well-being and clunks were accompanied by feelings of tenseness and/or mild anxiety.

Another effort (Baker, in preparation) to investigate the Automatic Monitoring Mechanism consisted of a research plan with two phases. To implement the first phase of the research plan, 10 three-paragraph passages on world history topics were written with deliberate confusions introduced into the middle paragraph of each passage. Types of text confusions included (a) pronouns with indefinite referents; (b) linguistic markers incorrectly signaling the nature of the text that follows (e.g., using *therefore* when *in addition to* is appropriate); and (c) presentation of new information relating to a previously developed topic that is inconsistent with earlier information. Each of the three types involved either a main point or a detail in the passage. Thirty-three college students were instructed to read the passages as editors might and to put a question mark by and/or explain any confusions they detected. It was hoped that these instructions would encourage the students to engage in a high degree of metacomprehension. Results showed that only 6% of the students were able to detect all of the planned confusions. Furthermore, the average percentage of the confusions detected per student was only 34%, which was lower than expected. Two plausible explanations were posed to account for this low percentage:

1. Some of the passages dealt with content that was difficult to understand (such as some of the philosophical aspects of history), which diminished the salient features of the planned confusions.
2. Students seemed able to impose plausible alternate meaning onto the

target areas of text and in so doing apparently solved any confusions they might have experienced.

In the second phase of the research plan, 26 college students were instructed to read the passages described above and were also told that they would receive a subsequent comprehension test over the material. For each of the 10 texts the test had one item (the target item) related to the confusion and two items from other places. These students were not informed that any of the texts had planned confusions.

Results from the comprehension tests showed that the presence or absence of confusions appeared to have no effect upon the performance of the nontarget items. When reading the target test items, from the confusing paragraphs, 51% responded with a recognized verbatim response from the passage (which is evidence that the inconsistency was not noticed and/or adequately resolved), whereas 45% recognized the correct answer (which is evidence of detecting an inconsistency). Four percent chose a third alternative, which was neither verbatim from the text nor a correct answer.

If subjects read a "consistent" passage, 76% responded with the correct alternative, 18% gave the "inconsistent" choice, and 5% chose the other alternative. In general, subjects responded more frequently with verbatim information when it was consistent with the passage (76%) than when it was inconsistent (51%). This difference indicates that many students were aware of the confusions in the text (at some level of processing) whether or not they could state so explicitly.

In a second study of Stage II, 37 subjects were presented a subset of the passages used previously: Two passages contained confusions (e.g., contradictions involving the main point of a paragraph), and two involved contradictions about passage details. The materials were presented sentence by sentence on the PLATO computer-assisted instruction system terminal screen (Bitzer, Sherwood, & Tenczar, 1973). The students controlled the amount of time they spent on each sentence. They were also given the opportunity to move around in the text; that is, they could look back or look ahead at any section of the passage when they so desired.

Another manipulation in the experiment involved the position of the contradictory target statement relative to its disconfirming context. In the case of the main-point passages, the contradictory statement was either the first or last sentence in the paragraph. The remaining sentences provided information that went against this statement. For detail passages, the context for the contradiction was but a single sentence, and both were embedded within the paragraph. Thus, the manipulation involved reversing the order of those two sentences. It was hypothesized that patterns of reading behavior depended on the position of the contradiction.

After reading the passages, subjects were given a series of on-line questions designed to assess their awareness of the contradiction. They were first asked to decide which of two alternatives was most consistent with each passage. The alternatives were paraphrases of either the contradictory target or its corresponding consistent control statement. Depending on which answer subjects gave, they were automatically branched by the computer to further questions probing their interpretations of the passages.

A significant result of the study was a paragraph type (main-point versus detail) by target type (contradictory or consistent) interaction. Subjects spent more time reading the entire paragraph when a contradiction was present if the contradiction involved a main point. However, on the detail passages, subjects spent more time reading the paragraph when the target statement was consistent rather than contradictory. This same pattern was also observed for (a) the amount of time spent on the target statement alone and (b) the number of lookbacks on the entire paragraph. Thus, the contradiction manipulation had the anticipated results only on main-point paragraphs. One plausible explanation is that subjects did in fact notice the contradiction on details but decided to gloss over it rather than attempt to resolve it. Thus, they actually spent less time studying the material than when it was written to make perfectly good sense.

Differences between main-point and detail passages were also apparent in the question-answering data. Overall, accuracy was greater on main-point questions than on detail, where accuracy is defined as the correct selection of the consistent, noncontradictory alternative. This held true regardless of whether the passage was consistent or contradictory. However, subjects were more accurate when they had read the consistent passage. This outcome is not at all surprising, since even if subjects had detected the contradiction, there would be a conflict between what they actually read and what the correct answer should be.

Finally, analysis of the time required to make a correct response showed that subjects required considerably more time answering detail questions when a contradiction was present. However, there was little difference in response times on main-point questions, suggesting that if subjects had resolved the inconsistency and identified the real main idea of the paragraph, they did so during initial reading. This interpretation is consistent with the observed differences in reading behavior on main-point passages.

As is obvious from the above accounts of research on the Automatic Monitoring Mechanism, the discovery process is just beginning. The research difficulty is compounded by the fact that many students are generally unable to keep a record of their monitoring activities without having the record keeping interfere with the monitoring. Consequently, we have had to use the indirect technique of having students study materials with planned confusions. To date, we have only a few results, all of which lead us to believe that the Automatic Monitoring Mechanism is quite complex, perhaps more so than we anticipated. It is able to distinguish between confusions that are potentially serious to successful comprehension, such as those involving a main point, and less serious ones, such as those involving passage details. However, confusions involving the improper use of transition words (e.g., *however* and *therefore*) never seemed to trigger the mechanism. The research paradigm, however, seems solid and it should have additional payoff in the not-too-distant future.

Response Judging and Feedback

After the episode has been interrupted by either the response-demand event or the Automatic Monitoring Mechanism and some response has been noted, the student makes a decision regarding the appropriateness of the response. Making this decision is, at best, a difficult task, and a realistic decision depends to a large extent on the explicitness of the criteria. After making the decision, rules concerning what to do next must be applied.

Decisions about What to Do Next

The tentative model of how skilled readers manage this what-to-do-next question will now be outlined. These conditional statements are the consequence of a logical analysis based on interview data of the actions students take when they fail to comprehend.

1. If a reader reads something that is not understood, some immediate action may occur or the information may be stored in memory as a pending question.
2. If the reader stores it as a pending question, a possible meaning (usually one) may be formulated, which is then stored as a tentative hypothesis.
3. If the reader forms a pending question, reading continues.
4. If a triggering event (i.e., too many pending questions, or repetition of the same pending question) occurs after the reader forms the pending question, some additional strategic action may be taken. By agreeing to take some strategic action, the reader may
   a. **Reread** some portion of the text in order to collect more information that will either answer a pending question or form a tentative hypothesis that is related to a pending question.
   b. **Jump ahead** in the text to see whether there are headings or paragraphs that refer to the pending question that might answer it.

c. **Consult an outside source** (e.g., dictionary, glossary, encyclopedia, expert) for an answer to a pending question.

d. **Make a written record** of a pending question.

e. **Think–reflect** about the pending question and relate it to information that is in memory.

f. **Quit reading** the text.

5. The reader may continue to read from the point at which comprehension failure was last encountered, whether the strategic action is successful or not.

And so the process continues in which the student manages episode after episode as each section of prose is processed.

STAGE III: POSTREADING ACTIVITIES

In this stage, activities are employed by the student to enrich the learning that has already taken place, to increase the probability that what has been learned will be retained, and to generate alternate texts (e.g., notes and outlines) that will be useful when the material has to be studied again later.

In what postreading activities should students engage? In one sense, any of the organizational (outline, mnemonics), translational (paraphrases, generate questions), and/or repetitional (recitation, rehearsal) schemes can help students remember what they have learned. However, there is the chance that to engage in these schemes will burden the students with unnecessary busywork and cause them to gain mastery of information that is unrelated to the criteria. Fortunately, Weinstein and Dansereau are researching interesting strategies related to this particular phase of study; they are discussed in other chapters of this book. These techniques have a very exciting potential of serving the student well during this stage of study.

At our Center, we have developed an idea mapping technique that is also potentially useful during this postreading stage. The technique is described as only "potentially" useful because it has not yet been field-tested with a large population of students. However, the underpinnings of the technique seem sound and are worthy of discussion here.

As is apparent in this chapter, studying involves complex behaviors in which the student imposes meaning on text material through a series of self-directed instructional episodes. Studying is not seen as a series of mechanical steps, but rather as an interactive process involving a student's prior knowledge, textbooks, study guides, etc. It is a process in which the student's comprehension of a text topic is expanded, sharpened, and made more relevant (or whatever else the studying criteria demand). When thinking about techniques to use in teaching students this complex process, a glaring hole in traditional study procedures is apparent. That is, there is no efficient way for students to represent concisely or record the meaning or the relationship among ideas found in lectures, notes, or text materials. Note-taking and outlining strategies are either too simplistic and insufficient for capturing the relationships or so elaborate that employing them is an inefficient use of student time.

Consequently, a new technique was designed that stresses the importance of students' ability to link ideas together **and** to represent the nature of the relationship between the ideas. As an illustration of the inadequacy of the traditional techniques, outlining only enables students to detect which sets of ideas are subsumed under others; however, outlines do not provide an adequate framework for showing why they are subsumed. Are the subsumed items merely properties of the superordinate ones? Or are they the outcomes of the superordinate items?

Some of our early thoughts about solutions to this problem came from an article by Hauf (1971), and from the work of John Merritt (Merritt, Prior, Grugeon, & Grugeon, 1977) at the British Open University. Hauf describes a mapping technique in which students can organize the main ideas from a text passage without the usual constraints found in a formal outline. She advocates that the central idea be written near the middle of a note page and the subsidiary ideas be attached in a concentric fashion, resulting in a product that resembles a city map. The main difference between this technique and outlining is that it breaks down the left-to-right and top-to-bottom conventions used in formal outlines. However, though it allows students to represent more faithfully the often complex interrelationships among ideas in a passage, it, like the outline, offers no easy way of expressing the nature of the relationships among the ideas.

In addition, some interesting work by Merritt (Merritt et al., 1977) influenced the development of our new technique, also called mapping. Merritt and some of his colleagues proposed an interesting hypothesis: For many, if not most, text passages, there is a preferred technique for succinctly representing their meaning. For example, some passages are best represented by either a Venn diagram, a flow chart, a double-entry (checklist) table, or a sketch. Data from the introspection activities of Merritt's team and from classroom students help support his hypothesis. Quite often students acting independently will design similar text representations from the same text passage. These outcomes suggest that there is some consistency in the way text can be represented. However, students would have to be taught a wide range of diagramming and charting skills in order to represent a variety of texts.

Any new mapping scheme, then, should have the flexibility and simplicity of the one discussed by Hauf (1971), but also should be capable of suc-

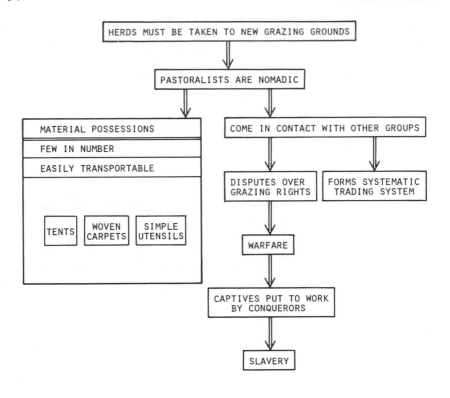

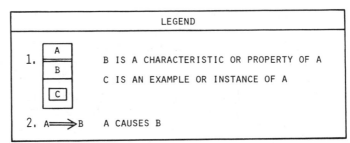

Figure 3.1 Map of Robertson (1977, p. 83) text.

cinctly representing a variety of relationships. Our new technique seems to
have these characteristics. To use this new scheme requires that the student
learn a set of relational conventions (symbols), which at the simplest level
indicate how two ideas are related, but at a text level can show the complex
relationships among many ideas. This scheme has seven fundamental relationships between two ideas, A and B: when B is an instance of A, B is a
property or characteristic of A, A is similar to B, A is greater or less than
B, A occurs before B, A causes B, and A is the negation of B. In addition,

two special relationships show when idea A is an important idea or a definition. The logical connectives *and* and *or* are also used.

An important feature of the maps, as illustrated in Figure 3.1, is that the shape of the map represents the organizational pattern of the ideas. For example, when the map based on text material is characterized by a series of embedded and segmented boxes, such as the box headed by "material possessions" in Figure 3.1, then the text is **describing** and **giving examples** of some perhaps fundamental ideas. Chapters in many introductory-level textbooks have these characteristic maps. On the other hand, when the map shows a series of boxes connected by arrows, such as those on the right side of Figure 3.1, then the text is concerned with a set of procedures (as in a technical manual), a chronology of events (as in a history text), or a causal chain of events (as in a concluding section of a chapter in a sociology text).

When and how often should students map ideas? Our experience with the technique is too limited to say for sure. However, we do know that mapping entire chapters, though often an enlightening process, requires a great deal of time, and realistically the student learns more from the exercise than is often necessary to know about the chapter content. Therefore, we are advocating that short maps be constructed for each important task outcome—that is, one for each item that might be on a chapter test. Roughly this translates into one map for each entry on the study guide, as described in an earlier section. The reader may note the similarities and differences with Dansereau's networking technique (see Chapter 1 of this volume).

SUMMARY

The process of studying is a criteria-related, self-directed form of reading text. The activities in this process are discussed in three phases, prereading, during-reading, and postreading. Prereading activities require the student to clarify the criteria for study. This is accomplished by collecting previously administered tests, lecture notes, and other evidence related to the criterion event, such as an examination, and then using these to construct a study guide by writing entries of key concepts from them onto appropriately labeled pages. Also during the prereading stage, the student surveys the text in an effort to determine how much of the text–topic is already known, how interesting it is, and how difficult or time-consuming it will be to learn what needs to be known.

The during-reading stage is characterized by periods of extended reading in which the students monitor their understanding of the text meaning and attempt to remediate any important comprehension failures as they occur.

When additional key concepts are encountered in the text, they should be entered in the study guide.

Finally, in the postreading stage, students employ activities to augment what has already been learned, to increase the probability that the learned material will be retained, and to generate useful alternate forms of the text materials. Concepts that have a high probability of being tested on a subsequent exam (e.g., those with entries on the study guide) should receive special attention by mapping the related ideas. Mapping is an elaborated outlining scheme in which not only are related ideas juxtaposed but the nature of their relationship is indicated by a symbol system.

ACKNOWLEDGMENTS

Ideas for this chapter came from several sources, but primarily from my many colleagues at the Center for the Study of Reading, University of Illinois at Urbana–Champaign. Those who contributed most are Stephen M. Alessi, Bonnie B. Armbruster, Linda Baker, Ann Brown, Alan Collins, Ernest T. Goetz, Leslie Moonshine, Diane L. Schallert, and Sally N. Standiford.

REFERENCES

Anderson, R. C., & Biddle, W. B. On asking people questions about what they are reading. In G. Bower (Ed.), *Psychology of learning and motivation* (Vol. 9). New York: Academic Press, 1975.

Anderson, T. H. Study strategies and adjunct aids. In R. J. Spiro, B. C. Bruce, & W. F. Brewer (Eds.), *Theoretical issues in reading comprehension*. Hillsdale, N.J.: Erlbaum, 1978.

André, M. E. D. A., & Anderson, T. H. *The development and evaluation of a self-questioning study technique* (Tech. Rep. No. 87). Urbana: University of Illinois at Urbana–Champaign, Center for the Study of Reading, June 1978.

Baker, L. *Strategies for dealing with comprehension difficulties: Recall and detection of text confusions* (Tech. Rep.). Urbana: University of Illinois at Urbana–Champaign, Center for the Study of Reading, in preparation.

Barton, W. A., Jr. *Outlining as a study procedure*. New York: Columbia University, Bureau of Publications, 1930.

Bitzer, D. L., Sherwood, B. A., & Tenczar, P. *Computer-based science education* (CERL Report X-37). Urbana: University of Illinois at Urbana–Champaign, Computer Education Research Laboratory, May 1973.

Brown, A. L., & Smiley, S. S. Rating the importance of structural units of prose passages: A problem of metacognitive development. *Child Development, 1977, 48,* 1–8.

Duell, O. K. *Overt and covert use of objectives of different levels*. Paper presented at the annual meeting of the American Educational Research Association, New York, April 1977.

Flavell, J. H. *Cognitive monitoring*. Paper presented at the Conference on Children's Oral Communication Skills, University of Wisconsin—Madison, October 1978.

Frase, L.T., & Schwartz, B. J. Effect of question production and answering in prose recall. *Journal of Educational Psychology,* 1975, *67,* 628–635.

Hauf, M. B. Mapping: A technique for translating reading into thinking. *Journal of Reading,* 1971, *14,* 225–230.

Merritt, J., Prior, D., Grugeon, E., & Grugeon, D. *Developing independence in reading.* Milton Keynes: The Open University Press, 1977.

Pauk, W. *How to study in college* (2nd ed.). Boston: Houghton Mifflin, 1974.

Reynolds, R. E., Standiford, S. N., & Anderson, R. C. *Distribution of reading time when questions are asked about a restricted category of text information* (Tech. Rep. No. 83). Urbana: University of Illinois at Urbana–Champaign, Center for the Study of Reading, April 1978.

Robertson, I. *Sociology.* New York: Worth Publishers, 1977.

Robinson, F. P. *Effective study* (rev. ed.). New York: Harper & Row, 1970.

Schmelzer, R. V. *The effect of college student constructed questions on the comprehension of a passage of expository prose* (Doctoral dissertation, University of Minnesota, 1975). *Dissertation Abstracts International,* 1975, *36,* 2162A. (University Microfilms No. 75-21,088)

4

Cognitive Psychology and Learning Strategies

GREGORY A. KIMBLE

The preceding chapters, which are the basis for this comment, all provide good examples of a particular approach to problems in applied psychology. In this strategy, the applied psychologist gets involved in some problem as it exists in its own context and then brings to bear whatever skills or techniques are available for the solution to that problem. This is a traditional approach in which the applied psychologist employs not so much the substantive content of psychology as the problem-solving skills of the field.

Actually there is a good reason for this tradition. Until very recently it always seemed to me that psychology—at least the part of it that I know about—had very little subject matter for which attempted applications were merited. What they taught me in graduate school, and what I have been teaching students since then, seemed to have very little potential for application.

Let me emphasize, however, that this was the state of psychology, but now I think that things have changed. Since the 1960s, developments in cognitive psychology, and the psychology of learning more generally, have come forth with ideas that seem to offer a stronger possibility of finding useful application. I want to present some of those newer ideas in this chapter.

PRELIMINARY SCATTERED THOUGHTS

Before turning to the main content of this comment, I would like to make some points that are incidental to the major themes I want to present.

I am reminded of my own small history of attempts to work in the field of applied psychology and the lessons that I learned along the way. Some of these lessons seem worth passing on.

Just after World War II, I managed a project at Yale that attempted to improve techniques of audiovisual instruction. My colleagues and I (see Wulff & Kimble, 1961) spent a great deal of time at Lackland Air Force Base doing experiments on the value of response guidance used along with such instruction. After a good bit of money and manpower was spent on the project, its entire positive outcome can be summarized in one brief sentence: In learning to read the slide rule (the task we employed) a moderate amount of guidance is optimal. Thus, the first lesson I learned in applied research was that the contributions can be disappointingly small, given the work it takes to make them.

There were, however, some other byproducts of this experience that strike me as more important. For one thing, this work gave me a high sensitivity to certain statistical problems that I was reminded of because they came up in the work reported in the prior chapters. There is, for example, the problem of initial differences between groups in the skills being studied. When that happens one is always left with the unattractive alternatives of using difference scores or analyses of covariance to attempt to make sense of data, or trying to argue the initial differences away on the grounds of statistical insignificance. None of these is a very satisfying solution to the problem.

The attempt to argue away may also be a Type II error (assuming the truth of the null hypothesis when it is in fact false). The abilities of different groups of participants in applied research may not be the same because they frequently are not randomly selected from a single parent population. In my early research at Lackland, this fact came forth with a vengeance. For the only time in my research career, I found myself dealing with a bimodal distribution of talent as measured by the Air Force Qualifying Test (AFQT). This fact came to light on retests carried out at Lackland: Although the recruits arrived with AFQT scores above an established cutoff point, their scores on retest were frequently below this criterion. This was the major source of the bimodality in the distribution, and it raised the question of how it occurred.

An insightful officer at Lackland made a shrewd guess and with a little detective work found the answer. A number of recruiting officers around the country, who had been unable to fill their quotas with qualified personnel, had given unqualified applicants enough help when they took the test to produce the required scores. Inevitably, this means that the low scores would be concentrated in particular groups of recruits who came to

Lackland at about the same time. Moreover, since (a) aptitude for mastering the slide rule task we were using was correlated with AFQT scores, and (b) we were testing the effects of different treatments on different groups of recruits, there was the problem of different initial levels of performance mentioned above.

There is also a subtler point to be made with the aid of this example. In question form: What statistical tests are appropriate in this situation? In spite of widespread opinion to the contrary, the problem is not with the nonnormality of the distribution. With samples of reasonable size, the central limit theorem guarantees normality of the distributions represented by the error terms in typical parametric tests (Kimble, 1978). The problem, rather, is with the assumption of randomness. Obviously, the individual subjects were not randomly assigned to conditions in this study. The only unit of sampling that has the feature of randomness is the **group** of recruits tested at the same time.

In the research on slide rule reading, we handled the problem by treating the means of group performances as the unit of sampling, something that was possible because we ran half a dozen groups in each experimental condition. When only N groups of subjects are run, however, each of them in the N different conditions of an experiment, this type of analysis is impossible. In my opinion, the results of such experiments are, at worst, unanalyzable. At best, they require the highly dubious assumptions that the failure to assign subjects at random did not affect the representativeness of the groups chosen. The appearance of initial differences in performance is a strong suggestion that the "at worst" situation holds. Numerical maneuvers that remove such differences in analysis provide no guarantee of also removing unequal susceptibilities to the treatments under study.

I have dwelt on this point, less because of the existence of such problems in the chapters that are the object of this comment than because the problem is currently widespread in experimental psychology. Much of the basic work in cognitive psychology is done on groups of subjects, sometimes with procedures that incorporate this error of design. It is, I think, important to be aware of the problem. Once one is aware of it, a number of possible solutions will suggest themselves: (a) running subjects one at a time; (b) selecting subjects by some haphazard procedure for assignment to groups to be run under one condition; (c) doing the experimental manipulation "within subjects"; and (d) if the variable can be manipulated by instructions, providing these instructions in written form and running different subjects in different conditions at the same time. Some of these suggestions solve the inherent problem less completely than others, but all of them represent an improvement over the techniques I am criticizing.

LEARNING STRATEGIES AND COGNITIVE PSYCHOLOGY

Having made these preliminary points, I will now present three key ideas in current interpretations of memory, asking in each case what these ideas might contribute to the development of effective learning strategies to apply in situations like those described in the prior chapters. The three key ideas involve (*a*) the distinction between episodic and semantic memory; (*b*) organizational factors in learning and memory; and (*c*) depth, breadth, or elaborateness of processing. I shall devote a short section to each.

Episodic and Semantic Memory

Tulving's (1972) distinction between episodic and semantic memory is as follows:

> Episodic memory receives and stores information about temporally dated episodes or events, and temporal–spatial relations among these events. . . . Semantic memory is the memory necessary for the use of language. It is a mental thesaurus, organized knowledge a person possesses about words and other verbal symbols, their meanings and referents, about relations among them, and about rules, formulas, and algorithms for the manipulation of these symbols, concepts, and relations [pp. 385–386].

In shorthand terms, episodic memory is memory for personal experience; semantic memory is knowledge about the world. From Ebbinghause on, laboratory work has concentrated on episodic memory. Only in recent times has there been much research on semantic memory. For the concerns of this book, that point is important. Knowledge available for an attempted understanding of learning strategies comes mainly from studies of episodic memory. But probably most of what goes on in practical learning situations is a reorganization of semantic memory.

To take just one example, most of you know the old jazz tune "The Sunny Side of the Street." If I ask you what that song is about, I am pretty sure that you will tell me that it advocates looking at the world through rose-colored glasses, being optimistic, in general taking a positive view of things. But suppose I tell you that the song means something quite different, that it is a black song and that the "crossing over" referred to in the lyric "This rover crossed over" is crossing the color line.

I picked "The Sunny Side of the Street" as an example because of its novelty, but I think that it is appropriate in reflecting what goes on in most educational situations. If this is true, a couple of implications are worth noting. The first is the fairly obvious point that it begins to help one understand a problem that teachers of social science tend to have all too frequently, the problem of being told that it is "all just common sense" or that "there's nothing there that would be news to my grandmother." Since mastering much of the content of a field like psychology entails little more than tinkering with the organization of semantic memory, such comments are often justified. Probably this is a cross we will have to bear until psychology develops to the point where it is more of a science than is now the case.

The second implication of this view of the educational process is more interesting in that it contains an invitation to research. To the extent that what a student "learns" on a topic is what he already knows, he is likely to have trouble keeping accurate track of his progress. Put somewhat differently, this problem will arise for the student because the elements of such learning are items of familiar information. What is new is the reorganization of these elements in semantic memory. When a student asks himself whether his experience is a "click" of understanding or a "clunk" of failure to understand (as Anderson puts it in Chapter 3), it is probably very easy to set criteria that are too low. When they are familiar with the raw materials, it is no doubt natural for students to mistake acquaintance with the materials for understanding the organization, and to think that they have mastered it when they have not.

The research related to this general issue will not be easy to do, although its general character seems clear enough. What we need to do is to find methods that allow us to separate criteria for having a "sense of knowing" from the actual possession of the knowledge. This sounds like an application of the theory of signal detectability. With such a separation accomplished, one could then determine the conditions that must exist for a student to set appropriate criteria of this type. The setting of meaningful criteria would represent an important learning strategy.

In a less ambitious context, I think that looking at the educational process as a matter of altering semantic memory says something important about "tricky" objective tests (e.g., true–false and multiple choice). They are tricky, one suspects, precisely because they offer as wrong answers answers that present accepted organizations of knowledge that we once accepted and now believe to be wrong. The wrong answers are part of the students' semantic memory. I mention this way of thinking because it fits in with the results of some experiments I have done.

Actually *experiment* is too strong a word. What I did was to give true–false tests covering the content of a psychology course to three different groups of subjects, analyzing the data in signal detection terms. In these analyses, a *hit* was responding "true" to a true statement. A *false alarm* was responding "true" to a false statement. The most important element of control was that two subgroups of subjects were presented with true statements that were in the false form for the third group. For example, two items for one group would be "Parents are **poor** at recognizing the emotions of their babies" (true) and "Co-twin control is a type of **power relationship**" (false). For another group, the items would be "Parents are **good** at recognizing the emotions of their babies" (false) and "Co-twin control is a type of **experimental design**" (true).

Analyses of the data yielded these two important results:

1. In their performances on these tests, 59 of 70 students gave more than 50% "true" responses. I suspect that this merely reflects the fact that somehow I have a knack for putting things in terms of "the memory necessary for the use of language [the] organized knowledge a person possesses about words, their meaning and referents," to use Tulving's (1972, p. 385) definition of semantic memory. Apparently, these organizations convey a powerful sense of truth in situations where the true content of statements does not warrant that reaction.

2. With a month's delay, hit rate showed a small decline from 85% to 72%. The rate of false alarms rose by more than a factor of three, from 15% to 49%. Again this suggested that as memory for the course material declined, the structures in semantic memory were allowed to take over.

Organization

The first thing to say about organization is that it is hard to say anything about it unless one knows what is to be organized. This is more than just a flip remark. Various analyses of the organization of prose produce different results. Thus, there are difficulties at the basis level of definition. In spite of this, I believe that I have four things to say about organization prompted by the chapters on which I am commenting:

1. Looked at broadly, the context of learning might be a part of organization. I have a bit of experimental data and an interpretation to report on that point.
2. More important than these experimental materials is a methodological point about the generalizability of findings.
3. Probably we can find out something about the nature of organization by looking at patterns of recall.
4. The ceiling effect of some organizational factors may point to a final important methodological fact of experimental life.

I shall comment briefly on each of these topics.

Emotional Context

We have read in the prior chapters that it is important to set an appropriate framework for learning and that a part of this is getting the learner into the right mood. We were also admonished that a state of anxiety is not a desirable part of this mood. Such assertions put us into the field of emotion and memory, a subject that has a long but not very glorious history. The only part of this history that I can be blamed for is directing one dissertation in the area (Davis, 1977).

In his dissertation research, John V. Davis put subjects in a happy or unhappy mood, using what might be called the "found letter technique." Suppose you find a letter that happens to be a detailed letter of recommendation for two people—and one of them is you. Suppose further that the letter is strongly negative (or positive) in its evaluation of you. How would the emotional state thus produced affect your learning and memory for the entire content of the letter?

Davis was not so cruel as to carry out this manipulation in its most realistic form. He discovered that (a) students could identify with the individuals in such letters quite easily even when they knew that the letters were fakes; and (b) the students found themselves actually experiencing the appropriate emotions. These affective states had no general effect on retention, but there was an interaction that indicated state-specific learning, where the state was an emotion. When put back into an emotional state for retention, the subjects remembered better if the state was the same as that under which original learning occurred.

One important conclusion suggested by Davis's study is that we should be very careful when the meddle with the moods of our students. They may be habitual contextual crutches that the students rely on when they study. I agree that the point seems unlikely, but it appears to be worth further research.

A Methodological Point

The results I just described were statistically significant only when evaluated by traditional between-subjects analyses of variance. These days it is common in cognitive psychology to do the analyses a second way—between materials—and to accept as reliable only outcomes that are significant in both analyses. Davis's mood-specific-memory data were not significant in this second analysis. I mention this because of the relevance of this point to the generalizability of findings.

There is a simple rule, and an easy way to express it, that I learned from Lindquist when I was a graduate student at the University of Iowa. Significant results generalize only to the populations whose variabilities are estimated by the error term in an analysis. The significant interaction in the between-subjects analysis tells us that this interaction is (with a certain level of confidence) generally characteristic of all individuals in the population of which the subjects in Davis's experiment were a representative sample. But only for the materials used in this experiment. This latter conclusion is required by the fact that the interaction was not significant in the analysis with an error term based on variance between materials.

The point to get from this is that the methods of analysis that have gained recent popularity provide a partial solution to the problem of generalizability of the approaches in the prior chapters.

Organization of Paragraphs

As some of the chapters in this book have suggested, it is appealing to think of prose materials as a network of related ideas, and one way to consider organization is in terms of the structure of these networks. This structure might be revealed by asking such questions as the following: What cues provide the most efficient entry into semantic networks when one tries to remember a set of materials? What materials are most available? How does one get from one place to another in this structure?

Consider the following sentence, which I asked introductory psychology students to try to remember as a summary of materials they had learned in the introductory course: *JOHN B. WATSON, the early behaviorist, did CLASSICAL CONDITIONING studies on children in an attempt to show that FEARS were learned as was suggested by his strong ENVIRONMEN-TALIST position.*

The subjects saw 24 items, of which the example above is representative. In each, the capitalized expressions were what the subjects knew they would be tested on. The items to be tested were always four for each passage: (*a*) someone's name (Watson); (*b*) a very general statement about that person's contribution or position (environmentalist); and (*c,d*) two more specific points about the person's contribution (classical conditioning, fears). The tests provided one of the items and the students were required to produce the rest. The questions to which the data might give partial answers are these: What are the least and most effective cues to retrieval? Given a particular cue, what are the least and most available items of information? Does recall follow any particular path as it retrieves this information?

Using the Watson example to illustrate, the results of this study suggested the following:

1. The most useful retrieval cue is the most general item of information (environmentalist); the least useful is the person's name (John B. Watson).

2. The most available piece of information is the proper name (John B. Watson); the least available may be the most general item (environmentalist).
3. Given any other cue, the most characteristic route through this network is to go first to the proper name and then to the other items of information.

Another Methodological Point

To illustrate how a preliminary summary of materials may benefit recall, suppose that you are required to learn the following paragraph, with or without the summary that I will give you in a moment.

> The procedure, actually, is quite simple. First, you arrange things into different groups. Of course, one pile may be sufficient, depending on how much there is to do. If you have to go somewhere else due to lack of facilities, that's the next step. Otherwise, you're pretty well set. It is important not to overdo things. That is, it is better to do too few things at once than too many. In the short run, this may not seem important, but complications can easily arise. A mistake can be expensive as well. At first, the whole procedure will seem complicated. Soon, however, it will become just another fact of life. It is difficult to foresee an end to the necessity of this task in the immediate future, but then one never can tell. After the procedure is completed, one arranges the materials into different groups again, and then they can be put into their appropriate places. Eventually, they will be used once more, and the whole cycle will have to be repeated; however, that is a part of life [Bransford & Johnson, 1973].

You may recognize this passage from Bransford and Johnson's (1973) study. They found that subjects who knew that the paragraph was describing the process of washing clothes remembered about twice as much as those without that information. I suspect that we have a clue here to the difficulty in much research of obtaining beneficial effects of summaries. If subjects are given just a hint as to the theme of a passage, by a title, the context of a study, or something else, that may be enough to accomplish most of what summaries can do. Additional summarization will have little effect. If this is true, the problem is an old, familiar friend: a ceiling effect.

Depth of Processing

In recent years the well-known fact that studying for meaning is effective has been the object of a considerable amount of laboratory work. The results have been impressive. Such deep, or elaborate, processing, as it has come to be called, has been shown to produce better recall than superficial or shallow processing, sometimes by as much as a factor of 13 to 1. I assume that these results are so well known as to need no more than mentioning and perhaps a key reference or two such as Craik and Lockhart (1972) and Craik and Tulving (1975).

The message I want to convey can also be very brief: Studies with discourse have begun to appear, and they have an advantage of deeper processing with materials like those used in the classroom. The magnitude of the effect is smaller than with word lists, but this is to be expected. Even to understand a sentence or paragraph requires deeper processing, and this appears to happen automatically. Thus, to no one's surprise, study for meaning is a learning strategy strongly recommended.

One question that came to mind as I read the prior chapters was whether procedures that seem very much like those used to produce deeper processing are equally effective on all types of test. Some of the data presented made it look as if deeper processing might have a greater beneficial effect on short-answer tests than on multiple-choice tests. If one thinks of these as free recall and recognition tests, respectively, this is a little surprising because such a difference does not show up in laboratory studies. The question is worth pursuing.

REFERENCES

Bransford, J. D., & Johnson, M. K. Consideration of some problems of comprehension. In W. G. Chase (Ed.), *Visual information processing*. New York: Academic Press, 1973.

Craik, F. I. M., & Lockhart, R. S. Levels of processing: A framework for memory research. *Journal of Verbal Learning and Verbal Behavior,* 1972, *11,* 671–684.

Craik, F. I. M., & Tulving, E. Depth of processing and the retention of words in episodic memory. *Journal of Experimental Psychology: General,* 1975, *104,* 268–294.

Davis, J. V. *Emotion and memory.* Unpublished doctoral dissertation, University of Colorado, 1977.

Kimble, G. A. *How to use (and misuse) statistics.* Englewood Cliffs, N.J.: Prentice-Hall, 1978.

Tulving, E. Episodic and semantic memory. In E. Tulving & W. Donaldson (Eds.), *Organization of memory.* New York: Academic Press, 1972.

Wulff, J. J., & Kimble, G. A. "Response guidance" as a factor in film instruction. In E. E. Lumsdaine (Ed.), *Student response in programmed instruction.* Washington, D.C.: NAS–NRC, 1961.

II

AFFECTIVE APPROACHES TO LEARNING STRATEGIES

5

Test Anxiety Reduction, Learning Strategies, and Academic Performance[1]

CHARLES D. SPIELBERGER, HECTOR P. GONZALEZ,
and TUCKER FLETCHER

In research on learning strategies, it is essential to consider both cognitive and affective factors that influence the learning process. Whereas cognitive variables are the major focus of some of the contributors to this book, our main concern in this chapter is with the affective domain of learning and, more specifically, with the influence of test anxiety on academic performance. As we shall see, however, it is difficult to study affective variables without also dealing with cognitive factors, since the two are closely interrelated.

In research on learning strategies, performance on a particular task must be monitored in order to investigate the processes that influence learning, and researchers must also be concerned with learning outcomes in order to determine how well particular learning strategies are working. With respect to the learning process, one needs to take into account both general factors, such as the nature of the learning materials and the mode of presentation, and individual differences in cognitive and affective variables that influence performance.

Cognitive variables that have been widely investigated in research on the learning process include encoding, storage, and retrieval. Though affective variables such as motivational and emotional states have received some at-

[1] Work on this chapter was supported by a grant to C. D. Spielberger and W. D. Anton from the Advanced Research Projects Agency, United States Department of Defense (MDA903–77–C–0190). It was monitored by the Training Analysis and Evaluation Group, U.S. Navy. Views and conclusions expressed in the chapter are those of the authors and should not be interpreted as necessarily representing the policies, either expressed or implied, of the sponsoring agency or of the United States government.

tention, the role of conation (i.e., striving, trying, persistence, will power, etc.) has been largely ignored by most learning theorists. In this chapter, we are concerned primarily with affective variables that influence academic performance and, in particular, with test anxiety.

Test anxiety has been defined as a situation-specific personality trait (Spielberger, 1972). The research of I. Sarason (1960, 1972, 1975), Wine (1971), and others who have worked in this area for a number of years (e.g., Alpert & Haber, 1960; Mandler & S. Sarason, 1952, 1953; Suinn, 1969) suggests that the concept of test anxiety refers to individual differences in anxiety proneness in test situations. In responding to examination stress, test-anxious persons are more likely to experience (a) emotional reactions characterized by feelings of tension, apprehension, and nervousness; (b) self-centered worry cognitions that interfere with attention; and (c) activation or arousal of the autonomic nervous system.

This chapter is divided into two sections. First, a brief historical survey of research on test anxiety will be presented. Then, the findings in a series of three investigations concerned with applications of behavior therapy designed to modify the affective reactions of test-anxious college students will be described.

HISTORICAL SURVEY OF RESEARCH ON TEST ANXIETY

The research of Seymour Sarason and George Mandler (Mandler & S. Sarason, 1952, 1953; S. Sarason & Mandler, 1952) at Yale University in the early 1950s is generally regarded as the pioneering work on test anxiety. These investigators conducted a series of studies that demonstrated that test anxiety leads to performance decrements in evaluative situations. They also developed the first widely used measure of individual differences in test anxiety, the Test Anxiety Questionnaire (TAQ). As will be noted, however, important work on "examination stress" preceded the Yale studies.

In 1929, Walter Cannon observed that metabolic changes induced by the stress associated with an academic examination lead to the secretion of sugar into the bloodstream (Cannon, 1929). When the system cannot handle the excess sugar, it is passed in the urine. On the basis of similar findings in a number of studies, Cannon concluded that academic examinations provided an ideal situation in which to investigate the influence of real-life stress on physiological changes.

Alexander Luria, the noted Russian physiologist, also conducted important research on examination stress, and was perhaps the first investigator to call attention to manifestations of individual differences in test anxiety.

Luria (1932) classified students as "unstable" if they displayed speech and motor disturbances and became excited and disorganized before and during examinations. In contrast, students who remained relatively calm and showed well-coordinated speech and motor reactions were considered "stable." In comparing stable and unstable students Luria concluded that academic examinations evoked intense emotional reactions in the unstable (i.e., test-anxious) students, for whom these situations appeared to produce "unmanageable stress."

Individual differences in test anxiety were investigated in the late 1930s in a series of studies at the University of Chicago (C. Brown, 1938a, 1938b; C. Brown & Gelder, 1938; Fiedler, 1949; Hastings, 1944; Waite, 1942). C. Brown (1938a) developed the first scale for identifying test-anxious students, noting that questions dealing with "subjective feelings of nervousness" and being irritable and worried about examinations were most highly correlated with scores on his scale. On the basis of his research findings, C. Brown (1938b) concluded that "students who become excited before examinations tend, on the whole, to do a little poorer in the examination than those students who are calm before the examination [pp. 30–31]." Thus, although most current research on test anxiety stems directly from the early studies at Yale, the importance of examination stress and test anxiety was recognized much earlier.

In the Yale studies, S. Sarason, Mandler, and their colleagues (Doris & S. Sarason, 1955; Mandler & S. Sarason, 1952; S. Sarason, Davidson, Lighthall, Waite & Ruebush, 1960; S. Sarason & Mandler, 1952; S. Sarason, Mandler, & Craighill, 1952) observed that evaluative situations have differential effects on the examination performance of high and low test-anxious students. These investigators demonstrated that failure feedback and other stressful instructions interfered with the performance of high test-anxious students compared with students low in test anxiety, and that high test-anxious subjects did better under conditions in which evaluative stress was minimized.

I. Sarason (1958, 1960, 1961, 1965) has been concerned with identifying situational factors that contribute to the differential performance of high and low test-anxious persons in evaluative situations. In a series of studies, he has demonstrated that (a) high test-anxious persons perform more poorly than individuals who are low in test anxiety when achievement is emphasized (I. Sarason, 1960, 1961); and (b) high test-anxious subjects show improved performance and low test-anxious subjects perform more poorly on tasks with instructions designed to allay anxiety (I. Sarason, 1958). On the basis of his research, Sarason concludes that test-anxious persons are more self-centered and self-critical than individuals low in test anxiety, and are more likely in examination situations to emit personalized, derogatory, self-critical worry responses that interfere with attention and test performance.

Most of the research literature on test anxiety has been concerned with the conditions under which test-anxious persons show performance decrements. There is also a more recent but substantial literature on the treatment of test anxiety in which behavior modification procedures have been employed as a means of reducing test anxiety and facilitating academic achievement. However, until recently, as Wine (1971) has noted, the test anxiety treatment literature has developed relatively independently of research on test anxiety and performance.

One major point of contact between the empirical investigations of the impact of test anxiety on performance and research on the treatment of test anxiety is that the same instruments have been used to assess test anxiety. The measures employed most often in both types of research are the Sarason–Mandler Test Anxiety Questionnaire (Sarason & Mandler, 1952), I. Sarason's (1972) Test Anxiety Scale (TAS), Suinn's (1969) Test Anxiety Behavior Scale (STABS), and the Liebert–Morris (1967) Worry–Emotionality Questionnaire.

A variety of therapeutic procedures have been employed in the treatment of test anxiety, including individual and group counseling, systematic desensitization, implosive therapy, rational–emotive therapy, and study-skills training. Of these approaches, systematic desensitization has been used more often than any other procedure, and positive evidence of the reduction of test anxiety was found in 27 of 31 desensitization studies evaluated in a recent review of the test anxiety literature (Gonzalez, 1976).

In research on the treatment of test-anxious students, the effectiveness of desensitization and other behavioral methods is generally determined by comparing changes on measures of test anxiety and academic performance. Reductions in test anxiety and improvement in grades are the desired outcomes. In the following section, the findings in a series of three investigations of the treatment of test anxiety with behavioral methods are briefly described.

SYSTEMATIC DESENSITIZATION, RELAXATION TRAINING, AND STUDY COUNSELING IN THE TREATMENT OF TEST ANXIETY

The subjects in these studies were undergraduate students who requested treatment for test anxiety at the Counseling Center of the University of South Florida. None of the subjects were currently receiving any other form of psychological treatment, and none had previous experience with behavior therapy. The therapists were all advanced graduate students in clinical psychology, with substantial training and experience in the behavioral treatment techniques that were employed.

Comparison of Systematic Desensitization and Group Counseling in the Treatment of Test Anxiety

Anton (1975) compared the effectiveness of systematic desensitization and group counseling in the treatment of test anxiety. The primary treatment outcome measures employed in this study were the Test Anxiety Scale (TAS) and changes in grade point average (GPA). A total of 54 students were assigned to desensitization ($N = 32$), group counseling ($N = 8$), and no-treatment ($N = 14$) control conditions. The subjects in these three experimental conditions were comparable with regard to mean TAS scores and cumulative GPAs prior to the beginning of the treatment program, and the distributions of male and female subjects in each experimental condition were similar.

Students assigned to the desensitization condition were further divided into four treatment groups, consisting of eight subjects each. In this condition, the subjects participated in eight 1-hour treatment sessions, two each week for a period of 4 weeks. The desensitization procedures were adapted from those developed by Donner (1968). The eight students assigned to the group counseling condition met once each week, for approximately 1 hour, over a 4-week period. Group discussion focused on test anxiety and the attitudes and feelings of group members with regard to course examinations. The group leader encouraged the students to discuss the methods they used to cope with anxiety during tests, and attempted to clarify any questions or issues that arose. The subjects in the no-treatment control group were informed that more students had signed up for the test anxiety program than could be accommodated, and they were promised they would be given an opportunity to participate in the program during the following quarter.[2]

All subjects participated in a posttreatment group-testing session in which the TAS was readministered. At the conclusion of the academic quarter in which treatment was provided, GPAs were obtained for each subject for the courses taken during the quarter. The mean pre- and post-treatment TAS scores for the desensitization, counseling, and no-treatment control groups are presented in Figure 5.1. It can be noted that the mean TAS scores for the three groups were essentially the same prior to treatment. After treatment, the mean TAS scores for the desensitization group

---

[2] Approximately 80% of the students in the no-treatment control group requested and received treatment during the following term.

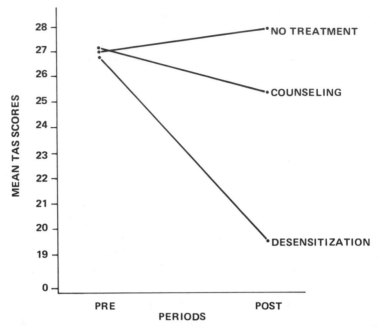

Figure 5.1 Pretreatment and posttreatment mean Test Anxiety Scale (TAS) scores for the desensitization, group counseling, and no-treatment groups. Reprinted with permission from Spielberger *et al.* (1976).

were markedly reduced, whereas the TAS scores for the counseling and the no-treatment control groups were essentially unchanged. Statistical analyses of the test anxiety data indicated that only the desensitization group showed a significant pre- to posttreatment decline in TAS scores.

In his analyses of the data for academic performance, Anton compared the individual student's cumulative GPA attained in all courses taken prior to the study with the GPA attained by the student for the quarter in which the study took place. No statistically significant effects were found for grades, suggesting that the experimental conditions had no impact on academic performance. Thus, although Anton's desensitization group showed a significant decline in test anxiety, this reduction was not associated with any improvement in grades.

Lin and McKeachie (1970) have observed that grades are influenced by many factors, and Allen (1972) has questioned the legitimacy of using GPA as an outcome measure in test anxiety treatment research. We reasoned, therefore, that tests of intellectual ability or aptitude administered before and after treatment might be more sensitive to changes brought about by reductions in test anxiety. In the next study, tests of intellectual achievement were used as outcome criteria. Performance on these measures was expected to improve with reductions in test anxiety.

Systematic Desensitization, Relaxation Training, and Suggestion in the Treatment of Test Anxiety

Bedell (1975) compared the relative effectiveness of systematic desensitization and relaxation training in the treatment of test anxiety. A total of 50 students participated in this study. Of these, 40 were randomly assigned to one of four treatment groups, and 10 students who met all of the selection criteria but were unable to participate in the treatment groups because of scheduling problems were assigned to the no-treatment control group. The subjects in the control group were given an opportunity to participate in the test anxiety program after the conclusion of the study.

In the pretreatment testing session, Bedell's subjects were given the TAS, the Wonderlic (1973) Personnel Test, and the arithmetic subtest of the Wide Range Achievement Test (Jastak & Jastak, 1965). The treatment and control groups were equated as closely as possible on the TAS and the Wonderlic. The relaxation and desensitization groups met twice each week for 4 weeks. Each session lasted approximately 1 hour, and there were seven sessions. During the first two sessions, all students were trained in deep muscle relaxation, using the procedures developed by Donner and Guerney (1969) as modified by Anton (1975). After the second session, students assigned to the relaxation condition continued training in deep muscle relaxation, while those in the desensitization condition were presented with the test anxiety hierarchy, using the same procedures that Anton (1975) employed.

Students assigned to the desensitization and relaxation training conditions were given instructions that were either high or low with respect to the suggestion for therapeutic gain. In the high-suggestion condition, students were told that the treatment was designed to enable them to overcome test anxiety by helping them to be more relaxed in testing situations. Students in the low-suggestion condition were told that the effectiveness of several techniques for reducing test anxiety was being evaluated, and that they would be given an opportunity to participate in another type of treatment if the program in which they were participating did not help them.

After the final treatment session, all subjects participated in a group testing session in which the same tests were given as in pretreatment group testing. In order to evaluate the general effects of treatment versus no treatment, Bedell's four treatment conditions were combined into a single treatment group and scores on each of the outcome measures for this combined treatment group were compared with those of the no-treatment control group. The mean pre- and posttreatment TAS scores for Bedell's treatment and no-treatment control groups are presented in Figure 5.2.

In the analysis of the data in Bedell's study, the significant treatments-by-periods interaction indicated that the Test Anxiety Scale means for the treatment and no-treatment groups were approximately the same prior to treatment, as can be noted in Figure 5.2. After treatment, the mean TAS score for the treatment group was substantially lower than that for the no-treatment group, for which the TAS scores were essentially unchanged. The reduction in TAS scores for the treatment group in this study was quite similar to the results obtained by Anton in the previous study (see Figure 5.1).

The effects of desensitization versus relaxation and high–low-suggestion instructions were determined for each outcome measure. In the evaluation of the TAS scores, the only significant finding was the pre- versus post-treatment (periods) main effect, reflecting the fact that desensitization and relaxation training were equally effective in reducing TAS scores from pre- to posttreatment. In the analysis of the effects of high- versus low-suggestion instructions, no statistically significant findings were obtained for any of the outcome measures.

In the analyses of the data for the measures of intellectual achievement, there was no evidence that treatment influenced test performance. Scores on the Wonderlic test were essentially unchanged from pre- to posttreatment. Scores on the Wide Range Achievement Test increased slightly more for the treatment group than for the no-treatment control group, but the

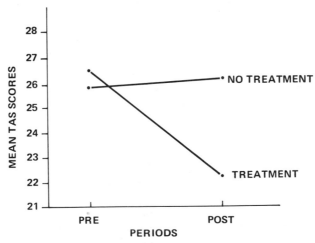

Figure 5.2 Pretreatment and posttreatment mean TAS scores for the treatment and the no-treatment groups. Adapted with permission from Spielberger *et al.* (1976).

statistical analyses suggested that the improvement in performance in both groups was a practice effect due to previous experience with this test.

In summary, the findings in Bedell's study were quite similar to those obtained by Anton. In both experiments, systematic desensitization produced marked reductions in test anxiety, and Bedell found that relaxation training alone was effective in reducing test anxiety. Although desensitization and relaxation treatments reduced test anxiety in both studies, the reduction in test anxiety did not lead to improvement in grades or to better performance on measures of cognitive–intellectual functioning.

Present evidence indicates that most behavioral approaches are effective in reducing test anxiety, but improvements in grades are only rarely observed (Spielberger, Anton, & Bedell, 1976). In six test anxiety treatment studies in which a combination of systematic desensitization and some form of study counseling was employed (Allen, 1971; Cohen, 1969; Doctor, Aponte, Burry, & Welch, 1970; Katahn, Strenger, & Cherry, 1966; McManus, 1971; Mitchell & Ng, 1972), significant reductions in test anxiety and improvements in academic achievement were reported. A study that combined desensitization or relaxation training with study counseling in the treatment of test-anxious college students is described in the next section.

Desensitization and Study Counseling in the Treatment of Test Anxiety

Gonzalez (1976) investigated the effectiveness of study counseling in combination with systematic desensitization and relaxation training techniques in the treatment of test-anxious students. The impact of study counseling alone was also evaluated, and a no-treatment group served as a control for test-retest effects and the passage of time. The 37 undergraduate students who participated in this study were randomly assigned to the desensitization plus study counseling (D + SC), relaxation plus study counseling (R + SC), study counseling only (SC), or the no-treatment (NT) conditions.

All of the students particpated in a pretreatment testing session in which they were given the Test Anxiety Scale and the Brown–Holtzman (1955) Survey of Study Habits and Attitudes (SSHA). Cumulative grade point averages (GPAs) were obtained for each student from official university records. Prior to treatment, the four groups were well matched with respect to GPA and scores on the TAS and the Survey of Study Habits and Attitudes (SSHA).

Each treatment group met twice weekly over a 4-week period, for a total of seven sessions. Students in the D + SC and R + SC groups received the desensitization and relaxation procedures while reclining in lounge chairs.

These procedures were presented on preprogrammed audio tapes, and were essentially the same as the procedures used by Anton and Bedell in the two studies described above. However, 8 of the 29 test anxiety scenes from Anton's desensitization hierarchy were eliminated because of apparent inconsistencies in the arrangement of the hierarchy items (Spielberger *et al.*, 1976).

Study skills training was given to all three treatment groups while the students were seated comfortably in padded armchairs. The study counseling procedures used in this study were similar to the procedures employed by Allen (1971). The following topics were discussed: motivational factors that interfere with academic performance; functional analysis of study behavior; monitoring and graphing study time; positive reinforcement and the Premack principle (Poteet, 1973); improvement of reading efficiency; and how to prepare for and take examinations. The students were given notes, charts, and guidelines for the materials covered in the study counseling sessions. Approximately half of the study counseling period was devoted to the discussion of study methods and the experiences of the students in implementing newly learned study skills.

Gonzalez's SC group received 65 minutes of study skills training, whereas students in his D + SC and R + SC groups spent only the first 30 minutes of each session in study counseling. In the last 35 minutes of each treatment session, the D + SC and R + SC groups received desensitization and/or relaxation training. All students participated in a posttreatment group-testing session in which the same scales were readministered. The GPA for the term during which the treatment took place was obtained for each student from the university registrar's quarterly printout.

The D + SC, R + SC, and SC treatments in Gonzalez's study were all effective in reducing test anxiety in contrast to the NT control group, for which test anxiety remained unchanged. The mean pre- and posttreatment TAS scores for the D + SC, R + SC, SC, and NT groups are presented in Figure 5.3. Statistical analyses of these data indicated that significant reductions in test anxiety were obtained for all three treatment groups, whereas no changes were found in the TAS scores of the NT control group. The finding that Gonzalez's treatment techniques reduced test anxiety was consistent with the results of other studies in which desensitization or relaxation training was combined with study counseling.[3]

The mean pre- and posttreatment study habits (SH) scores for the D + SC, R + SC, SC, and NT groups are presented in Figure 5.4, in which it can be noted that the scores for the four groups were approxi-

[3] The literature on the effects of study skills counseling alone on the reduction of test anxiety is inconsistent. In the nine studies in which this treatment was employed, significant reductions in test anxiety were found in four (see Gonzalez, 1976).

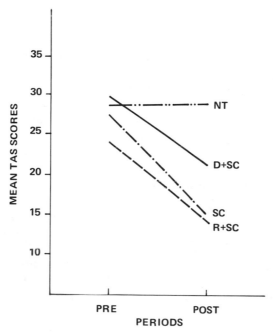

Figure 5.3 Pretreatment and posttreatment mean TAS scores for the desensitization plus study counseling (D + SC), relaxation plus study counseling (R + SC), study counseling only (SC), and no-treatment (NT) groups. Reprinted with permission from Gonazalez (1976).

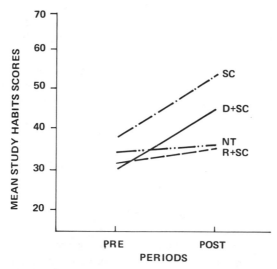

Figure 5.4 Pretreatment and posttreatment mean study habits scores for the desensitization plus study counseling (D + SC), relaxation plus study counseling (R + SC), study counseling only (SC), and no-treatment (NT) groups. Reprinted with permission from Gonzalez (1976).

mately the same prior to treatment. Statistical analyses indicated that the SH scores for the D + SC and SC groups increased significantly from pre- to posttreatment, whereas the scores for the R + SC and NT groups were essentially unchanged. Thus, study counseling alone and in combination with desensitization was effective in improving study habits, whereas relaxation combined with study counseling had no effect on study habits.

The improvement in study habits in Gonzalez's D + SC and SC groups was consistent with the results of Doctor et al. (1970), Mitchell and Ng (1972), and Garcia (1975). Failure to find improvement in study habits for the R + SC group was surprising, since this group received essentially the same study skills training as the D + SC and SC groups. It should be recalled, however, that the R + SC group received approximately 35 minutes of relaxation training in each of the seven treatment sessions. We may speculate that this treatment influenced students to become interested primarily in learning how to relax in order to reduce their emotional reactions in testing situations. It is also possible that the relaxation responses induced in students in the R + SC group resulted in lower arousal levels (Paul, 1969) that interfered with attention and information processing. In contrast, subjects in the D + SC group visualized scenes during desensitization that may have helped these students to stay more alert in learning new study skills. Although the importance of developing new study skills was equally emphasized in the three treatment groups, the amount of time devoted to relaxation training in the R + SC group may have contributed to the failure of these students to show any improvement in study habits.

Contrary to expectation, Gonzalez found no improvement in GPA for any of his treatment groups. As previously noted, desensitization or relaxation training combined with study counseling had resulted in improvement in the academic performance of test-anxious students in six studies (Spielberger et al., 1976). The failure to find improvement in GPA in Gonzalez's D + SC group was especially surprising since this treatment was effective in decreasing test anxiety and in improving study habits. A major difference between Gonzalez's D + SC treatment and the study counseling procedures employed in previous studies was that Gonzalez emphasized topics related to study skills while providing only minimal training in coping with anxiety. In most previous studies, considerable time was devoted to the discussion of specific anxiety coping techniques.

Another important difference between the Gonzalez study and previous investigations in which desensitization combined with study counseling resulted in improvement in academic achievement was the length of the academic term. Gonzalez conducted his study at a university operating on the quarter system, whereas five of the six studies in which improvements in GPA were observed were conducted at institutions that operated on a semester term (Allen, 1971; Cohen, 1969; Doctor *et al.*, 1970: Katahn *et al.*, 1966; Mitchell & Ng, 1972). In the single study conducted in the context of a quarter system (McManus, 1971), treatment was initiated at the beginning of the quarter, whereas Gonzalez did not initiate treatment until the fifth week of the 11-week academic term. Thus, there was relatively little time in Gonzalez's study for the observed changes in study habits to have any influence on grades.

Although Gonzalez found no improvement in GPA as a function of treatment, it was possible that the anxiety reduction found in all three treatment conditions had a differential impact on GPA for students with above- and below-average pretreatment study habits. Since Gonzalez's treatment groups showed comparable reductions in test anxiety, the data for these groups were combined in order to investigate the influence of reductions in test anxiety on GPA.[4] For this analysis, the subjects were divided into above- and below-average study habits groups. Students with pretreatment study habit (SH) scores above the median for this scale (34.5) were assigned to the good-study-habits group, and those with scores below the median were assigned to the poor-study-habits group.

The mean pre- and posttreatment GPAs for the good and poor SH treatment groups, and for the no-treatment group are presented in Figure 5.5. These data were analyzed by an unweighted-means analysis of variance that yielded a significant groups-by-periods interaction effect. This interaction reflected a substantial increase in GPA for students in the treatment groups with good study habits, whereas there was a slight drop for treated students with poor study habits. The grade point average for students in the no-treatment control group remained essentially unchanged.

Further evaluation of the groups-by-periods interaction showed that the increase in GPA for the good study habits group was significant, whereas the changes for the poor study habits and no-treatment groups could be attributed to chance. Thus, the treatment conditions appeared to help students with good study habits to improve their academic performance, but had no influence on students with poor study habits.

As previously noted, Gonzalez's three treatment conditions were equally effective in reducing test anxiety, but there was substantial variation among the subjects with respect to the magnitude of change in their test anxiety scores. Some students experienced little or no reduction in test anxiety, whereas others showed substantial declines. The optimal combination for

---

[4] Gonzalez's SC and D + SC groups showed improvement in study habits, but this did not facilitate their academic achievement. Since Gonzalez's treatment groups were functionally equivalent with regard to their impact on test anxiety and academic achievement, the three treatment groups were combined in evaluating the effects of large and small reductions in test anxiety on the grades of students with good and poor pretreatment study habits.

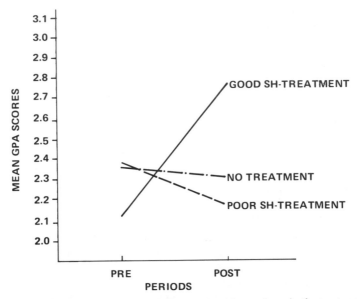

Figure 5.5 Pretreatment and posttreatment mean GPAs for students in the treatment groups with good and poor study habits and for the no-treatment group. Reprinted with permission from Gonzalez (1976).

improvement in GPA would seem to be a substantial reduction in test anxiety in students with good pretreatment study habits.

In order to examine the possibility that reductions in test anxiety influenced the changes in GPA that were observed for students with good study habits, the treatment groups were further divided into subgroups with large or small reductions in test anxiety. TAS change scores (delta TAS) were computed for each student by subtracting posttreatment scores from pretreatment scores. The students were then assigned to large or small TAS reduction groups on the basis of change scores that were above or below the median for the delta TAS score distribution.[5] Taking both study habits and reduction in test anxiety into account, the following four groups were formed: (*a*) good SH–large TAS reduction ($N = 5$); (*b*) good SH–small TAS reduction ($N = 6$); (*c*) poor SH–large TAS reduction ($N = 6$); and (*d*) poor SH–small TAS reduction ($N = 5$).

Pre- and posttreatment GPA means for students with good or poor pretreatment study habits and either large or small reductions in their TAS scores are presented in Figure 5.6. These data were evaluated by an

---

[5] Since this analysis is post hoc and the number of subjects in each group is quite small, the findings must be interpreted with caution. However, since the results are consistent with common sense and theoretical expectations, they are presented to stimulate further research.

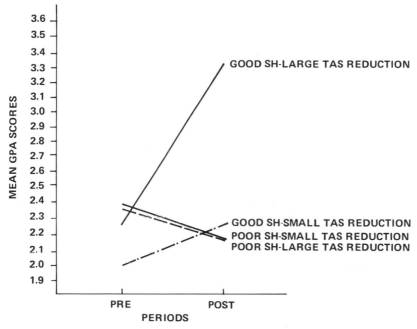

Figure 5.6 Pretreatment and posttreatment mean GPAs for students in the treatment groups with good SH–large TAS reduction, good SH–small TAS reduction, poor SH–large TAS reduction, and poor SH–small TAS reduction. Reprinted with permission from Gonzalez (1976).

ANOVA in which the groups-by-periods interaction approached significance ($p < .10$). This interaction reflected the tendency for students with good study habits and large TAS reductions to show a greater increase in GPA than students with good study habits and small TAS reductions, who showed only a slight increase in GPA. Interestingly, students with poor study habits tended to show a slight decline in GPA, irrespective of the amount of reduction in test anxiety that they experienced. Further evaluation of the data revealed that the increase in GPA for the good study habits–large TAS reduction group was statistically significant, whereas there was no significant change for any of the other groups.

In summary, Gonzalez's D + SC, R + SC, and SC treatments were all effective in reducing test anxiety as compared to the no-treatment condition, for which test anxiety remained unchanged. Study counseling alone, and in combination with desensitization, was effective in improving study habits, whereas relaxation plus study counseling had little or no effect on study habits. Though none of the treatment conditions had any direct impact on academic performance, improvement in GPA was found for treated students with good pretreatment study habits. Furthermore, students with good study habits and large reductions in test anxiety showed a greater improvement in GPA than did students with good study habits and small reductions in test anxiety. These findings suggested that good study habits and large reductions in test anxiety are required in order for behavioral treatments to facilitate improvement in the academic performance of test-anxious college students.

DISCUSSION AND CONCLUSIONS

The research literature on the treatment of test-anxious students demonstrates that desensitization and other behavioral treatments are effective in reducing test anxiety, but there is little evidence that behavioral treatments alone can facilitate academic achievement. On the other hand, improvement in grade point average was reported in six of seven studies in which desensitization or relaxation training was combined with some form of study counseling. The success of these combined treatment approaches has been attributed to their effectiveness in both reducing test anxiety and improving study habits (Mitchell & Ng, 1972).

Study habits correlate negatively with test anxiety (e.g., Wittmaier, 1972) and positively with academic achievement (W. Brown & Holtzman, 1955), and appear to contribute to academic performance independently of ability (Lin & McKeachie, 1970). Therefore, it would seem to be essential to take students' study habits into account in the treatment of test anxiety. At least 45 test anxiety treatment studies have been published over the past decade, and some form of study counseling was employed as a treatment component in 13 of these investigations. Yet study habits were actually measured in only five of these studies (Doctor *et al.,* 1970; Garcia, 1975; Gonzalez, 1976; Mitchell, Hall, & Piatkowska, 1975; Mitchell & Ng, 1972). Clearly, a major shortcoming in test anxiety treatment research has been the failure to measure and evaluate study habits.

Since students with test anxiety generally have poor study habits (Desiderato & Koskinen, 1969; Wittmaier, 1972) and devote less time to studying than low anxious students (Allen, Lerner, & Hinrichsen, 1972), it would seem important to provide study skills training in combination with desensitization in the treatment of test-anxious students. Wolpe, Brady, Serber, Agras, and Liberman (1973) have come to a similar conclusion with regard to applications of behavior therapy in other contexts. They contend that desensitization alone cannot be effective in the treatment of anxiety-related problems unless the client has adequate skills for coping with these problems, and they recommend that behavioral treatments be combined with the development of appropriate coping skills.

A careful examination of the test anxiety treatment studies in which significant improvements in grades were reported reveals that the participants in these studies were highly motivated to use relaxation as a means for coping with anxiety **during** examinations. Student motivation to use the techniques they learned in treatment appeared to be enhanced by active participation in group discussions of success and failure experiences with these techniques in a variety of stressful situations. The group discussions also appeared to facilitate "cognitive restructuring" (Goldfried, Linehan, & Smith, 1978), which seemed to reduce the tendency for test-anxious students to experience self-doubts and self-depreciating thoughts in evaluative situations.

To the extent that treatment reduces the amount of time and energy that test-anxious students spend in ruminating about personal shortcomings and perceived inadequacies, the students are better able to concentrate during examinations and to devote more attention to test requirements. Group discussions of anxiety coping techniques appear to increase the self-confidence of test-anxious students by reducing self-critical cognitions and helping them to control their emotional reactions in test situations.

In 1967, Liebert and Morris introduced an important theoretical distinction with regard to the nature of test anxiety that has not been given adequate attention in research on the treatment of test-anxious students. They conceptualized test anxiety as consisting of two major components, worry and emotionality, and reported evidence that worry was associated with performance decrements on cognitive–intellectual tasks, whereas emotionality was unrelated to performance on such tasks (Morris & Liebert, 1970). As previously noted, I. Sarason (1972, 1975) has also emphasized the critical role of worry in contributing to the performance decrements of test-anxious students. According to Sarason, high test-anxious students are more self-centered and self-critical than students who are low in test anxiety, and more likely to emit worry responses that interfere with information processing and attention to task-relevant cues (I. Sarason & Stoops, 1978).

In two studies in which cognitive behavior modification procedures were used in the treatment of test-anxious students, significant reductions in test anxiety and improvement in grades were found (Holroyd, 1976; Meichenbaum, 1972). Although the cognitive treatment procedures used in these studies appeared to facilitate the academic performance of test-anxious students by alleviating or reducing the intensity of their worry cognitions, no effort was made to measure changes in worry. In future studies designed to evaluate the effectiveness of cognitive behavior modification procedures in the treatment of test-anxious students, the assessment of worry cognitions would seem to be essential.

Building primarily on the work of I. Sarason (1972, 1975) and Liebert and Morris (1967), Spielberger (1972) has conceptualized test anxiety as a situation-specific form of trait anxiety, and has developed a new psychometric instrument, the Test Anxiety Inventory (TAI), to measure this construct (Spielberger, Gonzalez, Taylor, Algaze, & Anton, 1978). Although the TAI consists of only 20 items, the scale has excellent internal consistency and is highly correlated with other widely used test-anxiety measures. A unique feature of the TAI is that it has subscales for assessing individual differences in the worry cognitions and emotional reactions experienced by students in test situations. Derived by factor-analytic procedures, the TAI worry and emotionality subscales are both inversely related to study skills, but only the worry subscale correlates negatively with academic achievement (Spielberger et al., 1978). Extensive normative data for the TAI are available for both high school and college students.[6]

The TAI appears to have excellent potential for the assessment of test anxiety as a situation-specific personality trait, and would seem to be useful for investigating the effectiveness of various therapeutic approaches in the treatment of test-anxious students. The TAI worry scale would appear to be appropriate for evaluating the impact of cognitive behavior modification on worry responses, and the TAI emotionality scale appears to be potentially useful for assessing the effectiveness of systematic desensitization and/or relaxation training in reducing emotionality in test situations.

In future research on the treatment of test anxiety it would seem to be important to obtain a careful diagnostic assessment of the specific deficiencies of the test-anxious student. This will require the assessment of individual differences in the disposition to experience worry cognitions and emotional reactions in test situations and the measurement of study habits and attitudes. It will then be possible to tailor treatment programs to meet the specific needs and problems of the student. Since most test-anxious students have poor study habits and attitudes, treatment programs that combine systematic desensitization and/or cognitive therapy with study skills training are likely to be most effective. Future research on test anxiety should also investigate the role of the conative variables that influence the degree to which test-anxious students are motivated to apply the anxiety coping strategies and study skills that they learn in the course of treatment.

Summary

Research on the nature and treatment of test anxiety was examined in historical perspective and the results of three test anxiety treatment studies

[6] The Test Anxiety Inventory Test Form and the Preliminary Test Manual, for the scale, can be obtained by writing to Charles D. Spielberger, Center for Research in Community Psychology, College of Social and Behavioral Sciences, University of South Florida, Tampa, Florida 33620.

were reported. Systematic desensitization and relaxation training were found to be effective in reducing test anxiety, but these treatments failed to bring about any improvement in academic achievement. A combination of desensitization and study skills training was also effective in reducing test anxiety and in improving study habits but did not facilitate academic performance. However, students with good pretreatment study habits who participated in the test anxiety treatment program obtained better grades than test-anxious students with poor pretreatment study habits. There was also evidence that students with good study habits who responded to treatment with greater reductions in test anxiety showed more improvement in grades than students with comparable study habits who experienced little or no reduction in test anxiety. These findings were discussed in terms of the importance of taking study habits and attitudes into account in future research on the treatment of test-anxious students. It was further emphasized that treatment programs should be tailored to meet the specific needs and problems of the student, and that individual differences in worry and emotionality should be employed as outcome measures in test-anxiety treatment studies.

REFERENCES

Allen, G. J. Study counseling and desensitization in test anxiety. *Journal of Abnormal Psychology,* 1971, *77,* 282–289.

Allen, G. J. The behavior treatment of anxiety: Recent research and future trends. *Behavior Therapy,* 1972, *3,* 253–262.

Allen, G. J., Lerner, W. M., & Hinrichsen, J. J. Study behaviors and their relationships to test anxiety and academic performance. *Psychological Reports,* 1972, *30,* 407–410.

Alpert, R., & Haber, R. N. Anxiety in academic achievements situations. *Journal of Abnormal and Social Psychology,* 1960, *61,* 207–215.

Anton, W. D. *An evaluation of process and outcome variables in the systematic desensitization of test anxiety.* Unpublished doctoral dissertation, University of South Florida, 1975.

Bedell, J. *Suggestion in the systematic desensitization of test anxiety.* Unpublished doctoral dissertation, University of South Florida, 1975.

Brown, C. H. Emotional reactions before examinations: II. Results of a questionnaire. *The Journal of Psychology,* 1938, *5,* 11–26. (a)

Brown, C. H. Emotional reactions before examinations: III. Interrelations. *The Journal of Psychology,* 1938, *5,* 27–31. (b)

Brown, C. H., & Gelder, D. V. Emotional reactions before examinations: I. Psysiological changes. *The Journal of Psychology,* 1938, *5,* 1–9.

Brown, W. F., & Holtzman, W. H. A study-attitudes questionnaire for predicting academic success. *Journal of Educational Psychology,* 1955, *46,* 75–84.

Cannon, W. B. *Bodily changes in pain, hunger, fear, and rage.* New York: Appleton, 1929.

Cohen, R. The effects of group interaction and progressive hierarchy presentation on desensitization of test anxiety. *Behavior Research and Therapy,* 1969, *7,* 15–26.

Desiderato, O., & Koskinen, P. Anxiety, study habits and academic achievement. *Journal of Consulting Psychology,* 1969, *16,* 162–165.

Doctor, R. M., Aponte, J., Burry, A., & Welch, R. Group counseling versus behavior therapy in treatment of college underachievement. *Behavior Research and Therapy,* 1970, *8,* 87–89.

Donner, L. *Effectiveness of a pre-programmed group desensitization treatment for test anxiety with and without a therapist present.* Unpublished doctoral dissertation, Rutgers, The State University, 1968.

Donner, L., & Guerney, B. G., Jr. Automated group desensitization for test anxiety. *Behavior Research and Therapy,* 1969, *7,* 1–13.

Doris, J., & Sarason, S. B. Test anxiety and blame assignment in a failure situation. *Journal of Abnormal and Social Psychology,* 1955, *50,* 335–338.

Fieldler, F. E. An experimental approach to preventive psychotherapy. *Journal of Abnormal and Social Psychology,* 1949, *44,* 386–393.

Garcia, J. *The comparison of two methods of treating test anxiety: Group systematic desensitization and group study counseling.* Unpublished doctoral dissertation, Nova University, 1975.

Goldfried, M. R., Linehan, M. M., & Smith, J. L. Reduction of test anxiety through cognitive restructuring. *Journal of Consulting and Clinical Psychology,* 1978, *46,* 32–39.

Gonzalez, H. P. *The effects of three treatment approaches on test anxiety, study habits and academic performance.* Unpublished master's thesis, University of South Florida, 1976.

Hastings, J. T. Tensions and school achievement examinations. *Journal of Experimental Education,* 1944, *12,* 143–164.

Holroyd, K. A. Cognition and desensitization in the group treatment of test anxiety. *Journal of Consulting and Clinical Psychology,* 1976, *44,* 991–1001.

Jastak, J. F., & Jastak, S. R. *WRAT Manual.* Wilmington, Del.: Guidance Associates, 1965.

Katahn, M., Strenger, S., & Cherry, N. Group counseling and behavior therapy with test-anxious college students. *Journal of Consulting Psychology,* 1966, *30,* 544–549.

Liebert, R. M., & Morris, L. W. Cognitive and emotional components of test anxiety: A distinction and some initial data. *Psychological Reports,* 1967, *20,* 975–978.

Lin, Y. G., & McKeachie, W. J. Aptitude, anxiety, study habits, and academic achievement. *Journal of Counseling Psychology,* 1970, *17,* 306–309.

Luria, A. R. [*The nature of human conflicts*] (W. H. Gantt, trans.). New York: Liveright, 1932.

McManus, M. Group desensitization of test anxiety. *Behavioral Research and Therapy,* 1971, *9,* 51–56.

Mandler, G. & Sarason, S. B. A study of anxiety and learning. *Journal of Abnormal and Social Psychology,* 1952, *47,* 166–173.

Mandler, G., & Sarason, S. B. The effect of prior experience and subjective failure on the evocation of test anxiety. *Journal of Personality,* 1953, *21,* 336–341.

Meichenbaum, D. H. Cognitive modification of test anxious college students. *Journal of Consulting and Clinical Psychology,* 1972, *39,* 370–380.

Mitchell, K. R., Hall, R. F., & Piatkowska, O. E. A group program for the treatment of failing college students. *Behavioral Therapy,* 1975, *6,* 324–336.

Mitchell, K. R., & Ng, K. T. Effects of group counseling and behavior therapy on the academic achievement of test anxious students. *Journal of Counseling Psychology,* 1972, *19,* 491–497.

Morris, L. W., & Liebert, R. M. Relationships of cognitive and emotional components of test anxiety to psysiological arousal and academic performance. *Journal of Consulting and Clinical Psychology,* 1970, *35,* 332–337.

Paul, G. L. Outcome of systematic desensitization I: Background, procedures, and uncontrolled reports of individual treatment. In C. M. Franks (Ed.), *Behavior therapy: Appraisal and status.* New York: McGraw-Hill, 1969.

Poteet, J. A. *Behavior modification: A practical guide for teachers.* Minneapolis: Burgess, 1973.

Sarason, I. G. Inter-relationships among individual difference variables, behavior in psychotherapy, and verbal conditioning. *Journal of Abnormal and Social Psychology,* 1958, *56,* 339–344.

Sarason, I. G. Empirical findings and theoretical problems in the use of anxiety scales. *Psychological Bulletin,* 1960, *57,* 403–415.

Sarason, I. G. Test anxiety and the intellectual performance of college students. *Journal of Educational Psychology,* 1961, *52,* 201–206.

Sarason, I. G. The human reinforcer in research in verbal behavior. In L. Krasner & L. Ollman (Eds.), *Research in behavior modification.* New York: Holt, Rinehart and Winston, 1965.

Sarason, I. G. Experimental approaches to test anxiety: Attention and uses of information. In C.D. Spielberger (Ed.), *Anxiety: Current trends in theory and research* (Vol. 2). New York: Academic Press, 1972.

Sarason, I. G. Anxiety and self-preoccupation. In I. G. Sarason & C. D. Spielberger (Eds.), *Stress and anxiety* (Vol. 2). New York: Hemisphere/Wiley, 1975.

Sarason, I. G., & Stoops, R. Test anxiety and the passage of time. *Journal of Consulting and Clinical Psychology,* 1978, *46,* 102–109.

Sarason, S. B., Davidson, K. S., Lighthall, F. F., Waite, R. R., & Ruebush, B. K. *Anxiety in learning school children: A report of research.* New York: John Wiley, 1960.

Sarason, S. B., & Mandler, G. Some correlates of test anxiety. *The Journal of Abnormal and Social Psychology,* 1952, *47,* 810–817.

Sarason, S. B., Mandler, G., & Craighill, P. G. The effect of differential instructions on anxiety and learning. *The Journal of Abnormal and Social Psychology,* 1952, *47,* 561–565.

Spielberger, C. D. Anxiety as an emotional state. In C. D. Spielberger (Ed.), *Anxiety: Current trends in theory and research* (Vol. 2). New York: Academic Press, 1972.

Spielberger, C. D., Anton, W. D., & Bedell, J. The nature and treatment of test anxiety. In M. Zuckerman & C. D. Spielberger (Eds.), *Emotions and anxiety: New concepts, methods, and applications.* Hillsdale, N.J.: Erlbaum, 1976.

Spielberger, C. D., Gonzalez, H. P., Taylor, C., Algaze, B., & Anton, W. D. Examination stress and test anxiety. In C. D. Spielberger & I. G. Sarason (Eds.), *Stress and anxiety* (Vol. 5). New York: Hemisphere/Wiley, 1978.

Suinn, R. M. The STABS, a measure of test anxiety for behavior therapy: Normative data. *Behavior Research and Therapy,* 1969, *7,* 335–339.

Waite, W. H. The relationship between performances on examinations and emotional responses. *The Journal of Experimental Education,* 1942, *11,* 88–96.

Wine, J. Test anxiety and direction of attention. *Psychological Bulletin,* 1971, *76,* 92–104.

Wittmaier, B. C. Test anxiety and study habits. *Journal of Educational Research,* 1972, *65,* 352–354.

Wolpe, J., Brady, J. P., Serber, M., Agras, W. S., & Liberman, R. P. The current status of systematic desensitization. *American Journal of Psychiatry,* 1973, *130,* 961–965.

Wonderlic, E. F. *Wonderlic personnel test manual.* Northfield, Ill.: Wonderlic & Associates, 1973.

6

Time Management
as a Learning Strategy
for Individualized Instruction[1]

WILSON A. JUDD, BARBARA J. McCOMBS,
and JACQUELINE L. DOBROVOLNY

Innovations in instructional technology offer substantial promise not only for improving the effectiveness of education, but also for improving training efficiency. Advances in individualized instructional materials and procedures are particularly noteworthy in this regard. At the simplest level of individualization, materials such as programmed texts allow students to complete instruction at their own pace. The addition of computer-based instructional procedures enhances the individualization benefits of self-paced instruction by providing the information management capabilities required to implement more adaptive individualized instruction on a large scale.

The promises of both individualized instructional materials and computer-based instructional systems for improving training effectiveness and efficiency have been recognized by the Department of Defense as viable means for reducing military technical training costs. Perhaps in no other instructional environment is it more apparent that time equals dollars, since students are paid while in school. Every day of training time saved by innovations in materials or procedures translates directly into considerable savings of training dollars and more efficient utilization of manpower in the field.

Within the framework of large-scale military technical training, the benefits to be derived from computer-managed instruction are particularly

[1] This research was sponsored by the Defense Advanced Research Projects Agency under Contract No. MDA903 77 C 0144 and monitored by Air Force Human Resources Laboratory/Technical Training. The views and conclusions contained in this chapter are those of the authors and should not be interpreted as necessarily representing the official policies, expressed or implied, of the funding agencies or of the United State government.

promising. Computer-managed instruction can be defined as an instructional system in which the majority of the students' instructional activities are completed off-line, in contrast to computer-assisted instruction, where all instructional activities are conducted on-line at an interactive computer terminal. The computer's role in computer-managed instruction is that of evaluator, diagnostician, prescriber, and manager of instructional events. Although considerable effort has been devoted to improving the hardware, software, and instructional materials that support computer-managed instructional systems, the problem of preparing the student to utilize the system effectively and efficiently has received little attention.

Though the problem of helping students use instructional innovations effectively is not unique to military technical training, a computer-managed, individualized military training environment does provide a rich arena in which to explore materials and procedures designed to ease the students' transition into this new training experience. It must be assumed that until various forms of individualized instruction become common in our public school system, military trainees will find computer-managed instruction to be a novel learning environment. Few of these trainees will possess skills that enable them to use the capabilities of computer-based systems efficiently. Although there are certainly some basic skills that transfer from one learning environment to another, many trainees either will not have these skills or will not know how to adapt them to computer-managed training. If the computer-managed instructional systems being designed and built are to be most effective, students must be oriented to novel system capabilities and equipped with minimum skills to capitalize on these capabilities.

PROJECT GOALS

The overall goals of our research were to (a) determine the characteristic problems that students encounter in a computer-managed instructional system and to determine or define effective learning strategies for helping students cope with or adapt to these problems; (b) design, develop, implement, and evaluate a small set of self-contained instructional modules for increasing the effectiveness with which students adapt to and perform in a computer-managed instructional environment; and (c) investigate procedures for individualizing assignment of these modules so as to minimize total completion time and hence training cost.

This chapter describes the design, development, implementation, and evaluation of one specialized student skill module: a Time Management module that addresses the topic of students' rate of progress through a course of individualized instruction. The problem of time management is critical because (a) many students have little motivation to complete a course quickly and in some instances are actually motivated to prolong their training; and (b) a substantial number of students lack the self-management skills for effectively pacing themselves through an extended course of training.

To a great extent, the problem of time management has been aggravated by the belief that computer-managed instruction is "self-paced" instruction and that therefore students can complete the course at a pace of their own choosing, regardless of ability. Such a situation is at variance with emphasis on cost effectiveness in military technical training. The general objective of the Time Management module, therefore, was to motivate students to complete the course quickly by providing them with a set of effective time management tools.

RELATED LITERATURE

The literature pertaining to the problem of student skill training can be categorized into three areas of increasing specificity: (a) problems encountered by students in individualized and/or computer-managed instructional systems; (b) strategies or treatments for offsetting or remedying these problems; and (c) teaching time management skills.

Student Problems in Individualized and/or Computer-Managed Instructional Systems

On the basis of the literature describing military (Fletcher, 1975; Hansen, Ross, Bowman, & Thurmond, 1975; Kimberlin, 1973; McCombs & Siering, 1976; Middleton, Papetti, & Micheli, 1974) and nonmilitary (Allen, Meleca, & Myers, 1972; Cooley & Glaser, 1969; Countermine & Singh, 1974; Danford, 1974; Hagerty, 1970; King, 1975; Ullery, 1971) computer-managed instructional environments, the factors that are most novel to the student and hence of greatest concern may usefully be categorized along three dimensions: (a) a physical dimension involving the student's interaction with the physical aspects of the environment; (b) a learning process dimension including those training features in the environment that, either through design or accident, have a direct impact on the student's rate of learning; and (c) a social dimension involving those interpersonal dynamics directly related to the preceding factors.

Novelties that the student must cope with or adapt to in the physical environment include (a) a variety of multimedia materials: (b) learning centers containing 10 to 100 student carrels; (c) a variety of carrel designs, from individual to multiperson carrels, which may contain sophisticated equipment; (d) instructor stations or resource centers for obtaining learning materials; (e) testing rooms equipped with reader–printer computer terminals and/or interactive terminals; and (f) mark-sense answer sheets used for testing and requesting student assignments.

In the learning-process dimension, the student's new experiences may include (a) a broader concept of instructional materials, encompassing various media assigned on the basis of the student's characteristics or performance; (b) availability of organizers such as objectives, embedded questions, spaced and massed reviews; (c) frequent criterion-referenced testing; (d) individualized pacing; (e) computer scheduling of learning activities and equipment; and (f) unanticipated equipment or computer failures that interrupt the learning process.

The novelties inherent in the social dimension can include (a) less opportunity to discuss course content with peers since students are at varying points in the course; (b) less opportunity to assess one's own performance relative to others because of the absence of group, norm-referenced testing; (c) objective (computer) performance evaluations rather than subjective (instructor) evaluations; (d) individual interactions with instructors rather than group–instructor interactions; and (e) computer-assigned seating patterns rather than patterns based on peer relationships.

The problems that students encounter in adapting to the novel aspects of a computer-managed instructional environment are both affective and cognitive in nature. On the affective side, King (1975) discusses several potentially anxiety-producing aspects of computer-based instruction. Some students perceive computer evaluation as threatening. Individualized study carrels, materials, and procedures may lead to feelings of isolation and depersonalization that induce anxiety. Computer errors in test scoring, unpredictable system response times, and the varying quality of feedback are all sources of frustration and anxiety to some students. These contentions are supported by the work of Spielberger and his associates (e.g., Spielberger 1975, 1977; Spielberger, O'Neil, & Hansen, 1972) as well as recent work reported in Sieber, O'Neil, and Tobias (1977).

Cognitive problems that students encounter in individualized or computer-managed instructional environments appear to center around deficiencies in self-management skills (e.g., Seidel, Wagner, Rosenblatt, Hillelsohn, & Stelzer, 1975). These skill deficiencies include the inability to study, review, practice, accelerate, self-evaluate, and—what would appear to be most critical for computer-managed instruction—to manage time effectively. Poore and Pappas (1974) point out that ineffective study skills is one of the most serious and persistent student problems in any learning situation, and it is reasonable to expect that this problem would be compounded in the novel environment of computer-managed instruction.

Strategies for Remedying Student Adaptation Problems

A number of studies (e.g., Bond, 1971; Carpenter, 1971; McCombs & McDaniel, 1978; McCombs & Siering, 1976; Smith, 1973; Spielberger *et al.*, 1972) support the need to take both affective and cognitive characteristics into account in helping students perform effectively in an individualized or computer-based instructional system. There have been, however, relatively few attempts to identify specific skills that can be taught and effective methods for teaching these skills.

The work of Dansereau and his associates (see Chapter 1 of this volume as well as Dansereau, 1978; Dansereau, Actkinson, Long, & McDonald, 1974) and Weinstein (1975, 1978, and Chapter 2 of this volume) are exceptions in that these researchers suggest a number of viable techniques for teaching students new cognitive strategies. Dansereau's work deals with general strategies for all aspects of the learning process. He has developed instructional materials for teaching students (*a*) how to create a good mood for learning; (*b*) self-coaching skills; (*c*) concentration management techniques; (*d*) several general study skills and strategies; and (*e*) test-taking skills. On the other hand, Weinstein has concentrated on cognitive strategies in the area of memory skills and has developed materials and procedures for teaching students the use of various mnemonic devices, sentence and imaginal elaboration techniques, analogies, and paraphrasing, as well as techniques for drawing implications and creating relationships. Thus, this research has demonstrated the feasibility of developing materials that can modify students' approaches to a learning situation.

Groveman, Richards, and Caple (1975) conducted a thorough review of contemporary approaches to improving students' study behaviors. They concluded that behavioral self-control techniques (e.g., self-monitoring, progressive relaxation, self-instruction, self-reinforcement) and to a lesser degree the study skills counseling approach (e.g., counseling on study scheduling, textbook reading, note taking, test taking) were capable of significantly improving the performance of underachieving students. Although evaluated in the context of conventional, group-paced instructional environments, the generality of many of these skills for a computer-managed, individualized instructional environment seems apparent. Similarly, the work of Richardson (1978) emphasizes the importance of training students to use self-assessment and self-monitoring activities in behavioral self-control or cognitive self-change programs. Thus, there appears to be evidence for the viability of training techniques in effecting change in students' perceived locus of responsibility or self-regulatory behavior—necessary changes for successful performance in a computer-managed instruction environment.

Finally, there has been some work in the area of improving student attitudes toward computer-based instructional systems. Kopstein and Seidel (1972) discuss factors for alleviating the perceived dehumanizing aspects of an instructional system. These factors include changing the students from a state of "can't do" to a state of "can do," giving the students a feeling of choice in the management of their learning activities, and helping the students learn that the system is adaptive to their abilities and needs. It is suggested that materials with a degree of warmth and sensitivity to student needs provide critical ingredients for altering the perception of dehumanization. Khan and Weiss (1973) also suggest that materials be differentially designed for internal versus external locus of control students. The rationale is that the attitudes (and motivation) of students who believe that their degree of success is determined by sources beyond their control will improve if they use materials emphasizing self-management and/or self-determination (goal-setting) skills.

Strategies for Teaching Time Management Skills

There have been a number of interesting "self-help" books on time management techniques in the popular literature, such as Alan Lakein's (1974) *How to Get Control of Your Time and Your Life.* In the educational–psychological literature, however, approaches to teaching time management skills are sparse at best. One reason for this dearth of research is the traditional concern with level of achievement rather than learning times. When emphasis is placed on student efficiency in an individualized instructional situation, time management becomes more critical.

In addition to the work described previously on strategies to help students become more responsible for their learning, the effects of giving students data on completion times in a self-paced system is of relevance. Johnson, Salop, and Harding (1972) found that Navy students given predicted times and incentives based on whether they completed lessons in less time than was predicted completed the course in 17% less time than the control students, with no differences in final performance. There were, however, attitude differences between the two groups that suggest that quite different motivational factors may have been operating. Colton (1974) compared time and achievement scores of college students who were or were not given information about how long it took other students to finish 22 self-paced, criterion-referenced tasks. Students given time information completed 6 tasks in significantly less time but performed significantly less well on the criterion tests than did students not receiving the completion time information.

Two related studies investigated the effects of goal-setting instructions on student achievement in conventional courses. Gaa (1971) gave one group of tenth-grade English class students weekly individual goal-setting conferences, during which they set goals for the next week's activities and received feedback on their performance and progress in attaining previously set goals. A control group did not have the conferences but received the same in-class instruction. Students in the goal-setting group had higher scores on criterion-referenced achievement tests and better attitudes toward the course than did control group students. In his discussion of the attitude differences, Gaa interpreted the data to mean that the goal-setting group had higher motivation. In addition, the goal-setting students increased the internality of their feelings of locus of control as compared with the control students. Freeman and Niemeyer (1974), on the other hand, found no significant differences in criterion-referenced achievement test scores as a result of goal-setting instructions.

Anderson (1976) investigated the differential effectiveness of mastery and nonmastery learning strategies in altering students' time-on-task-to-criterion. When provided extra help (student tutors) in early course units and a mastery learning strategy (85% on within-unit tests) with built-in review procedures, students with lower entering skills attained equality with higher-ability students on both attainment levels and amount of on-task time to criterion by the end of the third unit. In addition, students in the mastery learning condition spent less time-on-task following this early tutorial help than did students in the nonmastery condition. These findings imply that early task-relevant skill training "costs" are amortized quickly when students begin using these skills to improve their performance. This suggests that early training in time monitoring and management can, on its own merits, reduce total training time by increasing the time students spend on task-relevant versus task-irrelevant activities. Combining this skill training with completion time predictions and progress feedback (as described by Johnson *et al.,* 1972) could then be expected to result in even greater time reductions.

PROJECT CONTEXT: THE ADVANCED
INSTRUCTIONAL SYSTEM

The context for the Computer-Managed Instruction Skill Modules project was the Air Force Advanced Instructional System (AIS): a prototype, multimedia, computer-based instructional system designed to improve the effectiveness and efficiency of Air Force technical training and to provide an operational research facility for assessing innovations in instructional technology. The system supports four technical training courses representative of the range of cognitive and performance skills required by enlisted Air Force personnel. An adaptive instructional decision model utilizes state-of-the-art computer hardware and software, as well as currently available statistical methodologies and instructional procedures, to provide instructional management and individualized assignments to alternative instructional materials.

The remainder of this section briefly describes the general structure of the courses and then outlines a typical student's experiences with the Advanced Instructional System, from course entry through graduation.

Course Structure

Each Advanced Instructional System course is divided into "blocks" of instruction that may require anywhere from 1 to 10 days to complete. Each block contains a number of lessons and a comprehensive end-of-block test. Within a block, lessons are arranged in a hierarchy based on their prerequisite relationships. A typical hierarchy resembles a set of parallel chains diverging and converging on certain pivotal lessons and a student may alternately work on lessons in two or more parallel chains.

The basic unit of instruction is the lesson. Each lesson consists of a set of objectives, two or more forms of a criterion test, and, typically, a self-test used by students to evaluate their understanding of the lesson before taking the criterion test.

A lesson's instruction is provided by one or more modules, each of which teaches the complete lesson content. Where two or more modules are present, they represent alternative instructional treatments. Depending on the lesson content and the nature of the treatment, a module may be a programmed text, an elaborated technical order, or an audiovisual presentation.

An Advanced Instructional System Student Scenario

A student's first experience with the Advanced Instructional System is when he or she is administered a preassessment battery consisting of a number of scales designed to assess cognitive and affective factors considered to be predictive of a student's performance in the course.

Following preassessment, the student requests a first assignment by submitting a "forward-going assignment" request at a management terminal. At this point, the student is enrolled in the course but has not yet entered a block containing actual course content. First, therefore, the system selects the block in which the student is to start work. Since the student has not yet completed any work in the course, only those blocks that have no prerequisites are considered. If there is more than one such block, the one containing the fewest students relative to the desired number in that block will be selected. The student is then assigned to an appropriate learning center and a home carrel. Finally, the student is assigned a specific lesson and one of the alternate forms of that lesson's criterion test.

Lesson assignment decisions are determined by two major components of the system—the Adapter and the Resource Allocation Model. The Adapter attempts to select, for each assignable lesson, the one module that is most appropriate for that student. This decision can be based on a variety of rules—for example, select the module that the student is predicted to complete in the shortest time, given that the student is also predicted to pass the criterion test. Each alternative module is given a weight indicating its relative preference. The Resource Allocation model assigns preference weights to modules for which the required resources are available in order to minimize the assignment's impact on the availability of instructional resources. Final lesson and module selection is based on a compromise between the two sets of preference weights. The form of the criterion test is chosen at random.

Having received the first printout, called a "student status report," the student reports to the instructor in a learning center, obtains the instructional resources required for the assigned lesson, and begins work at a home carrel.

After studying the lesson materials, the student completes a multiple-choice lesson self-test and reviews the material pertaining to any questions answered incorrectly. The student then completes the lesson criterion test and submits the test form to a management terminal. The resulting student status report details the student's performance on the criterion test (percentage total score, items missed, objectives failed, and the pass or fail decision) and the student's next assignment. If the test criterion was not met, the student is reassigned the same lesson and an alternative form of the criterion test. Otherwise, the lesson, module, and test selection procedures are repeated and the student is given a new lesson assignment.

After completing all content lessons in the block, the student is assigned a block review lesson. When ready for testing, the student is randomly assigned one of the alternate forms of the block test. Whereas lesson tests can be viewed as primarily diagnostic tools, end-of-block tests serve a certification function. There is no end-of-course test and performance on the block test is the basis for certifying mastery of the objectives contained in the block. If the student does not meet the block-test criterion, reassignment is made to the block in a status whereby assignments are made by the instructor rather than by the system. If the block decision is "Go," the block selection logic is repeated and the student is assigned to the next block of study.

The student's continued progress through the course is essentially a repetition of these events, with the exception that following the first and last blocks, questionnaires designed to assess students' attitudes toward the Advanced Instructional System are assigned.

PROBLEM DEFINITION

Analysis of Student Problems and Skills

Observations of student behaviors and informal discussions with students and instructors led to a number of hypotheses regarding the problems students experience in the Advanced Instructional System, problems that would be likely to generalize to other computer-managed environments.

Many problems appeared to derive from demands for more responsibility on the part of the learner than would be the case in a conventional classroom. Students appeared unable to manage their time and many seemed to feel that they were working in a vacuum; without the structure of group pacing and peer competition, they had little feeling for how they were progressing. Many were afraid to ask questions, including questions about their progress and standing, and some reacted to this uncertainty by procrastinating before making the commitment to take a block test. Additionally, students did not receive a comprehensive orientation to the Advanced Instructional System and, hence, were often confused by the variety of materials available to them.

To more fully understand students' problems, a series of interviews were conducted. Twenty-six students, falling into one of two categories, were drawn from the last halves of the Inventory Management and Materiel Facilities courses[2]: (a) students completing the course faster than average with above-average grades, and (b) students working at a slower than average rate with below-average grades. The interviews centered around students' problems with the Advanced Instructional System and were directed so as to ascertain opinions on 18 specific questions, listed in Table 6.1.

In general, students liked the system and the self-pacing concept,

---

[2] The content of these courses consists primarily of clerical and accounting tasks requiring procedure following, memorization, and reading skills on the part of the student.

TABLE 6.1
Questions Posed in Structured Student Interviews

1. What do you think about AIS?
2. How do you like the idea of self-pacing?
3. Do you have a feeling for how you are progressing?
4. Do you think anyone cares about how you are doing?
5. What strategies do you use to plan your time? Is it easy or difficult to plan time?
6. Do students care about doing well?
7. If you wanted to do better, what would you do?
8. What is the biggest problem students have with this course?
9. If you were advising a student just starting this course, what would you tell him or her to do or not to do?
10. If you were in charge of this course, what changes would you make?
11. How do you feel about having to reach performance objectives?
12. Was there a point in the course where you felt unmotivated or lost interest?
13. How do you feel about the computer's grading your tests and giving you the assignment?
14. How do you feel about your instructors?
15. Tell me about your study habits.
16. How do you use the objectives?
17. What motivates you to complete the course?
18. How would you feel about having a target date set for you?

although several students from the below-average groups indicated that they preferred group-paced instruction.

Most students believed that their instructors cared about how they were doing, although, again, several of the below-average students doubted their instructor's concern. Many students indicated that they had been fearful of asking questions during the first half of the course but also stated that their initial fears had been unwarranted and detrimental to their initial progress.

A majority of students had devised some method of measuring their progress, such as competing with peers or counting the number of lessons completed as compared with those remaining. About half of the students also used some type of time management strategy, although this was less common among the below-average students. Most thought that giving each student a target date for finishing the course would be a good idea.

Most, but not all, students indicated that they used the embedded questions in the programmed texts to test their knowledge and used the objectives to review for tests. When asked what they would do to try to do better, most indicated that they would take more time.

Students' biggest problem appeared to be motivation and becoming depressed during specific times in the course. The third block was the most difficult in both courses, and almost all students mentioned this block when asked if there was a time when they felt unmotivated. Inventory Management students were often motivated by pride, whereas Materiel Facilities students had more external motivators such as the desire to be an honor graduate or felt that the course was "part of my military career." Many were motivated by being able to go home upon course completion. The following conclusions were drawn from these interviews:

1. Students need a method of measuring their progress that is uniform throughout the course.
2. In conjunction with this progress measurement, students need to be taught basic time management skills.
3. Students need to be given information on what to expect in an individualized, computer-managed course.
4. Students need to be told that trying for the best possible grades, to the exclusion of any concern for time, is not necessarily the way "to do better."

Student Progress Management Component

Steps were already being taken to address some of the problems discussed in the previous section. Specifically, software to support a Student Progress Management Component had been designed and was being developed. The Advanced Instructional System supported a simple form of student progress monitoring and reporting that was recognized as being inadequate, one major concern being that it was not individualized. In addition, three specific problems shaped the characteristics of the Progress Management Component. First, the general opinion was that students could, if motivated, complete more course work than they were doing during the regular 6-hour shift. A related concern was to increase the amount of work students completed off-shift. Lessons were sometimes voluntarily completed out of class and students who failed one or more block tests were assigned off-shift remedial training. If, however, a student passed the block tests and progressed at a "reasonable" pace, there was no pressure to continue work off-shift. The third problem concerned prediction of course completion dates. Students' anticipated course completion dates were needed 10 days in advance for "out-processing," but variability in time to complete was so great that useful predictions required unattainably high correlation coefficients.

The Student Progress Management Component was intended to address each of these problems. The Management Component software would generate a target course completion time for each student that was predicated on the student's ability and that assumed that some lessons would be completed as homework. Daily feedback would be provided to the student and to learning center instructors and remedial training was to be assigned on the basis of poor rates of progress relative to students' targets as well as following block-test failures. Course managers were to employ available positive and negative incentives to manage students to on-target course completion.

As the Progress Management Component was implemented, a student's course completion time is predicted by a multiple linear regression equation employing data from the preassessment battery. A "policy function" converts this predicted time to a target time. If, for example, course management has determined that course completion times can and should be shortened by 5%, students' target times are set to 95% of their predicted course completion times. After a number of additional steps that allow for variable paths through the course and changes in course content, the end result is an individualized target rate, in the form of a standard score, corresponding to the student's target course completion time.

Time spent in the course is updated when the student completes an assignment, and the target time for the amount of work completed is updated when progress feedback is requested. The difference between these two times is the extent to which the student has deviated from his or her target rate.

The initial Progress Management printout occurs when the target rate is first computed, following submission of the student's last preassessment form. Target time for each block and the student's total target course completion time are listed in units of days and tenths of days. This printout is delivered to the student's learning center instructor and used by the student in completing the Time Management module.

The student's first student status report of each day contains the days (and tenths of days) of course completed and the days (and tenths of days) spent in class. The amount of work constituting a "day" of the course is, of course, a function of the student's target rate. Each student's rate of progress is also reported on the learning center roster: the number of days (and tenths of days) remaining to the student's targeted course completion date and the number of days (and tenths of days) by which the student is ahead of target. A negative value for "days ahead of target" indicates that the student is behind target and provides a means by which instructors can detect students who are falling behind in their course work.

If an instructor decides that a student's target rate should be reset, a request is forwarded to the course database manager, who changes student targets through an interactive editor. Although it would have been feasible to alter students' target rates automatically on the basis of their actual rates of progress, specific intervention by the instructor was purposefully required. Given the variety of reasons why students may be behind or ahead of their target rates, it was reasoned that the instructor is in a better position to determine the correct action than is the system software.

Perceived Deficiencies in the Student
Progress Management Component

Although the Student Progress Management Component, as implemented, would provide students with tools for coping with many of the problems they experienced in the Advanced Instructional System environment, simply providing them with these tools was not thought to be sufficient for actually resolving their problems. Further, no provision had been made for promoting student acceptance of the Management Component targets. It was thought that students needed to be intimately involved with the problems of pacing themselves and managing their time in order to want to improve their performance and, in turn, to allow the Progress Management Component to help them with this task. Additional mechanisms deemed necessary, therefore, were a method of telling students what to expect in this new learning environment and the goals of military technical training and, by virtue of this information, gaining their active involvement in attempting to complete the course quickly; a means of maintaining student concern with their rate of progress that would act in addition to (or in the absence of) the negative incentives being considered; and a means of improving the interactions between students and instructors concerning rate of progress. The additional mechanisms developed are described in the following section.

MODULE DESIGN AND DEVELOPMENT

Module Design

It was hypothesized that the most promising mechanism for maintaining student involvement with the target rate would be a means by which students would chart their daily progress relative to their target rate. It was reasoned that whereas it would be easy to dismiss adverse rate-of-progress information if it were simply listed on the student status reports, it would be much more difficult to ignore if the student were required to plot his or her daily deviation from the target rate. It was further reasoned that students would be more accepting of the course completion targets if they were actively involved in initiating the tracking chart.[3]

Because of the problems that students had expressed concerning approaching their instructors, scheduled "progress counseling sessions" were planned in which the student and instructor would periodically evaluate the student's progress. It was reasoned that, by scheduling such meetings early

---

[3] This logic was adopted from the behavioral modification literature (Richardson, 1978).

in the course, students would quickly find out that they did not need to fear discussing their progress with the instructors.

The major design goal of the module was reduction in course completion times beyond any reduction attributable to the Student Progress Management Component. Subordinate goals were that (*a*) students would maintain their progress tracking charts on a daily basis; (*b*) students and instructors would meet for progress counseling sessions; and (*c*) students would express positive affect regarding their experience with Student Progress Management.

Major concepts to be covered in the module were (*a*) the importance of completing the course quickly via efficient time management; (*b*) why and how each student is given a specific number of days to complete the course; (*c*) how the students should manage their study time using the progress charting technique; and (*d*) how to schedule progress counseling sessions.

Initial Product

The time management product developed consisted of the module itself, the criterion test instruments, a short attitude questionnaire, the student's daily progress charting process, and a set of procedures to be followed by the learning center instructors.

The objectives, stated in the front of the module, were as follows:

1. You (the student) will be able to identify good techniques for managing your time.
2. You will be able to use the computer to help you see how you are progressing toward your graduation day.
3. You will be able to keep track of your daily progress on a chart.
4. You will be able to identify when to enter into a progress counseling session with your instructor.

The module was written in a narrative style and explicit directions and examples were provided for the performance portions of the instruction. The vocabulary, grammar, and syntax were kept as simple as possible and frequent cartoons and diagrams were used to clarify details, to give the text low density, and to avoid the appearance of a technical document. The concept of time management and its importance in military technical training were described. The importance of speed, as opposed to high grades, was discussed briefly and Student Progress Management and the module's progress charting technique were described. Problems that could lead to the student's failing to keep up with his or her target rate and ways of dealing with these problems were discussed. The progress counseling session concept was introduced and the student was told how to schedule these meetings. Finally, the student was encouraged to set a "goal rate," a completion rate faster than the target rate, and taught how to draw it on his or her map.

The selected progress charting technique centered around a graph called a "course completion map," shown in Figure 6.1. The graph's axes, "Days Spent in Class" and "Days of Course Completed," correspond to the rate of progress information listed on the students' first daily student status reports. The graph is divided into fifths of days (not reproduced on Figure 6.1) and the student's course completion rate is shown as a 45-degree line extending from the origin to the number of days targeted for course completion. Plotted daily progress data that result in points falling below the line means the student is behind target. Points above the line show the extent to which the student is ahead of schedule.

The module contained detailed instructions on how to set up and maintain the map, and the student was stepped through the process of making and maintaining a map for a "typical" student before setting up his or her own map.

The criterion instruments included a 16-item postmodule test and an attitude questionnaire. The lesson test was designed to sample the students' knowledge and understanding of each of the four module objectives, and each objective was tested by at least three questions. Additionally, two performance questions tested the students' understanding of the procedures for creating and maintaining the course completion map. The attitude questionnaire consisted of five open-ended questions dealing with the student's opinion of the Time Management concept, the module format, and the lesson test.

The Time Management module created five new instructor-monitored procedures. The first formalized the intent of the Progress Management Component, requiring the instructor to check the learning center roster periodically to determine which students were either 2 days ahead or 2 days behind schedule and to initiate progress counseling sessions with these individuals.

In the counseling session, the instructor was to help fast students establish a goal rate—the student's personal goal for completing the course. To assist slow students, the instructor could initiate a "performance contract" indicating that the student agreed to make up X number of days by a specific date.

To assure that all students would have some interaction with their instructors to evaluate their progress, two scheduled progress counseling sessions with an instructor were designed to occur at the student's completion of the first block and 10 days prior to his or her target course completion date.

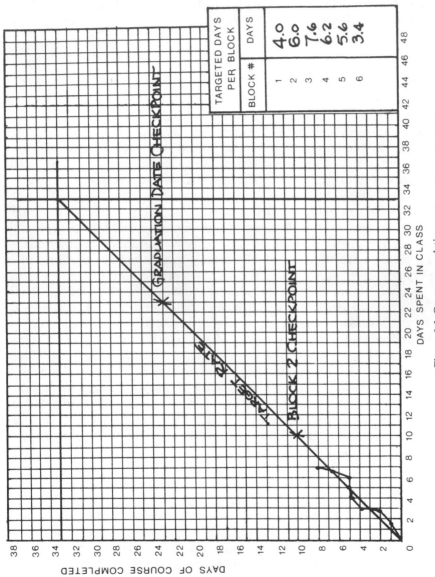

Figure 6.1 Course completion map.

149

The instructor could also change a student's target rate if it was deemed appropriate. To monitor the frequency and direction of the target changes, instructors were to contact the module developers to initiate such changes.

The final new procedure required instructors to check students' maps periodically to ensure that they were being maintained accurately.

Formative Evaluation

Formative evaluation of the Time Management module was conducted in the Inventory Management course and began with two small-group tryouts in which the primary concern was with the mechanics of the module itself. The evaluator worked one-on-one with a total of 42 entering students. In addition to the module, students were administered one form of the criterion test and the five-item attitude questionnaire to ascertain their attitudes toward the module and the time management concept in general.

As a result of these tryouts, a number of minor wording and grammatical changes were made, additional explanations and examples of daily progress plotting were added, two questions were added to the criterion test to evaluate understanding of this topic further, and the wording of a troublesome test question was revised.

This was followed by an operational evaluation in which the questions of interest concerned whether students could complete the module successfully without supervision, whether specified procedures would be followed, whether students expressed positive attitudes about their experiences, and whether course completion times were reduced. The Time Management Module was installed as the first lesson in the first block of a special, formative evaluation version of the Inventory Management course. The module questionnaire was not administered, since a standard "student attitude questionnaire" was administered at the end of Block 1. During this stage, 64 students entered the evaluation version of the course and of these, 28 completed the first four blocks. The number completing the remaining two blocks of the course was too small for meaningful analysis.

First-attempt scores on the module criterion test had a mean of 88.3%. Only one student failed to meet the criterion of 60% correct. The alpha reliability of the test was found to be quite poor, only .603. The decision was made, however, not to change the test until more data were available. First-attempt lesson times were found to be unreliable because of the lesson's position as the first assignment in the course. Administrative activities required at course entry were being charged against the lesson, and the lesson's position was later changed to avoid these timing errors.

Students maintained their maps with little difficulty, and many indicated

that they enjoyed keeping track of their daily progress. Some students failed to schedule progress counseling sessions, and instructors were encouraged to note when a student was approaching one of these milestones and remind the student of these responsibilities. Instructor-initiated counseling for students more than 2 days ahead or behind schedule occurred routinely with few problems. Only 10 target changes were requested, 3 of which were to shorten course completion times.

Student's completion times and end-of-block test scores on the first four blocks were compared with those of a group of students entering the course during the same period. Though none of the time or score differences were statistically significant, the results were considered promising, since the mean of the evaluation group's cumulative time for the four blocks was 3.75 hours (or 3.4%) less than that of the control group.

Eight items, considered likely to reflect attitude differences resulting from Progress Management and/or the Time Management module, were selected from the attitude questionnaire administered at the end of the first block. (The wording of these items is shown in Table 6.4.) As compared with the control group, the evaluation group's responses indicated that they felt more pressure to complete the course quickly and less able to work at their own pace. They also perceived their interactions with the instructors to be less satisfactory than did the control group.

Thirteen evaluation group students were also interviewed. The most useful information derived from these interviews was that when students were asked to complete the course as quickly as possible with minimal passing grades they did not really understand this concept, and, therefore, it was necessary to explain it to them again. Generally, students did not like this compromise.

Final Module Characteristics

A number of revisions were made on the basis of the operational evaluation. A page was added to the module elaborating the differences between the goals of military technical training and the goals of public school education. Directions for a practice exercise on the course completion map were clarified.

To assist students pace themselves, a handout was prepared listing average completion times for each lesson and a page explaining the use of the handout was added to the module. Summarized directions for plotting daily progress, reminders about scheduled progress counseling sessions, and the definition of a "goal line" were printed on the back of the handout.

Other than raising the criterion to 70% correct, no changes were made to the criterion test. A second form of the test was developed but, due to experimentor error, it was not implemented at the start of the summative evaluation period.

Learning center procedures remained essentially unchanged.

SUMMATIVE EVALUATION

Summative evaluation of the Student Progress Management Component and of the Time Management module was conducted in two phases. During Phase I, the complete Advanced Instructional System was undergoing an extensive evaluation (Integrated System Test) and the utility of the Progress Management Component was a major consideration in this evaluation. The Time Management module had come to be considered an integral part of the Progress Management Component and, thus, Phase I of the evaluation addressed the combined effects of Student Progress Management and the Time Management module. Following completion of the Integrated System Test, Phase II of the evaluation addressed the effects of the Time Management module per se in the presence of the Student Progress Management Component.

Phase I: Evaluation of Student Progress Management and the Time Management Module

During the Integrated System Test, students entering the Inventory Management course were randomly assigned to one of three versions of the course: a "main track" version, in which all students were assigned the instructional mode originally developed for that lesson; an "individualized instructional assignment" version, in which students were assigned one of two to five alternate instructional modules on the basis of their predicted time and score under each alternative treatment; and a "random" version, in which students were randomly assigned one of the alternative modules. Since main track and individualized instructional assignment were considered representative of two modes in which computer-managed instruction might be used for military technical training, a question of interest was whether students would react differently to the combined Progress Management and the Time Management module under these two differing conditions.

Student Progress Management and the Time Management module were introduced halfway through the Integrated System Test. The "no progress management" period lasted a total of 57 class days. A comparable 57-class-day period was defined beginning with the implementation of the Progress

Management Component (and Time Management module). Students who began the course and completed one or more blocks in the main track or individualized instructional assignment versions during the no-management and management periods constituted the control and evaluation groups, respectively. During the management period, the management component policy function was set to 90%.

Time Management Module Performance Data

The Time Management module was moved to the position of second lesson in the first block in order to avoid contamination of the lesson timing data. After about a month, however, course management moved the first two lessons out of the first block and administered them as part of the preassessment day activities. Consequently, collection of Time Management module performance data was restricted to the first 20 class days of the evaluation period.

Mean first-attempt lesson time (based on the data of 106 students) was 87.6 minutes with a standard deviation of 21.6 minutes.

Item-level criterion test data were available for 126 students. On the basis of these data, the alpha reliability of the test was found to have decreased to only .440 primarily because of six test items. Five of these six items had very low error rates and the sixth (pertaining to the frequency with which rate of progress data is provided) had a high (45%) error rate. These items were subsequently revised and satisfactory alpha reliabilities (i.e., .88 and .90, respectively) were found for both forms of the test.

Total first-attempt criterion test scores were available for 136 of the evaluation group students who also completed the first block of the course. For those students, the mean first-attempt criterion test score was 86.5. Nine students (6.6%) failed to meet the criterion of 70% correct.

Block Completion Time and Score Data

The question of primary interest concerned the hypothesized reduction in block and course completion times under Student Progress Management. A question of secondary interest was whether students would react differently to Progress Management under the two modes of assignment: main track and individualized instructional assignment. The block time data (block elapsed time less absence time), a measure of total course time (cumulative times over six blocks for students having reliable data for all six blocks), and first-attempt block test scores were, therefore, evaluated by means of 2 × 2 analyses of variance. The F tests of interest in these analyses were the main effects for management versus no management and the interaction between management versus no management and assignment mode. Main effects for assignment mode were not of interest for this evaluation.[4]

None of the seven time comparisons or six score comparisons indicated a significant interaction between management versus no management and assignment mode. All of the seven time comparisons and four of the six score comparisons did, however, indicate significant ($p < .01$) main effects for management versus no management. It was concluded that the effects of Student Progress Management were not moderated by the two differing modes of assignment. Consequently, the data obtained under the two assignment modes were combined, and only the main effect of Student Progress Management will be discussed. The means and standard deviations of the block times and scores obtained under Progress Management (evaluation group) and prior to implementation of the Progress Management Component (control group) are presented in Table 6.2 with the time or score differences between the two groups and the percentage time changes.

As Table 6.2 indicates, the mean completion time for Block 1 was 20.00 hours for the evaluation group as contrasted with a mean of 23.75 hours for the control group. This is a savings of 3.75 hours, or 15.8%—$F(1,575) = 37.150$, and $p = .001$. This is not, however, a clean comparison because of the changing content of the block: addition of the time management module at the start of the evaluation period and removal of both the module and the first lesson 3 weeks later.

The next two blocks, 2 and 3, both demonstrated significant time savings: 10.3% for Block 2—$F(1,505) = 15.760$, $p = .001$—and 13.7% for Block 3—$F(1,435) = 14.145$, $p = .001$.

Though still significant, Progress Management had relatively little effect on Block 4 times, resulting in only a 6.6% reduction—$F(1,442) = 6.992$, $p = .008$. Though there is no obvious reason why Block 4 should be less susceptible to Progress Management, it may be that the "mid-course slump" was relatively impervious to the treatment.

The final two blocks, 5 and 6, return to the pattern demonstrated in the first three blocks: a 10.5% reduction in Block 5—$F(1,348) = 13.776$, $p = .001$—and a 14.2% reduction in Block 6—$F(1,342) = 29.019$, $p = .001$.

For comparing total course completion times, only data from evaluation or control group students who completed all six blocks with reliable times

---

[4] An evaluation of the individualized instructional assignment (as contrasted with main track) is reported in McCombs (1979). It should be noted that whereas only block-level data are reported here, the questions of primary interest in the McCombs evaluation involved lesson-level data.

TABLE 6.2
Block Times and Scores for Summative Evaluation and Control Groups

Variable	Evaluation			Control			Evaluation –control	Percentage change
	N	$\bar{X}$	SD	N	$\bar{X}$	SD		
Block 1 time[a]	300	20.00	6.93	276	23.75	8.12	– 3.75	– 15.8
Block 2 time	274	26.05	7.62	29.03	29.03	9.03	– 2.98	– 10.3
Block 3 time	246	34.10	9.55	190	39.50	11.68	– 5.40	– 13.7
Block 4 time	243	21.08	5.37	180	22.58	6.42	– 1.50	– 6.6
Block 5 time	197	23.15	5.52	152	25.88	8.12	– 2.73	– 10.5
Block 6 time	196	16.23	4.32	174	18.92	3.63	– 2.69	– 14.2
Total time								
Blocks 1–6	75	136.13	31.33	115	153.33	31.52	– 17.20	– 11.2
Block 1 score[b]	359	80.3	10.8	280	82.5	10.3	– 2.2	
Block 2 score	320	79.8	12.8	251	82.3	11.8	– 2.5	
Block 3 score	304	74.1	11.3	208	77.6	10.2	– 3.5	
Block 4 score	269	81.1	9.7	192	83.4	9.1	– 2.3	
Block 5 score	233	76.7	14.6	163	80.9	10.1	– 4.2	
Block 6 score	223	82.7	10.7	155	84.8	9.9	– 2.1	

[a] Times shown in hours.
[b] Scores shown as percentages.

155

were considered. A prolonged computer failure during the evaluation period rendered many of the evaluation group students' times unreliable and substantially reduced the available N. For the remaining 75 evaluation group students, the mean course completion time was 136.13 hours (22.69 6-hour days), a reduction of 17.20 hours (2.86 days) from the control group mean, an overall reduction of 11.2%—$F(1,189) = 13.445$, $p = .001$.

A reasonable question is the extent to which block time reductions were attributable to increased homework. The percentage of lessons marked as homework actually declined from 8.57% for the control group to 4% for the evaluation group. Although at least part of this apparent reduction may have been due to changes in homework reporting procedures, there is no evidence that the block time reductions can be attributed to increased homework. Thus, the major factor contributing to the time reductions would appear to be increased student productivity during the normal shift.

Implementation of Student Progress Management was found to have a negative effect on first-attempt end-of-block test scores. The evaluation group's scores were 2 to 4 percentage points lower than those of the control group. F tests of the score differences between groups indicated that only the Block 2 difference failed to achieve significance at the .05 level.

It can be argued that in a criterion-referenced testing environment a reduction in mean block scores is not necessarily undesirable if the test failure rate is not increased. The number of first-attempt block test failures in the evaluation and control groups were contrasted by chi square tests. The percentage of failures, by block, in each group, the chi square values, and the resultant significance levels are shown in Table 6.3. Although the percentage of failures was consistently higher under the evaluation condition, the differences were statistically significant ($p < .05$) in only two of the six blocks: Blocks 1 and 3. It should be noted, however, that the total time students spent in a block, including any time spent in remediation following a block test failure, was, on the average, less than the time to complete the block prior to implementation of progress management.

Student Attitude Questionnaire Data

The same eight student attitude questionnaire items used in formative evaluation were employed to evaluate attitude differences between the control and evaluation groups. In this case, data were available from both administrations of the questionnaire: following Block 1 and at the end of the course, following Block 6. Item responses are arranged in a 5 point scale ranging from "strongly disagree" to "strongly agree" and are scored such that the most positive response is given a weight of five and the most negative a weight of one. The items, median responses from both administrations, differences between the evaluation and control group me-

TABLE 6.3
Percentages of First-Attempt Block Failures for Summative Evaluation and Control Groups

Block	Evaluation		Control		Evaluation-control	Chi square	P
	N	Percentage failures	N	Percentage failures	Percentage failures		
1	375	16.0	293	8.9	7.1	7.436	.01
2	329	14.9	261	11.9	3.0	1.132	.30
3	302	29.1	216	19.4	9.7	6.288	.02
4	281	12.5	199	8.0	4.5	2.353	.20
5	244	22.5	170	18.8	3.7	0.823	.50
6	232	7.8	166	4.8	3.0	1.329	.30

dians, the chi square values ($df = 4$), and the chi square probability levels (if $p < .10$) are presented in Table 6.4.

The first three items pertain to students' perceptions of their pace through the first block (first administration) or the course (second administration). The evaluation group's pattern of responses to the first item, "I felt that I could work at my own pace," were significantly more negative than those of the control group at the end of Block 1, but the responses of the two groups were essentially equivalent at the end of the course. Whereas the median response of the control group declined over time, the evaluation group's median response increased as students gained experience with progress management. The evaluation group's responses to the remaining two items are all slightly more favorable than those of the control group but only one comparison was statistically significant.

The next two items, pertaining to students' perceptions of the instructional methods and the career field, did not differentiate between groups.

The final three items pertain to students' perceptions of their interactions with their instructors. In contrast to the formative evaluation all three items demonstrated a slight positive shift, significant at the .05 level in two of the six comparisons.

Revisions to the Criterion Test

Based on Phase I results, two of the five items having very low error rates were eliminated since the concepts they tested were covered by other items. Distractors were reworded for the remaining three items. The higher-error rate item, pertaining to the frequency with which rate-of-progress data are provided to the student, was also eliminated since students quickly learn this information in the first few days of the course. Corresponding changes were made to the second form of the test and both forms were implemented with a more stringent passing criterion of 80% correct.

Phase II: Evaluation of the Time Management Module in the Presence of Student Progress Management

In the second phase of the summative evaluation, the effect of the Time Management module per se was evaluated in the Inventory Management course. Two versions of the course were defined: an evaluation version, containing the Time Management module as the student's first assignment after entering the learning center; and a control version in which students were given a placebo handout explaining the operation of the Student Progress Management Component. Student progress management and individualized instructional assignment were in operation in both versions of

TABLE 6.4

Attitude Questionnaire Responses for Summative Evaluation and Control Groups

Question	Block	Evaluation		Control		Evaluation–control	Chi	P
		N	Median	N	Median	Median	square	
I felt that I could work at my own pace.	1	353	4.32	274	4.55	−.23	12.468	.014
	6	212	4.49	158	4.46	.03	3.540	
Since Denver is such a nice area, I was not in a hurry to finish the course.	1	354	4.15	275	3.99	.16	5.017	
	6	213	4.03	160	3.93	.10	2.006	
I saw no reason to hurry through the course.	1	347	3.83	273	3.28	.55	28.761	.001
	6	210	3.67	157	3.37	.30	8.857	.065
I found myself trying to get through the programmed texts rather than trying to learn.	1	354	3.77	275	3.85	−.08	3.295	
	6	210	3.52	158	3.80	−.28	7.300	
I am anxious to get to my first assignment after finishing tech school.	1	356	4.81	279	4.74	.07	4.414	
	6	211	4.63	159	4.53	.10	5.477	
The instructors helped me and encouraged me to do well.	1	349	4.22	275	4.11	.11	7.114	
	6	207	4.38	160	4.33	.05	1.705	
I felt that I was not given enough personal attention.	1	351	4.30	272	4.18	.12	11.921	.018
	6	214	4.17	156	4.12	.05	2.268	
I felt no one really cared whether I worked or not.	1	355	4.27	277	4.17	.10	6.719	
	6	213	4.35	158	4.21	.14	10.388	.034

159

the course. Course completion times had become somewhat shorter and the policy function was raised to 95%.

The evaluation and control versions of the course were each taught in two learning centers on each of two shifts. Though random assignment of students to versions within learning centers would have been a preferable experimental design, it was thought that the continuing visible effects of the course completion map would contaminate the control group. At the start of the evaluation period, all entering students were assigned to one of the two versions. It was intended that this procedure would continue for at least 2 months.

Intervening events, however, prevented completion of the full evaluation plan. First, it was determined that instructors in one of the evaluation group learning centers had misunderstood the procedures and had instructed students to skip the Time Management module and continue with their normal course work. These students were eliminated from the evaluation. To compensate for the reduced N, the proportion of incoming students assigned to the evaluation group was raised to 65%.

It was then learned that the Advanced Instructional System was to be submitted to a second evaluation, termed a *service test* in which the second shift would be run without computer support. The service test plan went into effect on the twentieth class day of the evaluation period, preventing further data collection for second-shift students. Since very little data were available in the latter half of the course, data collection was continued 1 more week for those first-shift students who had entered the course prior to the service test.

Time Management Module Performance Data

Reliable lesson times were available for only 68 of the students who completed the first block of instruction. For these students, the mean first-attempt lesson time was 97.0 minutes (standard deviation of 31.9 minutes).

Reliable item-level criterion test data were available for 82 evaluation group students: 44 on Form 1 of the test and 38 on Form 2. The alpha reliability of Form 1 was .883, whereas Form 2 registered an alpha of .903. This increased reliability was, however, obtained at the cost of increased difficulty. The mean percentages correct for the two forms were 74.5 and 68.8, respectively. Further investigation revealed that these low means were largely attributable to the fact that two performance items were not marked by the instructors for almost half of the students. If these missing scores had been present, the means for the two forms would have been 80.9 and 75.1%, respectively. Form 2 of the test was slightly more difficult. Given the test criterion of 80% correct, the first attempt failure rate would have been quite high even if the missing performance items had been marked.

Block Completion Time and Score Data

A total of 79 evaluation and 79 control group students began and completed the first block of the course during the evaluation period. The number completing each successive block declined, with only 16 evaluation and 28 control group students completing the full six blocks of the course. Students who completed the latter blocks tended, of course, to be faster workers, regardless of treatment group.

Students were found to be unevenly balanced across the evaluation and control groups with respect to predicted course completion times. Although this suggested analysis of covariance, a question of interest concerned whether the presence of the Time Management module had differential effects on the rates of students predicted to have fast course completion times as compared with those predicted to complete the course more slowly. That is, was there an interaction between predicted course completion time and the presence or absence of the module? To test for such interactions, a pair of linear models (Ward & Jennings, 1973) was defined for each block in which the criterion variable was block completion time (block elapsed time less absence time), the first predictor variable was predicted course completion time, and the second predictor variable was a binary vector representing the presence or absence of the Time Management module. For the "full" models, both the intercepts and the slopes of the two regression lines (representing the evaluation and control groups) were allowed to vary between groups, whereas in the restricted models, only the intercepts were allowed to vary. Comparison of the error sums of squares of the two types of models, by means of an F test, is a test for homogeneity of regression. That is, a significant F would indicate that the slopes of the two regression lines were not parallel.

No significant ($p < .05$) interactions were found for any of the six blocks. In fact, five of the six F values obtained were less than 1.0. Since the assumption of homogeneity of regression was met, analysis of covariance was employed to evaluate the effect of the Time Management module on block completion times and scores.

The means and standard deviations of the evaluation and control group block completion times (adjusted for differences in the covariable of predicted course completion time) and the raw and percentage differences between groups are shown in Table 6.5. Since so few students completed the full course during the evaluation period, cumulative times are also shown for students completing the third, fourth, fifth, and sixth blocks.

As shown in Table 6.5, reliable Block 1 completion times were available for 77 evaluation group students and 76 control group students. The adjusted mean block time for the evaluation group was 19.51 hours, not significantly different from the mean (19.54 hours) of the control group.

TABLE 6.5
Block Times for Phase II Summative Evaluation and Control Groups

Variable	Evaluation			Control			Evaluation -control	Percentage change
	N	$\bar{X}$	SD	N	$\bar{X}$	SD		
Block 1 time[a]	77	19.51	6.23	76	19.54	6.29	− .03	− .15
Block 2 time	59	23.77	7.52	66	26.10	7.93	− 2.33	− 8.93
Block 3 time	39	32.11	10.26	62	35.39	11.01	− 3.28	− 9.27
Block 4 time	28	18.45	5.76	48	21.70	5.64	− 3.25	−14.98
Block 5 time	20	19.01	5.91	36	22.36	5.96	− 3.35	−14.98
Block 6 time	16	11.75	2.63	27	15.12	4.72	− 3.37	−22.29
Total time								
Blocks 1-3	34	74.11	23.13	53	78.26	21.77	− 4.15	− 5.30
Blocks 1-4	21	86.10	24.64	38	95.54	25.23	− 9.44	− 9.88
Blocks 1-5	13	95.19	26.69	25	108.94	25.52	−13.75	−12.62
Blocks 1-6	10	101.22	18.23	19	118.76	23.64	−17.54	−14.77

[a] Times, in hours, adjusted for differences in predicted course completion time.

This indicates that evaluation group students had regained the time required for the Time Management module itself by the end of the first block.

For Blocks 2 and 3, the mean block completion times of the evaluation group were approximately 9% shorter than those of the control group, and both comparisons approached significance at the .05 level: Block 2: $F(1,122) = 3.864$, $p = .052$; Block 3: $F(1,98) = 3.483$, $p = .065$. The fact that these relatively large differences failed to achieve significance was due primarily to the high variability of the block completion times.

The Block 4 and 5 comparisons indicate even larger time savings, almost 15%, attributable to the Time Management module, both of which achieved significance: Block 4: $F(1,73) = 6.079$, $p = .016$; Block 5: $F(1,53) = 4.490$, $p = .039$.

The apparent time savings attributable to the module in the sixth block exceeded 20%, but the number of students completing this block with reliable times was so small as to make the comparison suspect. Despite the small N, the difference between the adjusted means was significant: $F = 6.674$, $df = 1/40$, $p = .014$.[5]

Since the Phase I and II evaluation groups both received the same treatment, one might expect the block times to be similar, but in fact the Phase II evaluation group times were consistently shorter. Two factors contributed to this difference: Course completion times tended to become shorter during the period between the two comparisons, and, since the Phase II evaluation period was only half as long as the Phase I period, data in the later blocks of the Phase II comparison tended to be from faster students.

Cumulative times were obtained for those students who had reliable block completion times on the first through third, fourth, fifth, and sixth blocks. These values, adjusted for differences in the covariable, are shown in the lower half of Table 6.5. Thirty-four evaluation and 53 control group students completed the first three blocks with reliable times on all three blocks. The mean of the evaluation group was 4.15 hours less than that of the control group, a difference that was not statistically significant. By the end of the fifth block, the number of students having become quite small, the 13.75 hour savings did at least approach significance: $F(1,35) = 3.954$, $p = .055$. Finally, for those students with reliable times on all six blocks, the apparent advantage for the evaluation group was 17.54 hours: $F(1,26) = 5.431$, $p = .028$. Despite the several comparisons that failed to achieve statistical significance, the consistency with which the control group means exceeded those of the evaluation group strongly suggests that

[5] Statistical analyses of the unadjusted block completion times yielded the same behavioral conclusions.

the Time Management module did indeed have the effect of decreasing block completion times.

The means and standard deviations of the six end-of-block test scores, adjusted for differences in the covariable, are presented in Table 6.6. As is shown by the rightmost column, there was no consistent pattern of differences between the two groups. Further, none of the differences were statistically significant as evaluated by analysis of covariance. The number of first-attempt evaluation and control group block test failures were also compared by means of chi square tests. None of the six comparisons approached statistical significance. It can be concluded that the time savings attributable to the Time Management module were not achieved at the cost of increased block test failures.

A comparison of the score means shown in Table 6.6 with those obtained during Phase I of the evaluation suggests that the negative effects observed when Student Progress Management was first implemented were only temporary. The across-block, unweighted mean score of the Phase I control group (prior to implementation of progress management) was 81.92, whereas that of the Phase I evaluation group was 79.12. The unweighted mean of the Phase II evaluation group, 81.95, returned to the level observed prior to implementation of progress management.

Student Attitude Questionnaire Data

The same eight student attitude questionnaire items (see Table 6.4) were again employed to evaluate differences in attitudes attributable to the Time Management module. For the first three items, pertaining to students' perceptions of their pace through the course, only one of the six chi square comparisons indicated a significant difference ($p = .037$) between the responses of the evaluation and control group. Evaluation group students more strongly disagreed with the statement, "Since Denver is such a nice area, I was not in a hurry to finish the course," than did control group students, but only on the first (Block 1) administration of the scale. The effects of the Time Management module in this area were apparently only slight and diminished over time.

The only other item that approached significance ($p = .060$) was for the end-of-course administration of the statement, "The instructors helped me and encouraged me to do well," on which the responses of the evaluation group were more positive than those of the control.

Soon after the Progress Management Component had been implemented, 20 items were added to the attitude questionnaires dealing specifically with Student Progress Management. A comparison of the evaluation and control group student responses to these items indicated that only 2 of the 40 chi square comparisons (the number to be expected by

TABLE 6.6
End-of-block Test Scores for Phase II Summative Evaluation and Control Groups

Variable	Evaluation			Control			Evaluation -control
	N	$\bar{X}$	SD	N	$\bar{X}$	SD	
Block 1 score[a]	79	82.7	9.72	81	81.3	10.58	+1.4
Block 2 score	63	81.3	13.29	79	81.3	11.47	0
Block 3 score	43	80.0	9.83	64	76.9	10.70	+3.1
Block 4 score	31	82.5	9.12	51	82.6	10.41	− .1
Block 5 score	22	81.1	10.85	39	81.7	10.64	− .6
Block 6 score	16	84.1	8.46	28	85.4	8.20	−1.3

[a] Scores, shown as percentages, adjusted for differences in predicted course completion times.

chance) registered significant differences at the .05 level. Evaluation group students more strongly agreed with the statement, "It was difficult concentrating when I knew I was behind (target)," than did control group students on both the Block 1 and end-of-course administrations of the questionnaire. This result could be interpreted in either of two ways. The Time Management module, and particularly the course completion map, may indeed have increased students' anxiety when they were behind target, or it may simply be that the control group students attached little importance to the target rate.

CONCLUSIONS AND DISCUSSION

The goals of the project described in this chapter were (a) to design and develop a specialized student skill module for providing rudimentary time management skills, and (b) to implement and evaluate the effectiveness of this skill module for reducing course completion times and promoting positive student attitudes in the context of the Advanced Instructional System's Student Progress Management Component. Conclusions that can be drawn from the summative evaluation of the Progress Management Component and the time management module will be discussed first, followed by a discussion of the general significance of these findings for the learning strategies area.

Summative Evaluation Conclusions

As will be recalled, the effectiveness of the Progress Management Component and of the Time Management module were assessed in two evaluative phases. In the first phase, the major question of interest was whether the combination of Progress Management and Time Management module skill training would result in significant reductions in block and course completion times. The major question of interest in the second phase concerned whether the Time Management module per se, in the presence of Student Progress Management, contributed significantly to training time reductions.

On the basis of the Phase I summative evaluation data, there can be little doubt that the combination of Student Progress Management and the Time Management module resulted in substantive time savings—an 11.2% reduction in the time required for students to complete the six blocks of the Inventory Management course. This 11.2% savings represents 17.20 fewer hours (2.87 days) spent in a learning center by the average student. Since the normal Inventory Management course entry rate is 60 students per week for 50 training weeks per year, the total yearly savings amounts to 8600 student training days. Using the training cost figure of $75.60 per day proposed by Gant (1975), this time savings amounts to a yearly dollar savings to the Air Force of $650,000. Thus, the Phase I evaluation results clearly indicate that the combination of Student Progress Management and the Time Management module met the goal of reducing training time—at a level of magnitude representing sizable cost savings.

The Phase I block score, block failure rate, and student attitude results demonstrated less positive, but not totally unanticipated, effects of the total Student Progress Management Component (software plus module). That is, block test scores were lower in all six blocks for students in the progress management condition than for those in the no-management condition. Block test failure rates were also higher, and student attitudes under the management condition tended to be less positive than for students in the no-management condition. These results are consistent with the findings of Johnson *et al.* (1972) (with respect to attitudes) and of Colton (1974) (for criterion test scores), who investigated the effects of giving students predicted completion time information. It appears that the increased emphasis on completing the course quickly caused students to accept a greater risk of failure on end-of-block criterion tests, and the lower attitude scores may reflect feelings of conflict about this new trade-off of shorter times for lower scores.

Another partial explanation for the less positive attitudes of students in the Phase I management condition is suggested in a study by McMillan (1977). The interactive effects of students' degree of effort and the nature of written instructor feedback on student attitudes toward the subject were investigated in four university classes. High- and low-effort assignments were studied within conditions of high-praise or no-praise comments. McMillan found that students in the high-effort, high-praise condition formed significantly more positive attitudes than did students in the other three groups. The poorest attitudes were found for students in the high-effort, no-praise condition. Praise did not appear to effect student attitudes in the low-effort conditions. These findings imply that the Progress Management condition (a high-effort condition relative to no management) students may not have received enough instructor praise or encouragement for their efforts in maintaining their target rates to provide the environment required for positive attitude formation.

Although the Phase I results were very promising as to the time savings that could be obtained by the combination of Progress Management and the Time Management module, the question of how much the module per se contributed to these time savings is of more interest for the area of specialized skill training. In Phase II of the summative evaluation, student performance was evaluated under conditions where Progress Management was implemented with and without the Time Management module. The data from this second phase indicate a substantial time savings attributable to the Time Management module—14.77% for students who completed all six blocks. A word of caution is in order, however, in interpreting these time savings. The samples in the later blocks were small and were composed of the faster students. Even though no interactions were found between the effect of the module and predicted course completion time, the data from the later blocks may not be representative. Disregarding the first block, which is confounded by the presence of the module itself, the comparisons made in the second and third blocks, both based on reasonably large Ns, probably provide the most reliable estimate of time savings attributable to the module—on the order of 9%.

Before discussing the Phase II test performance and attitude data, it is of interest to assess the time savings that can be attributed to the basic Progress Management Component, to the module, and to a third factor—the continued presence of Progress Management over time. Table 6.7 summarizes several comparisons based on cumulative times to complete Blocks 2 and 3 by Phase I and II evaluation and control group students (see Tables 6.2 and 6.5 for the raw values).

As indicated in Table 6.7, introduction of the combination of the Management Component and the Time Management module resulted in a 12.2% reduction in these blocks as measured during the Phase I evaluation. There is no available measure of the immediate effect of the Management

TABLE 6.7
Times Savings in Blocks 2 and 3 Attributable to Various Treatments

Treatment	Data source	Time difference in hours	Percentage time saving
Management component plus module	Phase I control– Phase I evaluation	8.38	12.2
Management component only	Not available	—	—
Module only	Phase II control– Phase II evaluation	5.61	9.1
Time: Given management component plus module	Phase I evaluation– Phase II evaluation	4.27	7.1
Time plus management component plus module	Phase I control– Phase II evaluation	12.65	18.5
Time plus management component	Phase I control– Phase II control	7.04	10.3
Time plus module	Not available	—	—

Component by itself. The module in the presence of the Management Component contributed a 9.1% reduction in time as measured during Phase II. Approximately 4 months elapsed between the end of Phase I and the beginning of Phase II, and comparison of the Phase I and II evaluation groups indicates that the combined effect of Management Component plus module resulted in an additional 4.27-hour reduction (7.1%) in these blocks during this period. Thus, the total effect of the full Management Component (including the module), after a period of time, was an 18.5% reduction in completion times for these two blocks. The final available comparison implies that the Management Component by itself would have resulted in a 10.3% savings, given time to have its full effect. This is probably an overestimate, however, since both the Management Component and the module were in effect during the intervening period.

Two major conclusions are drawn from these results. First, both parts of the total Progress Management Component contribute to improvements in student efficiency and, interpolating from the values presented in Table 6.7, the contributions of each appear to be roughly equivalent. Second, the effects of the total Progress Management Component continue to increase over time.

The phenomenon of improving performance over time could be attributed to several factors. First, initial negative reactions by students and instructors to Progress Management may have diminished as its effectiveness for improving trainee efficiency was demonstrated. Some support for this hypothesis can be found in the more positive Phase II student attitude data as compared with the Phase I attitude data. Second, the additional 4 months of Management Component operation may have resulted in greater expertise on the part of the instructors in the use of the Progress Management Component.

Course content and tests remained constant, and thus can be dismissed. The fact that the Phase I evaluation period was longer than Phase II allowed more slow Phase I students to reach the upper blocks, but this was probably not a serious bias in Blocks 2 and 3. The Management Component policy function was eased from 90 to 95%, thus tracking the shortening course time rather than driving it. A final possible factor would be seasonal variation in entering student characteristics. Experience with the Advanced Instructional System, however, indicates that trainees entering technical training courses in late summer and fall (Phase I students) tend to be of higher ability than students entering late and early in the year (Phase II students). Thus, this latter explanation would not appear feasible.

If the increased efficiency observed is indeed due to increased acceptance and experience with the system, it suggests that one positive side effect of specialized skill training and its associated procedures may be that initial benefits increase over time. This possibility, and its implications for the learning strategies area, will be discussed in more detail in the next section.

Data on score and block failure rates also support the contention that the initial benefits increased over time. That is, Phase II evaluation group students were generally found to score as well and experience the same number of block failures as students without the module. Further, this level of achievement was approximately that found for students prior to implementation of Progress Management. These findings suggest that the poor test performance effects observed when Progress Management was first implemented were only temporary. That is, as students and instructors gained more experience with and confidence in the Progress Management procedures, students adapted to the more demanding course schedule while returning to traditional levels of performance.

That perceptions of Progress Management improved as experience with it increased is also substantiated to some extent by the Phase II student attitude data. Those attitude items that were most negative in Phase I tended to become more positive in Phase II. Items of particular interest were those dealing with instructor help and encouragement. Whereas students in the Phase I management condition were less positive on these items, in Phase II more positive feelings were reported. These findings support those of McMillan (1977) in the sense that more positive performance outcomes would be expected in this high-effort, high (or moderate)-praise condition.

In addition, Michaels (1977) discusses characteristics of individual competition situations that make them optimally rewarding:

1. Rewards (e.g., completing quickly or on schedule) should have an intrinsic or extrinsic value or utility.
2. Rewards should be contingent on performance (e.g., completing on schedule contingent on effort relative to ability).
3. Performance gains should be at least intermittently reinforced (e.g., daily performance feedback and charting).
4. Reward criteria or contingencies should apply equally to all students (e.g., same performance standards and outcomes are applied to students who meet or fail to meet their predicted targets).

To the extent that these characteristics were met by the time the Phase II evaluation was conducted, consistently superior student performance would be expected.

A final point of interest concerns the time required for the skill training—that is, time to complete the Time Management module itself, relative to the savings attributable to this training. In Phase II, evaluation group students had recovered the time spent on the module by the end of the first block. This result is quite consistent with Anderson's (1976) conclusions that early skill training "costs" are amortized quickly when students begin using these skills to improve their performance.

Significance for the Learning Strategies Area

The goals of the learning strategies program have been (a) to investigate methods for teaching students cognitive, affective, or motor skills necessary for efficient performance in military and civilian training environments, and (b) to produce modular training materials that teach such skills effectively. The present work focuses on the specific skill of time management in the context of a computer-managed instructional system. The instructional methods and procedures employed were intended to be sufficiently general that they could be implemented in other individualized or computer-managed instructional environments that have some type of completion time prediction capability. Further, an implicit goal was to investigate and evaluate methods that would be applicable to teaching other skills in similar environments. Therefore, this section will focus on those more general features incorporated into the design of the Time Management module that were found to be particularly effective in improving students' training efficiency.

One interesting aspect of the Time Management module is the means by which it provides the practice required to effect behavioral change without being part of the course materials themselves. As originally conceived, the student skill modules were to be short instructional packages that could be added to the front of an arbitrary course but that would continue to effect students' behavior throughout the course. Because fundamental habits and skills are involved, it was recognized that additional practice and spaced review would be required if the desired behavior changes were actually to occur. It can be argued, however, that this is still too optimistic an expectation, that occasional review is not sufficient, and that students will require extensive practice if new learning skills are to be acquired and old habits discarded. Though the desired effect could be obtained if stimuli for practice and appropriate feedback were built into the instructional materials themselves, this is considered prohibitively expensive for most technical training materials.

The module's course completion map and progress counseling sessions constitute a workable compromise between the requirements of extensive practice and independence from course materials. Students' daily progress charting repeatedly directs their attention to the problem of time management. It seems clear that requiring students to attend to their progress relative to their target rates is critical to maintaining awareness of their behavior as it affects their rate of progress and assisting them to utilize their daily progress feedback effectively. In addition, the effect of this daily activity is reinforced by students' knowledge that they will be required to discuss their progress with their instructor at relatively frequent intervals.

It is suggested that this technique for incorporating extensive skill practice outside course materials is an appropriate model for maintaining active student involvement for learning other, more complex study skills. That is, given initial instruction in the skill(s) to be acquired, the instructional designer should arrange frequent events, independent of the instructional materials themselves, that serve to focus the student's attention on the problem addressed by the skill to be practiced. In the absence of a computer-managed instructional system where rate of progress predictions can be generated easily, one question for future research in individualized learning situations is whether goal setting, combined with progress charting and counseling sessions, would achieve similar or superior training time reductions.

Another general implication of this specific approach to skill training is that, as was previously discussed, the benefits attributable to the training appear to increase over time as the skill training becomes a integral part of course procedures. For the classroom conditions described here, at least, this phenomenon appeared to be due to (a) increased instructor and student acceptance of and experience with the materials and procedures, and (b) the nature of the learning strategies inherent in the materials and procedures—that is the repeated practice of the new skills, the progress counseling sessions, and the continuing motivational effects of the practice and feedback. This suggests that when skill training is introduced, efforts to facilitate and promote its acceptance are a critical part of the development process and that summative evaluation should be postponed until the new procedures have become fully integrated if the full benefits of the training are to be realized and measured.

An interesting follow-up study, suggested by the work of Kifer (1975), would be to examine the differential effects of the Time Management module and its procedures for students with differing histories of academic success and failure. Kifer's work supports the position that students' requirements for skill training of particular types are a function of their prior academic histories. It is quite likely that individual differences in students' success–failure histories would be predictive of the required amount and frequency of specialized training in skills such as time management and of the efficacy of alternative approaches to training.

One final comment appears in order. In the military technical training environment, there are few, if any, guidelines for determining the amount of time an individualized course of instruction should require. The requirements for setting student performance criteria are also often ambiguous. In the absence of guidelines, standards tend to be set on the basis of the norm and such standards do not necessarily require particularly efficient student learning behaviors. The shortened course completion times, initially higher block failure rates, and lower attitude scores resulting from implementation of the progress management software, procedures, and module can be viewed, to some extent, as the result of tightening up the course's instructional procedures and schedule, thus placing greater demands on the students for efficient study. It is anticipated, therefore, that the additional modules to be developed under our project will have a greater facilitating effect on student performance under these conditions than would have been the case before implementation of Student Progress Management.

Although problem area selection and design of additional skill modules must await more in-depth analysis of student problems in a computer-managed instructional environment, it appears that training to improve self-evaluation or test-taking skills, general study habits and skills, and/or concentration management skills are viable approaches to further improving students' block test and attitude scores. Whatever the area selected, the results presented here strongly suggest that skill modules such as the Time Management module can have a positive impact on reducing time spent in training and hence technical training costs. Of equal or greater importance, the present results substantiate that the costs associated with this specialized skill training are quickly amortized and that strategies which maintain active student involvement continue to promote improvements in efficiency well after the original training.

REFERENCES

Allen, M. W. Meleca, C. B., & Myers, G. A. *A model for the computer-management of modular, individualized instruction.* Columbus: The Ohio State University and Brookings: South Dakota State University, 1972.

Anderson, L. W. An empirical investigation of individual differences in time to learn. *Journal of Educational Psychology,* 1976, *68*(2), 226–233.

Bond, J. A., Jr. *Motivating the student in CAI technical courses* (Technical Report No. 68). Los Angeles: University of Southern California, June 1971.

Carpenter, C. R., Teleinstruction and individualized learning. In R. A. Weisgerber (Ed.), *Perspectives in individualized learning.* Itasca, Ill.: F. E. Peacock Publishers, 1971.

Colton, F. V. Effects of giving students data on task completion time in a college media course. *Audio-Visual Communications Review,* 1974, *22*(3), 279–294.

Cooley, W. W., & Glaser, R. An information management system for individually prescribed instruction. In R. Atkinson & H. Wilson (Eds.), *Computer-assisted instruction: A book of readings.* New York: Academic Press, 1969.

Countermine, T. A., & Singh, J. M. Instruction support system. In H. E. Mitzell (Ed.), *An examination of the short-range potential of computer-managed instruction: Conference proceedings.* University Park: The Pennsylvania State University, 1974.

Danford, J. Computer-Managed individualized instruction. In H. E. Mitzell (Ed.), *An examination of the short-range potential of computer-managed instruction: Conference proceedings.* University Park: The Pennsylvania State University, 1974.

Dansereau, D. F., The development of a learning strategies curriculum. In H. F. O'Neil, Jr. (Ed.), *Learning strategies.* New York: Academic Press, 1978.

Dansereau, D. F., Actkinson, T. R., Long, G. L., & McDonald, B. *Learning strategies: A review and synthesis of the current literature* (AFHRL-TR-74-70). Lowry Air Force Base, Colo.: Human Resources Laboratory, 1974.

Fletcher, J. D. *Computer applications in education and training: Status and trends* (TR 75-32). San Diego, Calif.: Naval Personnel and Training Research Laboratory, April 1975.

Freeman, D. J., & Niemeyer, R. C. *The impact of written comments on student achievement.* Paper presented at the annual meeting of the American Educational Research Association, Chicago, April 1974.

Gaa, J. P. *The effects of individual goal-setting conferences on achievement, attitudes, and locus of control.* Paper presented at the annual meeting of the American Educational Research Association, New York, February 1971.

Gant, C. R. *Preliminary AIS Cost Evaluation* (Unpublished AFHRL Report). Lowry Air Force Base, Colo.: Human Resources Laboratory, March 1975.

Groveman, A. M., Richards, C. S., & Caple, R. B. Literature review, treatment manuals, and bibliography for study skills counseling and behavioral self-control approaches to improving study behavior. *Catalog of Selected Documents in Psychology,* 1975, *5,* 342.

Hagerty, N. K. *Development and implementation of a computer-managed instruction system in graduate training* (Tech. Rep. 11). Florida State University: Computer Assisted Instruction Center, June 1970.

Hansen, D. N., Ross, S. M., Bowman, H. L., & Thurmond, P. *Navy computer managed instruction: Past, present and future.* Memphis: Memphis State University, July 1975.

Johnson, K. A., Salop, P. A., & Harding, L. G. *The effects of incentives on student-paced instruction* (STB 73-2). San Diego, Calif.: Naval Personnel and Training Research Laboratory, September 1972.

Khan, S. B., & Weiss, J. The teaching of affective responses. In M. W. Travers (Ed.), *Second handbook of research on teaching.* Chicago: Rand McNally, 1973.

Kifer, E. Relationships between academic achievement and personality characteristics: A quasi-longitudinal study. *American Educational Research Journal,* 1975, *12*(2), 191-210.

Kimberlin, D. A. *A preliminary instructional model for a computerized training system* (Interim Report). Fort Monmouth, N.J.: U.S. Army Signal Center and School, July 1973.

King, A. T. *Impact of computer-based instruction on attitude of students and instruction* (AFHRL-TR-75-4). Lowry Air Force Base, Colo.: Human Resources Laboratory, May 1975.

Kopstein, F. F., & Seidel, R. J. Informal education with instructional systems. *Educational Technology,* 1972, *1,* 35-39.

Lakein, A. *How to get control of your time and your life.* New York: New American Library, 1974.

McCombs, B. L. *Identifying individualization parameters, strategies and models that are user acceptable and feasible: Methodological considerations.* Paper presented at the annual meeting of the American Educational Research Association, San Francisco, April 1979.

McCombs, B. L., & McDaniel, M. A. *The effectiveness of instructional strategies designed to compensate for individual differences in student memory abilities and motivation.* Paper presented at the annual meeting of the American Educational Research Association, Toronto, March 1978.

McCombs, B. L. & Siering, G. S. *The design and development of an adaptive model for the Air Force Advanced Instructional System.* Paper presented at the Sixteenth International Ergonomics Association Meeting, College Park, Maryland, July 1976.

McMillan, J. H. The effect of effort and feedback on the formation of student attitudes. *American Educational Research Journal,* 1977, *14*(3), 317–330.

Michaels, J. W. Classroom reward structures and academic performance. *Review of Educational Research,* 1977, *47*(1), 87–98.

Middleton, M. G., Papetti, C. J., & Micheli, G. S. *Computer-managed instruction in Navy training* (TAEG Report No. 14). Orlando, Fla.: Training Analysis and Evaluation Group, March 1974.

Poore, R. P., Jr., & Pappas, J. P. *A criterion related validity study of the McGraw-Hill Inventory of Study Habits and Attitudes.* Paper presented at the annual meeting of the Rocky Mountain Psychological Association, Denver, May 1974.

Richardson, F. Behavior modification and learning strategies. In H. F. O'Neil, Jr. (Ed.), *Learning strategies.* New York: Academic Press, 1978.

Seidel, R. J., Wagner, H., Rosenblatt, R. D., Hillelsohn, M. J., & Stelzer, J. *Learner control of instructional sequencing within an adaptive tutorial CAI environment* (HumRRO Tech. Rep. 75-7). Alexandria, Va.: Human Resources Research Organization, June 1975.

Sieber, J. E., O'Neil, H. F., Jr., & Tobias, S. *Anxiety, learning, and instruction.* New York: Lea/Wiley, 1977.

Smith, J. D. Impact of computer-assisted instruction on student attitude. *Journal of Educational Psychology,* 1973, *64,* 366–372.

Spielberger, C. D. Anxiety: State-trait process. In C. D. Spielberger & I. G. Sarason (Eds.), *Stress and anxiety* (Vol. 1). Washington, D. C.: Hemisphere/Wiley, 1975.

Spielberger, C. D. Computer-based research on anxiety and learning: An overview and critique. In J. E. Sieber, H. F. O'Neil, Jr., & S. Tobias (Eds.), *Anxiety, learning, and instruction.* New York: Lea/Wiley, 1977.

Spielberger, C. D., O'Neil, H. F., Jr., & Hansen, D. N. Anxiety, drive theory, and computer-assisted learning. In B. A. Maher (Ed.), *Progress in experimental personality research: VI.* New York: Academic Press, 1972.

Ullery, J. W. Individualized instructional systems for vocational education. *Educational Technology,* 1971, *3,* 22–25.

Ward, J. H. Jr., & Jennings, E. *Introduction to linear models.* Englewood Cliffs, N.J.: Prentice-Hall, 1973.

Weinstein, C. E. *Learning of elaboration strategies.* Unpublished doctoral dissertation, University of Texas at Austin, 1975.

Weinstein, C. E. Elaboration skills as a learning strategy. In H. F. O'Neil, Jr. (Ed.), *Learning strategies.* New York: Academic Press, 1978.

7

Teaching Task-Oriented Selective Reading: A Learning Strategy[1]

JOSEPH W. RIGNEY†, ALLEN MUNRO,
and DONALD E. CROOK

Consider the plight of many adults who are not effective readers. This ineffectiveness is evident in a number of circumstances. It is characterized, in part, by an apparent inability to employ the variety of reading strategies that are available to effective readers. The effective use of such strategies helps to ensure that the reader is processing the text in a manner that is sensitive to his or her needs (that is, to his or her reasons for reading the text) and in a manner that is appropriate for the type of text being read. Ineffective readers often seem to behave as though they know of only one way to process text, and they make use of this single strategy whether they are reading for diversion or to learn how to solve an important problem, whether their reading matter is light fiction or a complex and densely written technical manual.

Our overall objective is to develop an integrated system that will teach students both selective and extractive multipass reading strategies, as

†Deceased.

[1] This research was sponsored by the Defense Advanced Research Projects Agency and monitored by the Office of Naval Research, Contract N00014-77-C-0328. Views and conclusions contained in this document are those of the author and should not be interpreted as necessarily representing the official policies, either expressed or implied, of the Defense Advanced Research Projects Agency, Office of Naval Research, or the United States government.

We thank Captain James R. Mills, commanding officer of the Naval Reserve Officer Training Corps at the University of Southern California and his associates, Commander Stoakes and Lieutenant Swinburnson, who assisted us both in the selection of materials for the practice problems used in the second experiment and in the recruitment of NROTC student subjects for that experiment. We also thank Kathy A. Lutz for assistance in the design of the second experiment and in data analysis.

discussed in Rigney and Munro (1977). The employment of selective reading strategies encourages readers to read only those portions of the material available that are likely to contribute to the attainment of their current goals. The use of extractive multipass strategies increases the amount of information acquired from text and enables students to use the text deliberately to fill in gaps in their own knowledge. Students trained on an integrated system designed to teach these skills should become more effective readers of various kinds of materials and in various circumstances. They should learn self-directional skills that help them first to analyze their requirements for learning from particular texts in particular situations, and second, to make use of their analyses to read selectively. Each student should also be able to apply extractive multipass strategies to acquire information efficiently from the passages selected.

This dual instructional system is intended to be useful for job-oriented reading training—in both civilian and military contexts—where the acquisition and utilization of information from text is driven by requirements to perform job tasks (Huff, Sticht, Joyner, Groff, & Burkett, 1977). It should be possible to combine this system with other instructional systems, such as trainer-simulators, in order to give students integrated training in job-oriented reading and in performing job tasks. For example, the dual instructional system described in this article could be integrated with the Generalized Maintenance Trainer-Simulator (GMTS) (Rigney, Towne, King, & Langston, 1972) for giving Naval electronics technicians practice in performing fault localization on a variety of electronic equipment.

One of the most important aspects of a training system such as that described here is that it moves reading training away from the classroom and one step closer to real-world requirements for text processing. Students in elementary and secondary schools are typically taught to read for only a limited repertoire of purposes (often, only to prepare for tests). In most cases, reading selection is a function performed by instructors rather than by students. In school, the student's responsibility is simply to learn (often in only a very restricted sense) what is assigned. Is it any wonder that the products of such an educational system are incapable of selective reading or of the use of other flexible text-processing strategies? It is the goal of our training program to help bridge the gulf between reading and other important aspects of life, such as effective learning on the job.

Not infrequently, on-the-job trainees such as electronics technicians find themselves assigned to jobs in which they have to maintain equipment or systems they have not seen before or may have encountered only briefly in school. They have, in such conditions, a strong need to learn more about these devices, using available technical documents as a source of information. The technical manuals they consult may, in some instances, presuppose prior knowledge that is incomplete or partially forgotten. Thus, the technician on the job may need to learn information at several lower levels of complexity as well as at the technical-manual level and to organize a sequence of acquisition. The information the technician needs may not be contained in a single place in any document, and the structure of the document—table of contents, index, and so on—may not help the technician locate the proper information. Under these circumstances, technicians who are not self-directed might try to read the entire technical document from cover to cover, obviously wasting valuable time. On the other hand, some technicians might ignore the information resources available and simply begin sticking test probes into the defective equipment, again wasting time. In either case, the technician would benefit from knowing some techniques of being self-directed, of determining which information is relevant to his specific task and learning only that information.

The system described in this chapter is a preliminary version of one of the major components of the integrated system for teaching selective and extractive strategies toward which we are working. The system described here is intended to teach selective strategies in particular. Figure 7.1 (adapted from Rigney, 1978b) presents some conceptual geography for cognitive learning strategies. The italicized items in this figure represent those aspects of the complete cognitive strategy picture that are involved in

Processing Resources	Orienting Tasks	Subject Matter
Representational:	Communication:	Information:
Perceptual	*Instructions*	Narrative
Imaginal	Questions	*Explanation*
Verbal	*Content Structures*	*Representation*
		Prescription
Procedural:	Location:	*Performance:*
Processing	*Preceding*	*High* or Low
Metaprocessing:	*Embedded*	Semantic–
Selectional:	Following	High or *Low* Motor
Attention		
Intention	Generality	
Self-directional:	Scope	
Self-programming	Complexity	
Self-monitoring		
Technology:	Implementation	Environment:
High	Populations:	Schools
Intermediate	Children	Conventional
Low	*Adults*	CMI
	Special	CBI
		OJT
		Experimental

Figure 7.1 Some conceptual geography for cognitive strategies.

the present system. The emphasis of this system is the training of students in metaprocessing and self-directional procedural processing resources. Particular emphasis is given to selectional processes, but the training also is designed to improve students' self-programming and self-monitoring resources. A high-technology medium is used to assist trained students in the application of the strategies they learn: they make use of an automated-aids system on the PLATO computer system (Bitzer, Sherwood, & Tenc-zar, 1973) to help them guide their learning from text. Orienting tasks in our experiments thus far have simply been instructions to solve the complex problems presented, using the selectional strategies and the aids system. These tasks precede the texts that must be used to solve the problems. (Sub-tasks are also activated during the solution of the problem; in many cases, these tasks are embedded in the texts read by the subjects.) The texts used by the students, who have all been adults in our studies, are nonnarrative, expository types of texts. The performances that are called for by the problems presented are low in motor skills but require high semantic skills.

Our training system should be effective because, in effect, it gives learners new procedural processing resources of the sort discussed in Rigney (1978b). Of course, these selectional and self-directional resources are already possessed by some sophisticated readers. Many more readers, however, do not have these abilities, or make use of them only in a haphazard manner. The training provided by our system should particularly benefit these less sophisticated readers.

This chapter describes the initial development of a system to train students in the use of selective reading strategies. Our research plan calls for several cycles of development and testing of the training system. In this report we discuss our first passes at such a system. The computer-based aid and the training sequence are described, and the results of two experiments on the effectiveness of the system are reported. Plans for modifications to the training system, based on the results of this experiment, are discussed.

A COMPUTER-BASED AID TO
SELF-DIRECTED LEARNING

Our training program (called Aids) is designed to teach students how to use a computer-based aid to self-directed learning that has been developed in our laboratory. A learning task is presented, and the student is given considerable information—too much information, in fact—to complete this task. The aids system is designed to allow the student to break down the task into a set of more easily attained objectives, to decide when a chapter of the technical manual is relevant to the objectives, and in general

to keep track of learning. This aids system can be thought of as consisting of a number of "pages," each of which presents certain types of information and provides the user with certain options. The four major components of this sytem are the task page, the objectives page, the contents page, and the relevant contents page. (The term *page* in this context indicates one or more screen displays on a PLATO–IV panel.) From any of these pages, the student can choose to go to any one of the others. The major components and their subcomponents are shown in Figure 7.2.

The task page states the overall task or learning goal for the student. The task changes for each session that the student uses the aids system, but in each case it involves learning enough material to trouble-shoot a defective device of some kind. (See discussion under Task Domains for the Training System later in this chapter.) The task page also gives the student access to the example output from the defective device. The student uses this output to help determine the source of the fault in the device. When ready to attempt the task, the student can go to a test accessible from the task page. This test requires that the student identify the faulty component of the device; failing this test, the student is sent back to the aids system to study additional material. The student can later return to the task page to attempt the task once again. Another important function accessible from the task page is the student's goal stack, an overt representation of dependencies

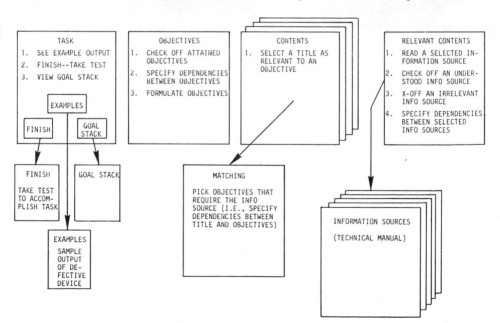

Figure 7.2 Automated aid to self-directed learning, functions of component specified.

that the student discovers among the various parts of the learning process—that is, task, objectives, and information sources.

The goal stack the student sees on the PLATO terminal screen looks something like the diagram in Figure 7.3. The arrows in the goal stack diagram show dependency relationships that hold among the student's objectives and the information resources available. For example, the curved line from Objective 1 to Objective 2 means that Objective 2 cannot be attained until Objective 1 is first attained; Objective 2 is thus dependent on Objective 1. Similarly, the line from Information Source 7 to Objective 4 means that Objective 4 requires the understanding of Information Source 7 for its attainment. The curved line from Information Source 3 to Information Source 1 means that 1 is dependent on 3; 3 should therefore be studied before 1.

The student is taught several heuristics as aids for effective use of the goal structure. For example, if the node on the goal tree that represents a particular goal has an arrow head impinging on it, then that goal should not be attempted until the goal at the other end of the arrow has been attained. This is a simple restatement of the principle that it is better to attempt the prerequisites of an action before attempting the action. Since the goal structure keeps a record of goals attained by means of check marks next to completed goals, this rule is easy to heed.

The second major component of the self-directed learning aid is the objectives page. The primary function of this page is to maintain a list of the learning objectives based on the task at hand. From the objectives page students can formulate new objectives that they believe are necessary to the accomplishment of the task. Once the student has entered an objective, it will be listed on the individual's objectives page. Two other functions available on the objectives page are checking off objectives that have been attained (after reading the relevant information) and specifying dependency relationships between objectives. When the student utilizes the latter op-

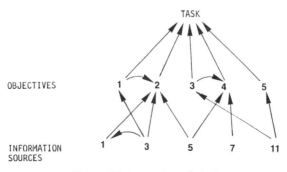

Figure 7.3 A sample goal stack.

tion, the aids system records the fact that there is a dependency between the two objectives named by the student. This dependency is shown whenever the student chooses to look at his goal stack (accessed from the task page), and an arrow is drawn from the required to the dependent objective on the goal stack. Thus, the arrows between any two objectives on the goal stack page are determined by what the student has done on the objectives page.

The contents page simply provides a list of the titles of "chapters," or information sources, of the technical manual that covers the device that the student is trouble-shooting. The student can scan this list of titles and make decisions about the probable relevance to the objectives of some of the topics mentioned. After deciding that the material under a certain title is likely to be relevant to some objective, the student exercises the choose-title option from the contents page. Picking a title has the effect of throwing control immediately to the matching page. On the matching page, the student is shown the list of objectives and the title just chosen; the student must specify which of those objectives requires learning the material named by that title. If the student does not want to match any of the objectives with the chosen title, then he or she must cancel the choice of the title. (The student can then choose to go to the objectives page, make up a new objective, and then return to the contents page to select the title again, planning to match the title with the new objective). In this way, the student is encouraged to select only those titles needed to solve the problem. As a result of the choices made on the matching page, the aids system remembers which of the chosen information sources are required by which of the objectives. This information appears whenever the student decides to look at the goal stack. It determines the arrows that are drawn from the numbers of the relevant information sources to their objectives. (See Figure 7.3.)

Choices made on the contents pages have one other consequence. Those titles that are chosen as relevant to some objective (and are matched with the objective) will appear on the relevant contents page. The relevant contents page is the student's personalized table of contents relevant to the trouble-shooting problem. When choosing to go to the relevant contents page, the student sees a list of all these chosen titles. A number of functions are available from this page. First, the student can decide to read any of the information sources listed there. Second, if a student has read and understood an information source, he or she can check off the title on the relevant contents page to signify that this subgoal was attained. If the student has read an information source and discovered that it was irrelevant, he or she can decide to remove it from the list of relevant information sources. A fourth option available is to specify dependencies between information sources. For example, if the student decides that Relevant Information Source 1 cannot be understood until Relevant Information Source 3 has been understood, then the student can specify that 1 is dependent upon 3.

The last three choices listed above all have consequences for the goal stack. If the student has checked off a title, then that title's number will have a check mark below it in the goal stack. If a title has been removed from the list because it is irrelevant, then it will not appear in the goal stack at all. And if a dependency between two information sources has been specified, then an arrow will connect the numbers of their titles in the goal stack.

The information sources, or chapters, themselves are quite simple. Each consists of a number of pages through which the student can progress. The student can page through an information source either forward or backward. In addition, from any page the student can elect to return to the relevant contents page.

TRAINING SEQUENCE

Students do not immediately begin with the complete self-directed learning aids system as it was discussed in the previous section. Instead, they are led to that version in a series of training sessions, each one having more of the features discussed in Section I than the previous session.

The complete training sequence used in a pilot experiment (discussed later) is shown in Figure 7.4. The initial session familiarizes the student with the PLATO terminal and introduces the aids system. The student begins by playing a few games of tick-tack-toe against the computer to introduce the idea of touching the terminal panel. The student then goes

1	FAMILIARIZATION WITH TERMINAL INTRODUCTION TO SIMPLIFIED AIDS SYSTEM
2	PRACTICE WITH SIMPLIFIED AIDS SYSTEM
3	INTRODUCTION TO MORE COMPLEX AIDS SYSTEM (WITH GOAL STACK)
4	PRACTICE WITH MORE COMPLEX AIDS SYSTEM
5	INTRODUCTION TO FINAL AIDS SYSTEM
6	PRACTICE WITH FINAL AIDS SYSTEM
7	POSTTEST WITH FINAL AIDS SYSTEM (NEW TASK DOMAIN)

Figure 7.4 Training sequence for use of self-directed aids system.

through a training lesson that teaches the use of the most rudimentary version of the aids system. (This version differs from the full system discussed in Section I in the following ways: First, students cannot formulate their own objectives but must make use of a set of objectives provided; second, the system does not provide a goal stack; third, the objectives page does not provide the option of making explicit the dependencies among the objectives; fourth, the relevant contents page does not provide the option of making explicit dependencies among chosen titles.) This first session has three parts. In the first part, the students are taught about the overall structure of the aids system and are given a quiz on their understanding of the system. Those students who score below the criterion must repeat this section of the lesson. In the second part of the lesson, the student is taught about the specific functions of each of the components of the system. This section of the training requires that the student step through each of these functions in a simulation of their actual use. In the third part of this session, the student has an opportunity to practice with the limited aids system on a very simple task (learning to use the PLATO keyboard to type and edit answers).

In the second session students are required to solve a trouble-shooting problem through the use of the simplified aids system they learned about in the first session. The task is quite complex, and most students require from 1 to 2 hours to accomplish it.

The third session introduces students to a more complex aids system. To the simplified system they have already learned about, the goal stack is added. In addition, the options to specify dependencies among objectives (on the objectives page) and to specify dependencies among information sources (on the relevant contents page) are included. The lesson requires the student to make appropriate responses in a simulation of the functions of these new options.

In the fourth session, the students practice with this more complex aids system. They are required to trouble-shoot the same type of device that they have already had a trouble-shooting problem on, but the problem and its symptoms are new.

The fifth session introduces the students to writing their own objectives on the automated aids system. When this lesson has been completed, a student has been introduced to the complete aids system depicted in Figure 7.2. This lesson is quite short and is usually combined with that of the sixth session for one long session.

In the sixth session, the student practices with the complete aids system. The new trouble-shooting task is, again, on the same type of device as were all the previous tasks.

The seventh session is a posttest session, although from the student's point of view it is simply another practice session with the full aids system. In this session, the trouble-shooting task is on a defective device of a different type from that with which the student is familiar. New information resources are, of course, provided.

TASK DOMAINS FOR THE TRAINING SYSTEM

Each time a student practices with some version of the aids system, a learning task must be solved. In the pilot experiment, the task was to trouble-shoot or debug a complex defective device. These devices produce outputs, some of which are incorrect; by examining these outputs and reading information sources on the various components of the device, a student can determine which component is faulty (that is, causing the improper output). The two devices used in the pilot experiments were a simulated sentence generator and a simulated essay generator. In the second experiment, simpler problems, largely having to do with using the maritime rules of the road, were used in the practice sessions. In the final test session, a sentence generator problem was used.

COGNITIVE MODEL FOR SELF-DIRECTED LEARNING

One way of viewing the goals of this research is to say that we intend to find the means to teach people how to do effective web-learning (described in Norman, 1973, 1974, in press). What is it that they will know when they have graduated from our training procedures? How will what they know guide their learning of complex materials in the future?

Our answers to these questions are couched in terms of schema theory (Munro & Rigney, 1977; Norman, Rumelhart, & LNR, 1975; Rumelhart & Ortony, 1977). The central tenet of schema theory is that knowledge guides thought. Stated baldly, this seems to be a truism. In schema theory, however, explicit claims are made about the means by which knowledge guides thought. Computer simulations of schema-theory models provide rigorous tests of the adequacy of the proposed mechanisms for the relations of concepts in memory (of knowledge). Knowledge, in turn, to a large extent, consists of "frozen" or fossilized activations—copies of other concepts in memory, with specific details determined by the particular contexts within which those concepts were activated (see Munro & Rigney, 1977, for further explanation).

In schema-theory terms, the knowledge that subjects acquire as a result of the training described elsewhere in this chapter is best represented in

terms of a *prescriptive schema.* A prescriptive schema is a conceptual structure that, when activated, gives people the impression that they are giving
themselves instructions. Prescriptive schemata are responsible for the effects that we attribute to "self-direction strategies." The set of schemata
that students acquire from our training program is an abstract conceptual
structure with considerable scope. (The uses of the terms *abstractness* and
scope with respect to schemata are discussed in Munro & Rigney, 1977.)
Here are the hypothesized schemata that we believe students acquire as a
result of their training (our explanation follows):

(1) SELF-DIRECTED-LEARNING (TASK)
        is when
    BUILD-GOAL-STRUCTURE (TASK)
    TASK-PURSUE (TASK)
        end.
(2) BUILD-GOAL-STRUCTURE (TASK)
        is when
    ANALYZE (TASK, for OBJECTIVES (TASK))[2]
    PREREQUISITE-SEARCH (for EACH (OBJECTIVE), in OBJECTIVES)
    PREREQUISITE-SEARCH (for EACH (OBJECTIVE), in CONTENTS)
        end.
(3) TASK-PURSUE (TASK)
        is when
    EXAMINE (GOAL-STRUCTURE)
    UNTIL (CHECKED (EVERY OBJECTIVE)), PURSUE (OBJECTIVE))
    TASK-ATTEMPT (TASK)
        end.
(4) TASK-ATTEMPT (TASK)
        is when
    IF (DO (TASK), then QUIT, else SELF-DIRECTED-LEARNING (TASK))
        end.
(5) PREREQUISITE-SEARCH (for GOALS, in SUBGOAL-SET)
        is when
    FOR-EACH (MEMBER, of SUBGOAL-SET,
        IF (PREREQUISITE (MEMBER, for GOAL),
        then (SPECIFY-DEPENDENCY (MEMBER, to OBJECTIVES-LIST))))
        end.
(6) PURSUE (GOAL)[3]
        is when
    FOR-EACH (SUBGOAL (NECESSARY (SUBGOAL, to GOAL)), in GOAL-
        STRUCTURE, WHILE (ANY (UNSATISFIED (SUBGOAL' (NECESSARY
        (SUBGOAL', to SUBGOAL)))),
            PURSUE (SUBGOAL'))

[2] The ANALYZE subschema has not yet been represented. How people are able to
discover the prerequisites or component actions of a task is not well understood.
[3] This structure is a variant of Rumelhart and Ortony's (1977) schema for TRYing, a
subschema of their PROBLEM-SOLVING schema.

```
        TRIAL (SUBGOAL))
            end.
(7) UNSATISFIED (GOAL)
        is when
    NOT (CHECKED (GOAL))
    NOT (ELIMINATED (GOAL))
        end.
(8) TRIAL (GOAL)
        is when
    ATTEMPT (ACTION, of GOAL)
    EVALUATE (GOAL)
        end.
(9) EVALUATE (GOAL)
        is when
    IF (NECESSARY (GOAL, to HIGHER-GOAL),
        then IF (SATISFIED (GOAL), then CHECK (GOAL),
            else TASK-PURSUE (TASK)),
        else ELIMINATE (GOAL, from GOAL-STRUCTURE))
            end.
(10)ATTEMPT (GOAL)
        is when
    IF (BELIEVE (CAUSE (ACTION, SATISFIED (GOAL))),
        then DO (ACTION),
        else when SUCCEED (PREREQUISITE-SEARCH (for GOAL)),
            ATTEMPT (PREREQUISITE (GOAL)))
        end.
```

According to the first of these schemata, the student believes that the way to achieve a task through self-directed learning is, first, to build a goal structure and, second, to pursue the task, using that goal structure. The second schema describes what is involved in building a goal structure. One analyzes a task for objectives (subgoals necessary for the performance of the task), and then one searches for prerequisite relationships among these objectives, between the available information resources and the objectives, and among the relevant available information resources. However, the schema does not contain explicit reference to the process of adding these relationships to the goal structure, because the goal structure is constructed for the student by the program that aids self-directed learning. The fifth schema is an essential part of the goal-structure-building schema, since it specifies how the search for prerequisites is conducted.

The second major part of self-directed learning, after building a goal structure, according to the above schemata, is to pursue the task. The third schema gives the top-level structure for task pursuit. One examines the newly constructed goal structure first; then one pursues the objectives included in that goal structure until every one of them has been checked.

(Checking is the process by which a student marks the attainment of a subgoal, using the aids program on PLATO.) When all the necessary objectives have been checked, the task is attempted. If the attempt fails (see Schema 4), then the student begins the self-directed learning process again, reconstructing or modifying the goal structure.

The pursuit of objectives is governed by the sixth schema. This is a recursive procedure that traces down dependency relationships in the goal structure. When a goal is found that has no prerequisites, that goal is subjected to a trial. This means (see Schemata 8, 9, and 10) that the student does an action to bring about the goal and then evaluates the results of that action. If the goal is satisfied, the student checks the goal and then pops back to the appropriate point in the procedure that is pursuing an objective. If it is not satisfied, the student looks for a new way to pursue his overall task. If the attempt reveals that the goal was unnecessary to the attainment of its higher goal, then it is dropped from the goal structure.

These schemata constitute working hypotheses about the nature of the conceptual changes brought about by training in the self-directed learning aids program discussed earlier.

The prose explanations of these schemata emphasize the way in which they call one another in a top–down, conceptually driven processing mode. Naturally, there is also a bottom–up, data-driven aspect to the activation of these schemata in normal circumstances. For example, when a student finds that a goal has been satisfied (say, as a result of reading one of the relevant information resources), this activates the subschemata in the fourth line of the ninth schema. The activation of these subschemata—IF (SATISFIED (GOAL), then CHECK (GOAL, . . .)—activates, in a data-driven fashion, its "parent" schema, EVALUATE. The activation of EVALUATE, in turn, can activate the schema that calls it, and so on, so that activation spreads in an upward as well as a downward direction.

PILOT EXPERIMENT

An experiment was conducted to test the effects of the self-directed learning aids system. A control aids system was established, containing only the task and contents pages of the system described earlier. A student in the control condition has the same learning task and the same information to read, but he has none of the aids system available to a student in the experimental condition. (Information sources in the control condition are accessed directly from the table of contents. As soon as the student touches a title, the corresponding information source is shown).

1	FAMILIARIZATION WITH TERMINAL INTRODUCTION TO CONTROL AIDS SYSTEM
2	PRACTICE WITH CONTROL AIDS SYSTEM
3	PRACTICE WITH CONTROL AIDS SYSTEM
4	PRACTICE WITH CONTROL AIDS SYSTEM
5	POSTTEST WITH CONTROL AIDS SYSTEM (NEW TASK DOMAIN)

Figure 7.5 Training sequence for control subjects.

Control Training Sequence

The training sequence for control subjects is similar to that for experimental subjects, except that the basic system is never modified for them, so that there is no need for teaching sessions other than the initial one. Consequently, all sessions are practice sessions using the control system. The complete sequence is shown in Figure 7.5.

The initial session begins in the same way as in the experimental condition, with a session in which the student is first given some practice using the touch panel of the PLATO terminal by playing tick-tack-toe. This is followed by a two-part PLATO lesson on the functions of the control aids system. As with the experimental group students, each part of this lesson is followed by a quiz that the student must pass in order to progress. This introduction is followed by a short practice session using a very simple learning task.

In the second, third, and fourth sessions, the student solves complex trouble-shooting problems (one for each session) using the control aids system. Each of these tasks involves a different problem with the same type of device, the sentence-generator. These sessions provide practice for the student in the use of the control aids system and in trouble-shooting problems on devices of the sort used for these exercises. In the posttest (Session 5), students are to use whatever learning skills they acquired during their training to perform a trouble-shooting task in the new domain of the essay generator. Several types of data are collected during this session, on both control and experimental subjects.

Data Collection

The data collected during the posttest were designed to measure both effective learning and self-directed learning. *Effective learning* is defined in terms of the time required to perform the task and the number of errors made in performing it. For each student data are collected on the number of erroneous attempts made to solve the problem and the total time taken to solve the problem after being presented with it. *Self-directed learning* is much more difficult to measure. It was decided that self-directed learning is typified by two phenomena: planning and selectivity in the use of information sources. The data collected reflect operational definitions of these phenomena.

Planning

It is not an easy matter to discover whether a student is engaged in effective planning. One type of data saved by our PLATO program is the sequence in which the student accessed the available information resources. Our analysis of the trouble-shooting task presented to the students in the posttest session has resulted in the formulation of a set of rules for scoring deviations from the order in which the information sources should be accessed. These rules, which we call *antiprecedence rules,* take the form of prohibitions of certain sequences. The extent to which a student has departed from sequences permitted by an ideal task analysis can be expressed in terms of the number of times the student's study sequence violates the antiprecedence rules.

Selectivity in the Use of Information Resources

Selectivity has to do with the ratio of the use of relevant information sources to the use of all information sources. A student for whom this ratio is high has read primarily only relevant sources. Three different ratios are computed by our program. The first is the ratio of number of relevant information sources read to total information sources read. The second is the ratio of the number of readings of relevant information sources to the number of readings of all information sources. The third is the ratio of time spent reading relevant information sources to the time spent reading all information sources.

Results

Mean scores on two measures for the effectiveness of the two groups of learners are presented in Table 7.1. In the final test session, in which students were required to trouble-shoot a faulty essay generator, those students who had not been exposed to the training in self-directed learning were slightly slower than those who had received the training. The experimental group subjects, on the average, solved the problem 9 minutes before the control subjects. The number of erroneous choices made by the

TABLE 7.1
Effectiveness of Learning in Posttest Session

	Means	
	Time to complete (minutes)	Errors
Experimental ($N = 7$)	65	2.9
	(31.90)[a]	(3.13)
Control ($N = 4$)	74	3.0[b]
	(25.15)	(0)

[a] Standard deviations are in parentheses.
[b] $N = 2$.

two groups of subjects before identifying the appropriate component as defective was about the same.

In Table 7.2 the evidence concerning the selectivity displayed by students trained under the two conditions is presented. The measures of selectivity that are ratios of the use of relevant information sources to total information sources show little or no difference between the two groups. Control subjects chose more than twice as many titles to read than did the experimental subjects, suggesting that students in the control condition were not as selective; however, this difference was not statistically significant.

Table 7.3 summarizes the measure used to detect planning. Planning, as described earlier, is evidenced by few violations of principles of efficient sequencing in reading the available materials. The means suggest that the ex-

TABLE 7.2
Selectivity in Posttest Session

	Means			
	Titles chosen	R_1[a]	R_2[b]	R_3[c]
Experimental ($N = 7$)	9	.73	.75	.73
	(3.79)[d]	(.11)	(.09)	(.12)
Control ($N = 4$)	20	.83	.72	.72
	(13.89)	(.15)	(.12)	(.08)

[a] R_1 = Ratio of number of relevant information sources read to number of total information sources read.
[b] R_2 = Ratio of number of readings of relevant information sources to number of readings of all information sources.
[c] R_3 = Ratio of time spent reading relevant information sources to time spent reading all information sources.
[d] Standard deviations are in parentheses.

TABLE 7.3
Planning in Posttest Session

	Means
	Violations of efficient sequencing
Experimental (N = 7)	1.8
	(3.08)[a]
Control (N = 4)	2.5
	(5.00)

[a] Standard deviations are in parentheses.

perimental subjects were better planners than the control subjects, since they made only 72% as many planning violations. Again, this difference was not statistically significant.

Discussion

Interpretation of these results is problematic. Although the students in the experimental group seem to be slightly more efficient planners in the posttest session and slightly more selective readers, they do not seem to be significantly more efficient learners. A closer examination of the students' behaviors in the posttest session, however, reveals that the nominal experimental treatment may not have been operational. The results cannot be interpreted as evidence that the use of the self-directed aids system is not helpful, because the experimental subjects were not really using the aids system. Only three of the seven experimental treatment students ever specified dependencies among information sources that they had chosen as relevant. Only two of them ever looked at their goal stacks. **None** of these students ever specified a dependency between objectives. A majority of these subjects (four of the seven) failed to formulate more than one objective. (Those who formulated only one objective simply restated their task in the form of an objective—e.g., ''Identify the defective part of the essay generator.'') Thus, the two groups did not really differ in functional treatment.

Not all students who were given the aids system found it to be useless or even a handicap, however. The subject JR, for example, made very effective use of it. She showed good planning by formulating useful objectives and then selecting information resources that could help her attain those objectives. By the measure of planning discussed in the results, her planning was perfect; she had no violations of our rules for efficient sequencing. She was also a selective user of information resources. She chose only nine titles for study, and her selectivity ratios (explained in Table 7.2) were very high (R_1 = .89, R_2 = .90, R_3 = .88). She was also an efficient learner. She took about an average amount of time to solve the problem; however, unlike many other students, she made no errors. She correctly identified the defective component on the first attempt.

The fact that this student was better able than others to exploit the functions of the automated aids system dramatically highlights the variation found in student performance. An examination of the standard deviations given in Tables 7.1, 7.2, and 7.3 confirms this variation. The large variation and the small sample size cause any differences between the group means to be nonsignificant.

A regression of scores on the Nelson–Denny test of reading ability on time taken to complete the task reveals an interesting difference between the experimental subjects and the control subjects. This difference is shown graphically in Figure 7.6. Note that the control subjects display the relationship that would be expected a priori: Students who score lower on the reading test take longer to complete the task. Experimental subjects, on the other hand, show considerably less effect of reading ability. However, experimental subjects scoring in the low range on the Nelson–Denny test require much less time to complete the task than control subjects scoring in this same range. Perhaps the automated aids system benefits poor readers to a greater extent than it benefits good readers.

The results of the pilot study suggested several necessary revisions for the next experiment. Some aspects of the aids system, such as the goal stack, needed improvement. More training was called for, with less confusing examples. A more thorough training program was certainly called for.

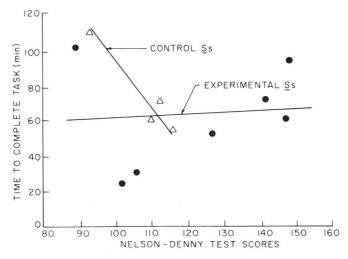

Figure 7.6 Regression of reading scores on task-completion time for each group.

Students in the experimental group were exposed to a very large number of aids-system functions but were given little opportunity to practice using most of these functions. Each function was demonstrated once in training, and the student was then required to mimic its use only once. Experimental students in the pilot experiment bore the burden of learning about two complicated systems—the automated aids system and the sentence generator—at the same time. It is clearly important that subjects should receive training drill on the use of the functions of the aids system in a context in which they are not burdened with the simultaneous need to puzzle out the workings of another complex system at the same time. We also decided that more interesting or personally relevant problem domains might improve motivation during learning and practice. Subjects in the second experiment were Naval Reserve Officer Training Corps students. The problems and examples presented in the training were more job-oriented problems dealing with Naval procedures, ship handling, and maritime rules of the road.

SECOND EXPERIMENT

Experimental Design

The experiment was designed to test the following two research hypotheses: (*a*) Students who are trained in self-direction strategies will solve a complex learning task more quickly and efficiently than students who are not trained, and (*b*) when students are trained in self-direction strategies, those students who are provided with the automated aids system to facilitate the use of those strategies will solve the task more quickly and efficiently than the students who are not provided with the aids system. The overall design is shown in Figure 7.7. Subjects were assigned at random to one of the following conditions:

I. Training plus aids system: Students were trained in self-direction strategies and in the use of the aids system. During the final session

	Condition		
	I	II	III
Training Sessions	AIDS SYSTEM	AIDS SYSTEM	CONTROL SYSTEM
Test Session	AIDS SYSTEM	CONTROL SYSTEM	CONTROL SYSTEM

Figure 7.7 Combinations of systems available to subjects in each condition.

(during which data on student performance were collected), they were provided with the aids system designed to facilitate application of the strategies.

  II. Training and no aids system: Students were trained in self-direction strategies and in the use of the aids system in the same way as Group I. During the final session, they were not given the aids system; instead, they had to accomplish the task using the same apparatus available to the group in Condition III.

 III. No training and no aids system: Students were given no training in self-direction strategies, nor did they have the aids system available during the final problem-solving session.

The first research hypothesis is tested by comparing the performance of students in Condition II with that of students in Condition III, whereas the second hypothesis is tested by comparing the performance of students in Condition I with that of students in Condition II. This design is similar to a 2 × 2 factorial except that the cell corresponding to "no training and aids system" was omitted because students could not be expected to use the complex aids system without prior training in its use.

During the testing phase, students in the training-only and control groups (Conditions II and III) use an automated system containing only the task and contents pages of the system described earlier. Students in these groups have the same learning task and the same information to read, but they have none of the aids system available to students in the training-plus-aids group (Condition I). (Information sources in this simplified system are accessed directly from the table of contents. As soon as the student touches a title, he is shown the corresponding information source.)

The training sequence for control subjects is similar to that for the other students, except that the basic system is never modified for them, so there is no need for teaching sessions other than the initial one. Thus, Sessions 2 and 3 are practice sessions using the control system, and Session 4 is the testing phase. The training phase for students in the training-only group is identical to that for students in the training-plus-aids group. During the final session, however, the training-only students use the control system rather than the self-directed learning Aids system. As noted before, the combinations of different systems used in all three conditions are shown in Figure 7.7.

Method

Subjects for the experiment were volunteers recruited from a lower-level, Naval Reserve Officers Training Corps (NROTC) course at a major university. Thirty-nine subjects were assigned at random to each of the three conditions just described. The students were told that they would receive exposure to junior-level NROTC course material by participating in the experiment as well as $20 for completing the experiment. During the test session, they were told that they could receive an additional $2 for solving the task correctly on the first attempt or an additional $1 for solving it on the second attempt. The reason for this bonus was to discourage random guessing and to encourage students to have a fair degree of confidence in their answer.

Data Collection

The data collected during the testing session were of essentially the same type as those collected during the pilot experiment. These included measures of effective learning (reading time and number of errors) and self-directed learning (planning violations and selectivity ratios). In addition, we attempted to validate the schema representations given earlier. Following the final session, students were asked to describe the "learning techniques or strategies" that they used in solving the complex troubleshooting task. Their summaries of these strategies were analyzed using a modified form of the method for scoring text recalls and summaries described in Gordon, Munro, Rigney, and Lutz (1978), to try to determine whether subjects in different treatment groups would summarize their strategies differently. This method of text analysis examines summaries for occurrences of statements of particular relevance for self-directed learning—that is, the schema representations. These were translated into short English statements, and three judges scored the summaries of strategies for the presence of these statements.

Results

For each of the three treatment groups, means and standard deviations were computed for the dependent measures. These are presented in Table 7.4. Visual inspection of the results reveals that the training-only group

TABLE 7.4
Means and Standard Deviations of Dependent Measures

Variables		Treatment conditions		
		Training + aids	Training only	Control
Reading time (minutes)	$\bar{X}$	20.05	41.89	27.44
	SD	(14.71)	(33.93)	(13.12)
Errors	$\bar{X}$	1.23	3.31	1.62
	SD	(1.54)	(3.20)	(3.02)

TABLE 7.4 (Cont.)

Variables		Training + aids	Training only	Control
		\multicolumn{3}{Treatment conditions}		
Selectivity in titles picked	$\bar{X}$	.77	.61	.68
	SD	(.17)	(.17)	(.22)
Selectivity in time allocation	$\bar{X}$	.71	.62	.67
	SD	(.20)	(.18)	(.24)
Planning violations	$\bar{X}$	1.39	1.54	1.58
	SD	(1.50)	(1.13)	(1.56)

performed worse than both the training-plus-aids and the control groups on almost every measure. In retrospect, this result seems unsurprising, since the training in self-direction that the subjects were given was, for the most part, either oriented toward or interpretable in terms of the functions of the aids system. Students in the training-only group were required to solve a complex problem in the final session using an aids system with which they were unfamiliar. The comparison of the training-plus-aids group with the control group will therefore be emphasized in the discussion that follows.

The number of errors made in solving the complex problem is a measure of the effectiveness of the learning strategies that students use to accomplish their task. Although a paired comparisons test did not reveal a significant difference between the two groups of interest, inspection of the descriptive statistics indicates that the control group made slightly more errors on the average and varied more widely in their performance. The variance of the control group is about twice that of the treatment group. This suggests that the treatment served to reduce individual variation in complex problem solving. A second measure of learning effectiveness is the amount of time spent reading the information resources. The training-plus-aids group spent less time reading the information than the control group, but again the difference did not reach significance.

The other three variables included in Table 7.4 are measures of self-directedness during problem solving that require the use of text. All differences between the two groups are in the predicted direction but are not significant. Students in the training-plus-aids group were somewhat more selective in choosing only relevant titles and also spent more of their time reading relevant information than did the controls. The treatment conditions also resulted in fewer planning violations than did the control condition.

Therefore, as assessed both by final performance and by behaviors during problem solving, the treatment condition produced slightly (but not significantly) more effective and self-directed learning.

Aptitude by Treatment Interactions

Correlations between variables were examined for the training-plus-aids and control conditions. These correlations appear in Tables 7.5 and 7.6. Visual examination of the data indicates an overall pattern of differences between the treatment groups. In general, the expected relationships between ability, time, and performance occur only in the control condition. For example, we would expect students of higher verbal ability to need less reading time to solve the problem (and lower-ability students to require more reading time). Yet, the expected negative correlation between these two variables (verbal ability and reading time) occurred only in the control condition, $r = .50$ for the training-plus-aids group, but $r = -.48$ for the

TABLE 7.5
Correlation Matrix for Training + Aids Group

	A	B	C	D	E	F	G
A. Reading time							
B. Errors	.35						
C. Selectivity 1 (title choice)	−.21	−.40					
D. Selectivity 2 (time allocation)	−.14	−.09	.83*				
E. Planning violations	.30	.03	−.61*	−.67*			
F. SAT: Verbal	.50*	−.18	−.12	−.38	.27		
G. SAT: Math	−.15	−.26	.41	.53	−.26	−.33	
H. SAT: Composite	.39	−.35	.16	−.01	.09	.77*	.35

* $p < .05$.
ª $N = 13$ (due to missing data).

TABLE 7.6
Correlation Matrix for Control Group

	A	B	C	D	E	F	G
A. Reading time							
B. Errors	.28						
C. Selectivity 1 (Title choice)	−.67*	−.55*					
D. Selectivity 2 (time allocation)	−.67*	−.62*	.97*				
E. Planning violations	.16	.59*	−.69*	−.72*			
F. SAT: Verbal	−.48	−.71*	.46	.55	−.50		
G. SAT: Math	.59*	−.21	−.18	−.17	−.03	.72*	
H. SAT: Composite	.03	−.67*	.08	.23	−.28	.78*	.68*

* $p < .05$.
ª $N = 13$ except due to missing data.

control group. The correlations between verbal ability and error scores also fail to be strongly negative except for the control group, $r = -.18$ and $-.71$, respectively. In other words, only in the control condition was the negative correlation significant ($p < .05$). Ability, then, is predictably related to the dependent measures only in the control condition.

The relationship between ability and self-direction also seems to fit our expectations only in the control group. We would expect students of higher verbal ability to be more selective and make fewer planning violations. Although we would predict that verbal ability and selectivity are positively related, a positive correlation between ability and selectivity in time allocation occurred only in the control condition, $r = -.38$ and $.55$, respectively. Similarly, the correlation between ability and selectivity in title choice was positive only for control subjects, $r = -.12$ and $.46$, respectively. Furthermore, we would expect that verbal ability is inversely related to violations in planning, yet the obtained correlations did not match that prediction except in the control condition, $r = .27$ and $-.50$, respectively. Hence, the expected relationships between verbal ability and measures of self-directedness did not hold except for students in the control condition.

Several other expected relationships held only for the control condition. We would expect that selectivity would decrease reading time, so that these variables should be negatively correlated. Although the correlations are negative for both groups ($r = -.21$ and $-.14$ for training-plus-aids and $r = -.67$ and $-.67$ for control), they are significant only in the control group. The final prediction is that planning violations should be related to errors because inefficient learners are probably ineffective as well. The correlations are $r = .03$ and $.59$, respectively. In other words, the naturally expected correlation between planning violations and errors is found only in the control condition.

The aptitude by treatment interactions (ATI) evidence shows that expected relationships between ability and performance held only for the control group. It seems likely that students of high ability in the experimental groups may have been hampered by the cumbersome mechanics of the aids system, which promoted less efficient strategies than they would have used on their own. Less capable students in the experimental groups, who may have had no useful strategies, were probably helped by the features of the aids system. This explanation is supported by the reduced variance in errors found in the training-plus-aids group as compared with the control group.

Strategy Summary Results

Means and standard deviations were computed for the scored strategy summaries. A two-factor analysis of variance (ANOVA) with repeated measures on the rater factor was performed on these data, and the results appear in Table 7.7. Differences among the treatment conditions are significant: $F = 5.34$, $p < .01$. Although differences among the raters are also significant, the interaction between the two factors is not significant ($F = 1.93$, n.s.), indicating that group differences in reported strategies are not a function of rater bias. Therefore, strategy scores were averaged across raters (the interrater reliability coefficient is .81). The resultant group means are shown in Table 7.8. Differences between the training-plus-aids and the training-only group are significant—t (24) = 2.93, $p < .01$.—and the differences between the training-plus-aids and the control group are also significant—t (24) = 2.38, $p < .05$. We may conclude, then, that students in the training-plus-aids group learned significantly more of the self-directed learning strategies than did students of either of the other two groups.

Why students in the training-plus-aids group should report different strategies than those in the training-only group is difficult to understand. One explanation that seems likely relies upon the fact that students were instructed to produce summaries "that you used to solve the problem you just worked on." As we have already seen in the performance data, students in the training-only group performed quite poorly. It seems likely that they were not making use of the self-directed learning strategies during the final session. The fact that they did not produce summaries of the self-direction strategies does not necessarily mean that they did not learn the

TABLE 7.7
ANOVA Summary Table for Strategy Summary Judgments

Source	df	MS	F
Between-treatment condition	2	19.56	5.34**
Error$_b$	36	3.67	
Within raters	2	35.41	37.55**
Interaction	4	1.821	1.931
Error$_w$	72	.94	

** $p < .01$.

TABLE 7.8
Averaged Strategy Summary Judgments

	Treatment condition		
	Training + aids	Training only	Control
$\bar{X}$	2.7	1.3*	1.6*
SD	(1.4)	(1.0)	(.9)

* $p < .05$ (for comparison with training + aids group).

strategies. Rather, they simply have been obeying the instructions by not describing the strategies that they failed to use.

Discussion

Our analyses of the data on self-direction and reading effectiveness found a nonsignificant tendency for those students who had both received training and had the use of the aids system during the test to perform better than the students in the other two groups. It is possible that with more training practice or with more subjects these results might have reached significance. It is noteworthy that the training-plus-aids group outperformed the other two groups on each of the performance measures we took. On only one measure, the scores for summarized strategies, did the performance of the training-plus-aids group significantly exceed that of the other two groups. It seems that one of the reasons that the training-plus-aids group did not do better was that, despite the improved training system, not all of the students in the group made use of all the facilities of the aids system. For example, only 8 of the 13 subjects ever accessed the goal stack. (On the average, those students accessed the goal stack twice during the last session.) This is an improvement over the performance of students in the pilot experiment, but it is clear that students were, on the whole, still not highly motivated to make use of the aids system facilities. Perhaps the training system should make use of a system of rewards for the use the aids system functions. Ideally, the administration of rewards for the use of such functions should be under the control of the subject himself. By following the principles of behavioral self-control set forth in Kanfer and Goldstein (1975), Mahoney (1974), Mahoney and Thoresen (1975), Thoresen and Mahoney (1974), and Watson and Tharp (1972), we should be able to help students develop learning habits that they can apply outside the experimental environment as well as within it. Those students who were both trained in the use of the self-directed learning aids system and given access to that system in the test session were able later to summarize the principles of the system in writing. Yet other students who had received the same training (the training-only group) but did not practice with it in the last session were no better than control subjects at expressing the strategies.

An unexpected aspect of our results was the (nonsignificant) difference between the control group and the group that was trained in the use of the aids system but did not have the use of that system during the test. We had predicted that the training-only group would perform less well than the training-plus-aids group but better than the control group. Instead, control group students did better than those in the training-only group. In retrospect, this result seems quite natural. Students in the training-only group received training in the use of one computer-based aids system but were tested on their facility with another. The switch in systems may well have been confusing, and this could have caused their performance to deteriorate.

The results of the research reported here lend support to two conclusions that we believe are also supported by other recent results in cognitive research. The first is that human learning and human thinking are not very general processes but are always closely linked to fairly detailed or specific situations. The second conclusion is that human learning strategies or skills are highly automatized; as a result, even inefficient learning strategies may lead to superior performance when they are compared with nonautomatic strategies. In the remainder of this chapter we will present evidence for these two claims and discuss their implications for training research.

A number of theorists in cognitive science (for example, Goldstein & Papert, 1977) have recently proposed that models of human thought should include few, if any, general processes. Rather, knowledge and thought are best represented as a collection of quite specific concepts, concepts that are bound to particular restricted entities in particular situations. If this claim has substance, it may be that the strategies that subjects in our training groups learned were somehow closely bound up in their minds with the topic matter of the example-learning problems that were used during training. In the training sessions, subjects were given problems on the rules of the road. The test session, however, used a very different (and much more complicated) problem of trouble-shooting a defective device. Subjects may have learned the strategies that they had been taught in such a way that they would apply them only to rules-of-the-road problems. Some of the comments made by the subjects in their written evaluations of the experiment seem to reflect this problem:

> To start with I made up 4 goals objectives to complete before I could complete the task. Then as I worked on the information I noticed that some (most?) of my objectives were not really suited to the subject.
>
> This problem was a little different in regards to strategy than others at 1 point.
>
> The third problem set, after learning goal stack, objectives, and dependency should place more emphasis on the use of those features. The two problems I had in this phase of the training were much too easy to incorporate all features of the system.
>
> If the practice [sic] problems were more difficult it would help repare [sic] the learner.
>
> More practice with tougher problems.
>
> A few of the problems (2nd and 3rd session) were pretty easy and I was able to have a few common-sense deductions about the answers. I think the experiment would have gone off much better if the areas studied were a little more difficult and challenging.

If this process (of learning strategies only with respect to certain topic-matter domains) is as widespread as we fear it is, a number of measures should be taken to improve the results in attempting to teach such strategies. Two methods come to mind. First, the applications for which the strategies are intended should be closely examined. If they belong to a restricted class, then the practice materials for training in the strategies should all come from that class. Second, if the applications are not members of a restricted class, then as wide a variety of practice problems should be used as is possible. The training process will most certainly have to be more protracted in such a case.

The second general conclusion about human learning that we have been led to is that adults' learning strategies have been highly automatized. Rigney (1978a) has reviewed evidence on this issue. If this claim is true, we should not be surprised to discover that our experimental subjects, who should have been using superior strategies, did not do significantly better than those subjects in the control group. First, it is possible that for many of our experimental subjects, the highly overlearned, old, inefficient strategies automatically went into action and competed with the new, less well-learned strategies we had taught them. Second, if some experimental subjects were able to use the new strategies we had taught them, they could have been at a disadvantage with respect to the control subjects who used their old strategies. The control subjects' strategies could be activated automatically and should have required little conscious control. The new, unfamiliar techniques used by the experimental subjects, however, would surely require considerable conscious control, thus reducing the processing resources available for learning and problem solving. Viewed in this light, the fact that experimental subjects did not do significantly worse than control subjects seems to support the essential validity of the learning techniques embodied in the aids system.

REFERENCES

Bitzer, D. L., Sherwood, B. A. & Tenczar, P. *Computer-based science education* (CERL Report X-37). Urbana: University of Illinois, Computer Education Research Laboratory, May 1973.

Goldstein, I., & Papert, S. Artificial intelligence, language, and the study of knowledge. *Cognitive Science,* 1977, *1,* 84–123.

Gordon, L., Munro, A., Rigney, J. W., & Lutz, K. A. *Summaries and recalls for three types of texts* (Tech. Rep. 85). Los Angeles: University of Southern California, Behavioral Technology Laboratories, May 1978.

Huff, K. H., Sticht, T. G., Joyner, J., Groff, S. D., & Burkett, J. R. *A job-oriented reading program for the air force: Development and evaluation* (HumRRO Tech. Rep.

AFHRL-TR-77-34). Alexandria, Va.: Human Resources Research Organization, May 1977.

Kanfer, F. H., & Goldstein, A. P. (Eds.). *Helping people change.* New York: Pergamon Press, 1975.

Mahoney, M. J. *Cognition and behavior modification.* Cambridge, Mass.: Ballinger, 1974.

Mahoney, M. J., & Thoresen, C. E. *Self-control: Power to the person.* Monterey, Calif.: Brooks/Cole, 1975.

Munro, A., & Rigney, J. W. *A schema-theory account of some cognitive processes in complex human learning* (Tech. Rep. 81). Los Angeles: University of Southern California, Behavioral Technology Laboratories, July 1977.

Norman, D. A. Memory, knowledge, and the answering of questions. In R. L. Solso (Ed.), *Contemporary issues in cognitive psychology: The Loyola symposium.* Washington, D.C.: Winston, 1973.

Norman, D. A. Cognitive organization and learning. In S. Dornic & P. M. A. Rabbit (Eds.), *Attention and performance V.* London: Academic Press, 1974.

Norman, D. A. Notes toward a theory of complex learning. *Proceedings of the NATO symposium on cognition and learning,* in press.

Norman, D. A., Rumelhart, D. E., & the LNR group. *Explorations in cognition.* San Francisco: Freeman, 1975.

Rigney, J. W. *Cognitive learning strategies and dualities in the human information processing system.* Paper presented at the Conference on Aptitude, Learning, and Instruction: Cognitive Process Analysis, San Diego, March 9, 1978. (a)

Rigney, J. W. Learning strategies: A theoretical perspective. In H. F. O'Neil, Jr. (Ed.), *Learning strategies.* New York: Academic Press, 1978. (b)

Rigney, J. W., & Munro A. *On cognitive strategies for processing text* (Tech. Rep. 80). Los Angeles: University of Southern California, Behavioral Technology Laboratories, March 1977.

Rigney, J. W., Towne, D. M., King, C. A., & Langston, E. T. *Computer-aided performance training for diagnostic and procedural tasks* (Tech. Rep. 72). Los Angeles: University of Southern California, Behavioral Technology Laboratories, October 1972.

Rumelhart, D. E., & Ortony, A. The representation of knowledge in memory. In R. C. Anderson, R. J. Spiro, & W. E. Montague (Eds.), *Schooling and the acquisition of knowledge.* Hillsdale, N.J.: Lawrence Earlbaum Associates, 1977.

Thoresen, C. E., & Mahoney, M. J. *Behavioral self-control.* New York: Holt, Rinehart and Winston, 1974.

Watson, D. L., & Tharp, R. G. *Self-directed behavior: Self-modification for personal adjustment.* Monterey, Calif.: Brooks/Cole, 1972.

8

A Person-by-Situation View of Computer-Based Instruction

IRWIN G. SARASON

The three preceding chapters seemingly deal with rather separate and distinct topics. Spielberger, Gonzalez, and Fletcher report and discuss studies of test anxiety that have clinical implications. Judd, McCombs, and Dobrovolny describe an effort to increase the efficiency of computer-managed instruction. Rigney, Munro, and Crook present ideas and preliminary evidence concerning a method intended to strengthen selective job-oriented reading. The three chapters differ in the theoretical domains to which they pertain, the first one growing out of a large literature on individual differences in personality, the other two part of an ambitious effort to achieve a breakthrough in educational technology.

Despite these differences, there are basic commonalities. One of these is interest in optimizing performance. Another is a concern for the cognitive correlates and antecedents of performance. The stimulus for the "cognitive revolution" in psychology has been the growing recognition that the O in the traditional S-O-R (stimulis–organism–response) paradigm is more complex than had often been recognized in earlier times. Questions about cognitive processes run throughout the three chapters. Rigney, Munro, and Crook ask: What are the mental products of training programs? Judd, Mc-Combs, and Dobrovolny speculate about the cognitive steps involved in achieving improved time management skills. Spielberger, Gonzalez, and Fletcher address themselves to the interaction between cognitive processes and what several authors in this volume refer to as *affective factors* and others call *personality*. Links among these issues, each important, have not yet been achieved.

One is reminded of the story of the reports given by blind persons who

COGNITIVE AND AFFECTIVE
LEARNING STRATEGIES

touched different parts of an elephant. As far as they went, each report was veridical, but there were many disparities. The realities of an elephant vary depending upon the part of its body explored, and the realities of the acquisition of cognitions are similarly complex.

Sorely needed in the study of cognitive processes is a theoretical structure that will provide the framework within which the problems posed and questions raised by the three preceding chapters can be interrelated.

A person-by-situation approach to educational technology may provide a useful set of guidelines. The reality of persons and situations is that they exist—but never in isolation. Personal characteristics of an individual, even if their reliability over time is high, interact with one another and with changing conditions of life. The restriction of scientific endeavors simply to the study of functional relationships between environmental variables and behavior seems at first glance to be consistent with the physical sciences paradigm after which many psychologists strive to model their science; but is it really? Eysenck (1967) has succinctly answered this question:

> No physicist would dream of assessing the electric conductivity, or the magnetic properties, or the heat-resisting qualities of matter, of "stuff-in-general." . . . Much energy was spent on the construction of Mendeleev's tables of the elements precisely because one element does not behave like another. Some conduct electricity, others do not, or do so only poorly; we do not throw all these differences into some gigantic error term, and deal only with the average of all substances. But this is what experimental psychologists do, in the cause of imitating physics! It may be suggested that the root of many of the difficulties in duplicating results from one study to another, may lie in the neglect of individual differences [p. 5].

The reality of human behavior is that it is modified by both environmental stimulation and stimulation the individual supplies for himself in the form of preoccupations, expectations, and interpretations of what is going on in the environment.

The person-by-situation paradigm applies to situations in which persons are presented with problems to be solved, tasks to be carried out. In the case of computer-based instruction, the task is highly novel. This fact makes understandable the challenges taken up by Spielberger, Gonzalez, and Fletcher. Highly test-anxious people usually respond poorly to novelty. For them, novelty often comes to be equated with difficulty. More needs to be uncovered concerning the test-anxious person's subjective response to novelty and the mechanism by which newness and differentness are transformed into difficulty. More specifically, more needs to be uncovered concerning the meaning of educational settings for learners. Though individual differences in test anxiety help to shape those meanings, surely other personal variables do so as well. For example, internal–external locus of control would certainly appear to be a relevant factor in computer-based instruction. On the one hand, the learner usually knows little about the mechanisms and technology involved in such instruction. On the other hand, the learner probably has a much more predictable learning environment in the computer–based situation. In either case, cognitive events would seem to play a central role in the instructional process. The cognitive events may be viewed as inputs in the information-processing system that shape the *psychological situation* to which the person responds. The list of cognitive factors that in all likelihood play important roles in learning is long and includes a variety of factors related to the way in which the individual perceives, interprets, and responds to the world:

1. Self-preoccupations, self-statements, and daydreams
2. Ambivalences and conflicts
3. Attributions, labeling habits, and appraisals
4. Expectations and assumptions
5. Problem-solving strategies
6. Cognitive rehearsal skills
7. Self-observations and introspections
8. Awareness of alternative response possibilities

Advances in the cognitive approach to personality seem to require means of identifying and quantifying individual differences in human information-processing systems.

What people bring to learning situations—regardless of the situation's novelty—are distinctive sets of needs, motivations, and dispositions. The word *affective* does not quite encompass those elements of personality that are often described as nonintellective. At least to this writer, affective refers to feelings and emotions. Motivations—which have affective implications—are aroused by goals of importance to the person. Dispositions—which also are not independent of affects—are acquired tendencies to attend and respond to perceived demands. Cognitive styles illustrate dispositions that influence behavior in many situations, including the tendency to see threats in academic examinations. Cognitive styles seem particularly relevant to the development of innovative educational technologies because they exert such an influence over how novel situations are perceived. Put another way, it is necessary to find out how learners interpret their task in the computer-based situation.

Of the three chapters under discussion, the one by Spielberger, Gonzalez, and Fletcher clearly recognizes the importance of identifying person-by-situation interactions in learning situations. However, neither they nor any other researchers have charted these interactions extensively over a wide range of situations. To say that test anxiety interacts with experimentally created threats (such as, "I'm now going to give you an intelligence test that will reveal whether you are college material") is really too general a statement. The environment or context in which the threat occurs plays a powerful role as a moderator, and this gets us back to the matter of the meaning of computer-based situations to the individual. Where do these situations fit within the population of meanings persons attach to situations?

In addition to these meanings are the relevant and irrelevant thoughts that preoccupy the individual during learning situations. This problem seems especially salient to researchers such as Rigney, Munro, and Crook, whose work deals with reading. What are the thoughts that help and hinder readers in their identification of important material and their efforts to make sense of and use it? To what are effective and ineffective readers attending when they examine linguistic symbols in books or other visual displays? Though it is very difficult methodologically to assess such strategies and styles while performance is in progress, postperformance assessment is possible. We can at least find out what learners **say** they thought about while working on a particular task. Table 8.1 contains excerpts from the writer's Cognitive Interference Questionnaire (Sarason,

TABLE 8.1
Excerpts from Cognitive Interference Questionnaire

I. We are interested in learning about the kinds of thoughts that go through people's heads while they are working on a task. The following is a list of thoughts some of which you might have had **while doing the task on which you have just worked.** Please indicate approximately how often each thought occurred to you while working on it by placing the appropriate number in the blank provided to the left of each question.

       Example 1 = never
                 2 = once
                 3 = a few times
                 4 = often
                 5 = very often

I. ____ 1. I thought about how poorly I was doing.
   ____ 2. I wondered what the experimenter would think of me.
   ____ 3. I thought about how I should work more carefully.
   ____ 4. I thought about how much time I had left.
   ____ 5. I thought about how others have done on this task.
   ____ 6. I thought about the difficulty of the problems.
   ____ 7. I thought about my level of ability.
   ____ 8. I thought about how often I got confused.

II. Please circle the number on the following scale which best represents the degree to which you felt your mind wandered **during the task you have just completed.**

Not at all 1 : 2 : 3 : 4 : 5 : 6 : 7 Very much

1978), which was devised to elicit clues to relevant and irrelevant cognitions in performance situations.

This type of post-performance assessment also seems applicable to research on time management similar to that described by Judd, Mc-Combs, and Dobrovolny. Time management involves, among other things, decisions and judgments with action implementations on the part of the person. Personal preoccupations for some people intrude on the time management process and may lead to performance decrements.

One final comment concerns the factor of efficiency in new technological developments. Considerable emphasis was placed in the chapters by Judd *et al.* and Rigney *et al.* on maximizing efficiency in performance using computer-based approaches. Although efficiency is a laudable goal, it is at least equally important to bear in mind the conceptual structure within which one's work is—or should be—conducted. From the person-by-situation interactional perspective, the research reported in these papers seems somewhat imbalanced in the sense that the technology of the situation has played such a central role relative to individual differences in personality and cognitive styles. This may not be a fair appraisal of the strategies of the authors or the chapters under discussion, since their work reported in this volume is quite preliminary. Still, in some ways, the technological dimensions of computer-based situations are the easiest to tackle. More challenging, in part because of the difficulties involved in assessing personality and cognitive variables, is the private world of the person as it interacts with the computer–based situation. Test anxiety is one type of individual difference variable that merits incorporation in the computer-based situation.

REFERENCES

Eysenck, H. J. *The biological basis of personality.* Springfield, Ill.: Charles C. Thomas, 1967.
Sarason, I. G. The Test Anxiety Scale. In C. D. Spielberger & I. G. Sarason (Eds.), *Stress and anxiety* (Vol. 5). Washington, D.C.: Hemisphere, 1978.

ALTERNATIVE APPROACHES TO LEARNING STRATEGIES

9

Learning Strategies, Cognitive Processes, and Motor Learning[1]

ROBERT N. SINGER and RICHARD F. GERSON

For years, motor learning research has been plagued with a lack of a unified orientation, as well as systematically designed research efforts leading to meaningful conceptual directions. Even worse, sufficient practical implications have been difficult if not impossible to evolve from these efforts. Fortunately, times have changed.

Adams (1971), Keele (1973), and Schmidt (1975), among others, have provided well-formulated models of motor behavior that in turn have generated an abundance of well-conceived investigations. Special control processes that underlie the acquisition of skill have been identified and analyzed. Much of the work has been focused on either the nature of the input or the processes leading to the reproduction of specific movements. However, the role of the variety of cognitive processes as potential control factors in motor behavior has been generally overlooked.

Therefore, the major focus of our research is oriented to the determination of the relationships among (a) hypothesized internal processing mechanisms; (b) cognitive (potential control) processes; and (c) learner strategies (externally and internally generated).

We have attempted to conceptualize about hypothesized *mechanisms* that appear to be activated sequentially in stages or in parallel as informa-

[1] Preparation of this chapter was supported by the Defense Advanced Research Projects Agency under contract MDA 903-77-C-0200, and monitored by the U.S. Army Research Institute for the Behavioral and Social Sciences. Views and conclusions contained in this chapter are those of the authors and should not be interpreted as necessarily representing the official policies, either expressed or implied, of the Defense Advanced Research Projects Agency, U.S. Army Research Institute for the Behavioral and Social Sciences, or of the United States government.

215

tion is processed leading to complex motor behavior. We define a *mechanism* as a real or hypothesized "location" or "structure" associated with the nervous system in which specified unique control processes and functions occur.

Likewise, a *cognitive process* (also referred to as a cognition or a control process by others) has been identified as to type and location, and is associated with a proposed mechanism. We define a cognitive process as a control process, which is self-generated, transient, situationally determined conscious activity that a learner uses to organize and to regulate received and transmitted information, and ultimately, behavior. The ultimate objective of our work is to describe alternative strategies available to learners–performers that may be available to help facilitate the processing of information and benefit performance. Our interpretation of a *strategy* is a self-initiated or externally imposed way of directing information leading to decisions for purposeful behavior.

We intend to examine the relationships among mechanisms, processes, and strategies in various ways to understand the learning of complex motor skills in a more comprehensive fashion in order to suggest techniques that will eventually contribute to the improved operation of pertinent processes, hence learning. Whereas previous efforts in the analysis of motor skill learning have been geared to relatively simple tasks that place minimal demands on a learner's organizational and decision-making capabilities, the acquisition of complex skills requires a learner to utilize cognitive processes in a more extensive manner than heretofore realized. The identification and the subsequent effective manipulation of these control processes by learners will enable them to use personal information processing capabilities to develop appropriate strategies for learning and performing a variety of psychomotor activities, in order to be able to problem-solve and to adapt to new but related situations with minimal guidance.

The enumeration of processes that may be under the control of the learner can lead to a more thorough analysis of potential alternative strategies that the learner can activate to meet task demands. In turn, this information can provide a meaningful basis for instruction designed to assist learners in the development and the selection of the best strategies applicable to the acquisition of different types of tasks. Instruction would then proceed at a more rapid pace and be more economical because the strategies that are most relevant and most effective for the learning of categories of psychomotor tasks have been determined. Ultimately, the ideal learning environment would be one in which strategies were **self-generated** by learners rather than externally imposed by instructors.

The identification of alternative learner strategies associated with the cognitive control processes a learner may use in conjunction with one or several internal mechanisms is the challenge we have established for ourselves. To accomplish this goal, an extensive, analytical review of the extant literature in the verbal and motor learning areas has been conducted. In this chapter, a brief description of the development of a proposed model of the human behaving system will be provided that contains specific considerations unique to motor behavior.

An extensive body of research and theoretical literature has been reviewed and has permitted us to gain a comprehensive perspective of the human behaving system in regard to motor skills. Although earlier efforts have been described elsewhere (Singer, 1975, 1978; Singer & Gerson, 1978), recent advancements in the contemporary body of knowledge as well as more extensive analyses on our part have resulted in the revised model proposed in this chapter.

To be congruent with the very latest developments in the literature, several refinements of and elaborations upon certain mechanisms and processes identified in the original and revised models have been made in order to prepare the most scientifically sound model of motor behavior, with consideration for instructional implications. Our information processing model may be interpreted as primarily a stage one, and a debate has raged between proponents of stage and levels of processing models, although the arguments and divisions between the two camps may be more academic than real (Glanzer & Koppenaal, 1977).

The primary emphasis in this chapter is on the identification of cognitive processes and strategies a learner may use during the acquisition of complex motor skills. Additionally, the potential for a classification scheme of tasks and strategies will be described, along with a description of the relationship between the categorization systems. Future directions in our planned experimentation and practical applictions in various situations will be examined at the end of the chapter.

A CONCEPTUAL MODEL OF MOTOR BEHAVIOR

Any behaving system becomes activated and functionally operative when sense receptors are stimulated by environmental and/or organismic cues. As is shown in Figure 9.1, this information is briefly retained in the sensory stores (Sperling, 1960). The person conducts a preattentive analysis (Neisser, 1967), which results in some subthreshold stimuli fading from the system while other stimuli are determined as ready for processing. On the other hand, some information is forwarded, without need for a referent, directly to the perceptual mechanism as the process of detection begins (Massaro, 1975).

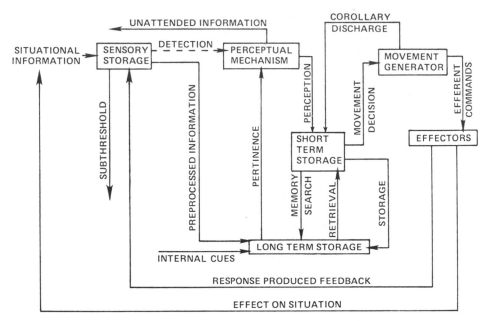

Figure 9.1 A conceptualization of information processing and motor behavior.

Other preprocessed information, as we term it, is transmitted forward to the long-term store to make memory contact with previously stored, similar, internal representations (cf. Norman, 1973).

Preprocessed information, which has contacted its memory representations in the long-term store, is then transmitted to the perceptual mechanism while the memory representations are forwarded as referents to the short-term store to facilitate the active processing that occurs in that mechanism. Meanwhile, a level of pertinence (relationships) is established by the learner based on these internal representations (Lindsay & Norman, 1977; Norman, 1968, 1976). Through the establishment of a level of pertinence or a perceptual expectancy set, the system is alerted to anticipate the ordered arrival of specific information from the long-term store into the perceptual mechanism, after which the inputs are forwarded to the short-term store as perceived information to facilitate both further processing and the decision-making process. Additionally, if an input does not contact an internal representation in long-term storage, that stimulus may still be transmitted through the system, although it is "unrefereed." When no memory representation is located, this information, or lack of it, will not have a referent in the short-term store if the unrefereed information reaches that mechanism.

The manner in which information is transmitted to the perceptual mechanism and the cognitive processes that occur within that mechanism contribute greatly to the potential output. Once the system has been alerted, the person selectively attends to the most pertinent, or relevant, information. The filtering process enables the learner to recognize important features of the display, and at this point the information begins to gain meaning.

After the system has begun to interpret the environmental and organismic cues, the information is then transmitted to the short-term store, where further processing occurs. Concurrently, as information is being processed by the perceptual mechanism, the memory representation that was contacted in the long-term store is advanced into short-term store. Long-term stored information is transmitted as referents to the short-term store to facilitate the active processing that occurs in that mechanism.

The short-term store may be considered as the working memory because the primary or active processing activities of the system occur within this mechanism (Schneider & Shiffrin, 1977; Shiffrin & Schneider, 1977). The short-term store receives information from both the perceptual mechanism and the long-term store and then organizes it for decision-making purposes or future storage. More specifically, there are identifiable and important control processes associated with the short-term store.

When information enters this mechanism, it is rehearsed and processed effectively so that it may be retained in the system, in long-term storage. The learner may also use this information to aid in any immediate decision-making process. Another way the learner can increase the utility of the information is by performing transformation operations so that an organizational structure can be imposed on the information (Bousfield, 1953; Gentile & Nacson, 1976; Mandler, 1967; Tulving & Donaldson, 1972). By structuring the input, the learner is capable of extracting additional meaning from the information, as well as increasing the available functional processing space (Chi, 1976).

An increase in capacity should result in the learner's being able to process incoming cues while working on information already in the mechanism. The information that has received more extensive processing can be used as a comparison base for the new input. The stored referents are used, along with the newly obtained information, by the learner to select a motor program from the long-term store and to plan the execution of the program (Keele, 1973). The purpose of these selection and planning cognitive processes (Klapp, 1977) is to transmit the specific program and the parameters in which the program is to operate to the movement generator.

Once the movement decision has been made, all the information used to formulate that decision is transferred to the long-term store to establish learning. The newly stored information will be used to determine future pertinence levels and as referents for comparisons of response-produced feedback and externally administered knowledge of results. The learner will be able to use this stored information to establish causal attributions following the receipt of performance outcome information. Thus, the major purpose of the long-term store is to hold information permanently for future use to establish pertinence levels; to aid in anticipation, expectancy formation, and perception; and to serve as a comparator between incoming situational demands and previous related experiences.

While information is being transmitted from short-term storage to long-term storage for future retrieval, a movement decision based on this information is being simultaneously transmitted from the short-term store to an hypothesized movement generator (Klapp, 1976). After the motor program is loaded into the movement generator, the performance commands that will initiate motor behavior are then sent to the effectors. These commands serve to cue or to tune the appropriate musculature in preparation for the response parameters of the upcoming movement (Keele & Summers, 1976). The movement generator also emits a feedforward signal along with the performance commands. The signal is a corollary discharge (Kelso & Stelmach, 1976), which is a copy of the efferent commands to the musculature that is transmitted to the short-term storage system to alert the organism to receive expected sensory information. The effectors then enact the programmed response.

The effectors yield an observable performance, which leads to response-produced feedback. The manner in which this feedback is recycled through the system to sensory storage and then to long-term storage for future use as a referent, and then to short-term storage to modify the present motor program or to select a new motor program is similar to the way any information is transmitted through the system. While processing the response-produced feedback, information about the nature of the movement, the learner may be concurrently receiving information about any situational changes due to the movement. The learner interprets these two sources of outcome information to formulate causal reasons (attributions) about the performance. Thus, feedback about performance, whether self-generated or externally provided, can serve several functions as we consider potential determinants of behavior.

Feedback information can be used to help to regulate ongoing behavior, to adapt a behavior to situational demands, to activate or to lower emotions, or to form the basis of evaluation of the performance. Feedback information may also be used by a learner through a nonconscious means of control, depending on the depth, or level, at which one investigates the mechanisms and control processes involved (Klapp, 1976). At the level of analysis that we are investigating, a learner applies conscious control processes to direct the transmission of feedback within the system. At a different level of analysis, the learner's use of feedback may involve the implementation of the gamma-efferent, or spindle receptor, system to control the execution of the motor program (Keele & Summers, 1976; Klapp, 1976), and this control may become refined with the development of skill. The refinement of the lower, nonconscious level of feedback control may serve as a partial explanation of the performance differences between beginners and highly skilled performers, as well as account for the apparent automaticity in the execution of skilled movement. However, the lower-level feedback system will not be discussed further here, as our concern is with the conscious control processes (psychological rather than neurophysiological) a learner may invoke to utilize feedback in the acquisition of skill.[2]

A brief description of the mechanisms, their interrelationships, and their contributions to complex motor behavior is illustrated in Figure 9.1. The figure summarizes the points made in this section of the chapter. Some form of control can be potentially exerted by the learner–performer from the time information enters the system until it is transformed into movement activity. Although these processes have been alluded to, we will now direct our attention to an in-depth exploration of the nature of cognitive processes, with special implications for motor learning and motor performance.

COGNITIVE PROCESSES IN THE
ACQUISITION OF SKILL

The formulation of a model of motor behavior, with heavy emphases on cognitive processes, has been described and provides the framework for the following material. To repeat, our basic thesis is that a great deal of information processing goes on when people attempt to learn complex motor activities. Much of it can be under the control of learners. The desirability of exerting deliberate conscious control depends on many factors. One of the primary differences between the highly skilled and the lesser skilled is the degree and type of conscious involvement prior to, during, and following motor performance. Therefore, conscious focus and intervention at a par-

[2] It should also be pointed out that deafferentation techniques do not permit the learner to use sensory feedback during the performance of a skill (see Kelso & Stelmach, 1976, and Taub, 1976, for reviews), but reasonable movement can occur anyway, based on previous information feedback stored in the long-term memory. These movements are crude and can approximate the skill to be performed.

ticular stage must be determined according to task demands, personal level of skill, and ultimate objectives of an instructional program.

The term *cognitive processes,* or *cognitions,* has been defined in many ways. In fact, it appears that each researcher who uses the term provides a personal definition for it (e.g., Battig, 1975; Hunt & Lansman, 1975; Neisser, 1967; Norman & Rumelhart, 1975). These numerous definitions can become confusing, considering the different contexts in which the term has been applied. For this reason, and for purposes of clarity in relation to this work, we offered our own definition earlier. Conscious control processes operate serially and in stages. Those that operate subconsciously, as with higher levels of skill, can operate in parallel with a conscious control process.

Many conscious control processes can be relegated to a subconscious level of control. This is what occurs when highly skilled behavior is initiated in complex motor activities. And, in the case of initial information contact to long-term memory without attention, consciousness may not be present in a person at any level of skill. A person can exert many forms of control to manipulate information and the effectors, nonetheless, thereby directing behavior. However, the person does not totally influence any situation, nor does the reverse probably happen. Whereas behaviorists might lead us to view human behavior as passively controlled by situational dictates, cognitive psychologists would suggest that people actively control their environments. The truth probably lies somewhere in the middle. Behaviors are not produced without cues or stimuli, and these behaviors are directed accordingly. But all people do not respond similarly to the same events, thereby demonstrating some degree of self-determination. In a sense, then, associative behaviors are indeed developed, but in a person's own way.

The interaction between the person and the environment is considered the foundation of cognitive psychology (Estes, 1970, 1975). Neisser (1967) elaborated on this view by suggesting that the focus of cognitive psychology is on the processes by which sensory input is transformed, reduced, encoded, stored, recovered, and used. The specific subject matter that is operational for investigative purposes encompasses mental states and processes (Butterfield & Dickerson, 1976). Several processes associated with cognitive behavior are perception, information representation in memory, use of knowledge (Norman & Rumelhart, 1975), sensation, imagery, retention, recall, problem solving, and thinking (Neisser 1967). The manner in which a learner employs these various processes in relation to personal cognitive capabilities for the efficient use of information, in activities such as comprehension, listening, and reading, is the major determinant of individual differences in the acquisition of skill (Battig, 1975; Gagné, 1967; Marteniuk, 1974; Reitman, 1969; Simon, 1975).

Differences in skill level may be better understood with a contrast of beginners and advanced performers and how they utilize information to formulate behavioral responses. A beginning learner may not know which situational cues are relevant or irrelevant and may process several cues as individual inputs. This would result in an increased short-term or working memory load and a decreased capacity to process additional information that might be present and useful, for little organization of the information has taken place. The beginner would probably be unaware of how to use the appropriate control processes for the transmission of information through the hypothesized mechanisms of the human system. Therefore, a motor response based on the selective use of much available information would be erratic, since the manner in which these cues were processed would require that they each be retrieved separately. In contrast, a highly skilled performer could abstract the commonality among the inputs and employ an encoding strategy for processing this information.

Encoding refers to a transformation of information from a general to a more abstract representation to facilitate storage and retrieval. Since the cues would be processed as a unit, more capacity becomes available to deal with new stimuli that can be used to update any response requirements. Consequently, this performer will emit efficient motor behaviors because of the quality of the encoding of the cues, and the more efficient retrieval of those cues (cf. Tulving & Thomson, 1973). Thus, the cognitive processes that a learner applies to the processing of information can account for many of the differences observed between skill levels.

Table 9.1 contains a description of a number of cognitive processes that can be associated the particular mechanisms. Possible functions of these processes are described as well.

Cognitive processes such as these are ongoing operations (Hunt & Lansman, 1975; Norman & Rumelhart, 1975) that the learner employs to enhance the acquisition, representation, and utilization of knowledge in memory. Other researchers have interpreted cognitive processes as controlling factors in the sequence of serially or hierarchically organized behaviors, a definition similar to ours (Atkinson & Shiffrin, 1968; Johnson, 1974; Kausler, 1974; Scandura, 1977). Atkinson and Shiffrin (1968) have defined a control process as a transient phenomenon under the control of the learner, rather than as a permanent feature of memory, indicating that the use of a particular control process is situationally determined. The learner, by using both internal and external inputs, is capable of activating a particular control process so that selected items in the task environment receive more attention and rehearsal time than other items. This process would facilitate both the placement of these rehearsed items in memory and their retrieval at a later time.

However, this is a somewhat restricted view of control within an infor-

TABLE 9.1
The Conceptual Relationship of Mechanisms, Potential Cognitive Processes, and Functions in Complex Motor Behaviors

Mechanisms	Cognitive processes	Functions and purposes
1. Sensory storage[a]	Receive	Briefly hold information
	Transmit	Forward it to long-term storage for memory contact or directly to perceptual mechanism
2. Perceptual mechanism	Detect	Realize existence of signal
	Alert	Anticipate
	Selectively attend	Filter
	Recognize	Analyze features
		Match (present cues with stored information)
		Make meaning of information
	Transmit	Forward information to short-term storage for action
3. Short-term storage	Rehearse and process information temporarily	Retain information for immediate use and decision making
	Compare	Retrieve information from long-term storage for analysis, decision making, and attributions following feedback
	Transform	Organize (chunk)
		Make more functional space available
		Provide additional meaning
	Appraise situation	Form performance and goal expectancies
		Establish emotional state
	Select programs from long-term storage	Transmit programs to movement generator
	Plan program execution	Determine parameters (location, speed, direction, timing, amplitude, force, effort) in which program is to operate
	Transmit information	Transfer information to long-term storage to establish learning

224

TABLE 9.1 (Cont.)

Mechanisms	Cognitive processes	Functions and purposes
4. Long-term storage	Store information permanently	Make information available for future use, establish pertinence, aid in anticipation, expectancies, and perception
5. Movement generator	Initiate program for motor behavior	Cue appropriate musculature to execute within response parameters
	Initiate corollary discharge	Alert sensory center of the brain, anticipate movement
6. Effectors	Receive command	Execute observable performance
	Activate feedback sources	Provide information for future usage (comparison, recognition) by making it available for long-term storage
		Provide information to peripheral organs to help regulate ongoing behavior, to adapt behavior to situational demands
		Provide information to influence arousal and attitudinal states

[a]Cognitive processes do not directly influence sensory storage but can affect orientation to stimuli.

mation processing system. Our viewpoint is that the control of motor behavior must be investigated beyond mere information representation. The cognitive control of such affective factors as arousal for stress adaptation, as well as the cognitive motivational factors of expectancies for the achievement of success related to causal reasons (attributions) for performance outcomes, must be placed into perspective with other cognitive processes that interact to direct and to regulate behavior. Thus, cognitions, or control processes, are involved in the learning and performing of skills in various ways (e.g., for motivation, stress adaptation, concentration, relaxation, and performance expectancies, as well as information processing).

Table 9.2 simplifies much of the material contained in Table 9.1. Here we can view a number of conscious activities that may operate somewhat sequentially in the learning of many psychomotor activities. As learners improve in their functional abilities with regard to these activities, we may assume that their skill level will improve as well.

TABLE 9.2

Explanations of Potential[a] Cognitive Activities and Functions in the Performance of Complex Motor Behaviors

Cognitive activities	Function
1. Convert instructional information	Transform sensory information for movement representation
2. Analyze relationships	Recognize similarities between present and past tasks, situations, and experiences (transfer)
3. Retrieve information	Facilitate recall and recognition, and interpretations and decisions
4. Understand task goals	Form goal image of intended performance
5. Select cues	Identify most relevant and minimal cues at any given time
6. Establish personal goals and expectations	Form performance expectancies
7. Concentrate	Focus attention, broad or narrow, depending on task demands
8. Maintain optimal arousal (motivational) state	Demonstrate conscious control over emotions where necessary
9. Analyze nature of task	Use fixed or adaptive behaviors as required
10. Mentally rehearse prior to and/or after performance	Strengthen images and potential motor responses
11. Adapt to stress	Use control over emotions and environment where appropriate
12. Analyze outcomes of decisions	Consider costs and payoffs
13. Make correct response decisions	Consider amplitude, speed, location, distance, and accuracy
14. Conserve energy	Minimize effort to deter possible fatigue to maximize performance
15. Evaluate ongoing performance (feedback) when appropriate and possible	Monitor, regulate, and adjust performance
16. Evaluate the results of performance (feedback)	Use in future decisions in similar activities
17. Attribute performance outcomes objectively	Influence motivation, expectations, and performance in subsequent similar activities

[a] Any of these cognitive processes may be activated, depending on the skill level of the person, the nature of the activity, and personal intentions.

226

The deliberate use of certain conscious control processes, or the capability of activating certain desirable subconscious control processes, will improve the functional capabilities of one or several of the hypothesized mechanisms in the human behaving system (cf. Belmont & Butterfield, 1977; Butterfield & Dickerson, 1976), such as increasing the capacity of the short-term store by imposing an organizational structure to information being processed in that mechanism (Rigney, 1978). We are hypothesizing that a definite relationship exists between a particular mechanism and associated cognitive processes. Although a one-to-one relationship between a mechanism and a cognitive process may exist, it should be realized that several cognitive processes may also be associated with a given mechanism.

This relationship may be explained best by returning to the previous example of the performance difference between beginning and highly skilled learners. Both these performers use many of the same cognitive processes, perhaps at different levels of operation, to perform a skilled action, although the motor actions of the advanced performer appear to occur more quickly, smoothly, and efficiently. It is as if performance becomes automatic with the development of skill—that is, when information passes through a particular mechanism, the control processes necessary to work on that information are invoked without much conscious effort. Also, the skilled performer processes less information, taking into consideration perceptual, decisional, and effector redundancies. **The appearance of automaticity is thus due to the application of appropriate control processes, operating optimally at the different information processing stages, along with the physical capabilities of the performer and the well-learned mechanics of the movement.** It seems, then, that the skilled performer must employ the appropriate cognitions associated with a specific cognitive stage, as well as possess the requisite physical qualities necessary, to yield superior performance. In contrast, the erratic and inconsistent performance of a beginner is due either to a lack of desirable physical condition and movement technique, to a lack of cognitive processing capabilities (Chi, 1976), or to some combination. However, given performers with equivalent movement skills, superior performance will probably be evidenced by the person more capable of demonstrating appropriate control processes relative to changing task requirements (Battig, 1975).

Evidence for the mechanism–cognitive control process relationship would be provided by showing that the effective use of a particular control process for a given task reduces the amount of information that must be transmitted through that mechanism (cf. Butterfield & Dickerson, 1976). Because of the existence of this relationship between cognitions and stages of processing (Trabasso, 1973), the learner is capable of developing a hierarchy of processing skills corresponding to each mechanism (Schaeffer, 1975). The hierarchy is based on the complexity of the cognition or processing operations the learner must employ to transform and to transmit information through the system. Thus, as information passes through each stage (cf. Sternberg, 1969), the corresponding control processes must be adapted by the learner to meet the changing task requirements so that information may continue to be transmitted through the system.

To integrate some ideas expressed so far, the learner–performer may invoke cognitive processes to perceive the nature of the task in the context of the environment, to recognize similarities between the present task and previous experiences, and to attend selectively to and identify the most relevant yet minimal number of cues necessary for a response to occur. Cognitions may be used to store permanently evaluative feedback and causal reasons of a performance outcome for future use. In conclusion, processes run sequentially and probably concurrently within the human system (especially when the second process can operate at a subconscious level), producing a profound effect on the learning and performing of complex psychomotor tasks.

The identification of various control processes and their importance leads to a discussion of learner strategies, for control processes do not operate directly on the information within the system. Rather, cognitive processes are facilitated by the learner's activation and implementation of the appropriate strategies (cf. Kausler, 1974). Several strategies may be available to the trainee, and the most productive one associated with a particular control process should be adopted. Strategies and cognitive processes are very much related in the acquisition of achievement in motor skills.

LEARNING STRATEGIES IN THE
ACQUISITION OF SKILL

An effective strategy has been described as the simplest and most efficient means of processing the information inherent in a situation (Newell & Simon, 1972). Rigney (1978) has stated that a strategy may be interpreted as signifying operations and procedures that a learner may use to acquire, to retain, and to retrieve different kinds of knowledge. Similarly, Bruner, Goodnow, and Austin (1956) have defined a strategy as a pattern of decisions in the acquisition, retention, and utilization of information that serves to meet certain objectives—that is, to ensure certain forms of outcomes and to ensure against certain others. To Gagné (1974), a strategy is a skill of self-management that the learner acquires to govern the processes of attending, learning, and thinking, and Gagné and Briggs (1974) have suggested that a cognitive strategy is an internally organized skill that governs the learner's own behavior (cf. Richardson, 1978).

More pragmatically, Dansereau (1978) proposed a definition in which a strategy was considered to be a learner-based technique that, when acquired, would enable the individual to function effectively when confronted with the (*a*) identification of important, unfamiliar, and difficult material; (*b*) application of techniques for comprehension and retention of circumstances; (*c*) efficient retrieval of information under appropriate circumstances; and (*d*) effective coping with internal and external distractions while these other processes are being employed.

A conclusion based on an interpretation of the preceding definitions would be that a strategy developed by a learner in accordance with cognitive abilities and situational demands would be most effective in relating new information to previously obtained experiences (Bruner, 1961).

From an information-processing point of view, the nature of a strategy is such that it enables a learner to form an organizational structure in which information can be stored and retrieved more efficiently (Bousfield, 1953; Bower, 1970; Mandler, 1967; Miller, 1956; Tulving, 1962). The composition of the order imposed by the learner depends on the inherent structure of the information and the cognitive capabilities of the learner (Gentile & Nacson, 1976). The fact that this organization is a result of the strategies employed by the learner to construct groupings, or relations, among the informational inputs to be learned leads to the inference that memory is a constructive and interactive process (compare the work of Bower, 1970; Mandler, 1967; Tulving, 1968). This process involves the learner's actively searching for contextual relationships between the input and information stored in the system in order that incoming material can be transformed and recoded into newer and larger internal units (Gentile & Nacson, 1976).

Whereas organizational processes have been frequently investigated in studies of verbal memory by examining the input–output relationship of to-be-remembered material (Bousfield, 1953; Bower, 1970; Mandler, 1967; Tulving, 1962, 1968), the concept of organization has been virtually ignored by motor learning researchers. However, interest in the organizational variables that may affect motor skill acquisition has increased. This is evidenced by the concern for central or peripheral mechanisms of motor control (Keele, 1968; Kelso & Stelmach, 1976; Schmidt, 1975), the processing characteristics of spatial information (Jones, 1972, 1974; Kelso, 1977; Laabs, 1973; Marteniuk, 1973; Stelmach, Kelso, & McCullagh, 1976; Stelmach, Kelso, & Wallace, 1975), and the general encoding properties of movement information (Gentile, 1967; Nacson, 1974; Nacson, Jaeger, & Gentile, 1973).

Without providing a detailed description of these studies, it will suffice to say that the general conclusion has been that **a learner imposes some type of structure on movement information** so that it is learned and retrieved more efficiently. Performance is dependent either upon the experimental structuring of the task in which the totality of the relations among the movement cues is emphasized (Gentile & Nacson, 1976), or on the subjective organization of the information, in which a structural context corresponding to the learner's cognitive capabilities is imposed on the movement cues. Thus, the development of the organizational strategies occurs in one of two ways.

The behavioral processes that a learner uses to select and to govern attentiveness in a learning situation, the management of information storage and retrieval skills, and the construction of a problem solution (Gagné & Briggs, 1974) are directed by the implementation of associated strategies. These strategies may be external, instructor-imposed strategies or internal self-generated strategies. These types of instructional strategies have been found to facilitate both verbal learning (Gagné, 1977) and motor learning (Roy & Diewert, 1975). An instructional strategy that is imposed by the instructor on the learner may be designed to help the learner to acquire a skill as quickly as possible or to facilitate transfer effectiveness or problem solving in the future. Though some imposed strategies may increase the rate of initial skill acquisition (Singer & Pease, 1976), they may not facilitate learning in transfer situations in which no instructor is present (Singer & Gaines, 1975). In the latter case, this can only be achieved when a learner becomes capable of self-generating learning strategies, whether they have been initially externally directed or self-generated.

A self-initiated strategy is one in which the learner is capable of determining a procedure that is compatible with personal cognitive capabilities and cognitive style for the learning of a task or a category of related tasks. Strategy choice is partially determined by the particular situation (Bruner *et al.,* 1956), so a sound educational practice would appear to be to instruct learners initially in the use of learning strategies. Once a learner comprehends the nature of and the reasons for the use of particular strategies for the acquisition of skill, he or she should be capable of self-generating strategies in related future learning environments.

This is the ultimate outcome, as we see it, of any meaningful instructional or training program, to instill in learners the ability to develop their own effective cognitive strategies without external guidance. Following an instructional program, a learner should be able to generate the strategies that were taught by the instructor, even if the instructor is no longer present, when these strategies are necessary to perform certain tasks. Learners should acquire the ability to generate strategies that are congruent with their cognitive capabilities for learning a task, or capabilities should be structured in a desirable direction.

The learning experience is governed by the use of strategies, which in

1. A situation activates potential alternative *strategies*
2. A particular *strategy* influences a corresponding *cognitive process*
3. A particular *cognitive process* is associated with a corresponding *mechanism*
4. situation → strategy → process → mechanism

Figure 9.2 The relationship among strategies, cognitive processes, and mechanisms.

turn activate conscious and subconscious processes. The hypothesized relationships would be that situations activate particular strategies, which influence cognitive processes associated with particular mechanisms (see Figure 9.2).

A particular example of these relationships is found in Figure 9.3. Here the task situation of having to hit a baseball activates a narrow focus of attention strategy on the part of the skilled performer to facilitate the need to concentrate. Concentration (to the right cue) improves the cognitive process of selective attention. According to our models, selective attention is associated with the perceptual mechanism.

Strategies, either self-generated or externally imposed, may be used by a learner in such ways as to attend to the learning environment, to manage information storage and retrieval, and to determine the requirements of a selected motor response. It may be concluded that strategies are selected and formulated to enhance the operation of a particular control process, and they are determined, in part, as a function of task requirements, problem content, and situational constraints. However, it is often quite difficult actually to observe the strategy a learner is actually using.

Bruner *et al.* (1956) contended that a strategy does not refer to a conscious plan for the acquisition and the utilization of information, since neither a strategy nor a plan can be observed. Rather, a strategy is to be inferred from the pattern of decisions one observes in a problem solver. Thus, the decisions a learner makes in regard to the selection of solutions for a problem can be interpreted as overt demonstrations of strategy usage.

The learning of a motor skill or a verbal skill involves a problem that must be solved. The behaviors involved in acquiring both types of skills are very similar (Adams, 1971) in that the learner must identify and interpret the problem, utilize strategies to facilitate the processing of information so

Hit a baseball
↓
Narrow focus (concentration)
↓
Selective attention
↓
Perceptual mechanism

Figure 9.3 Example relationship.

a plan may be devised that will lead to possible solutions, produce those solutions, and then **decide** which is the best solution (Posner, 1973).

Baldwin and Garvey (1973) have identified similar components of the problem-solving process. A learner must define the general problem, relate the problem to previously experienced situations, identify the essential and relevant information in the problem, synthesize and formulate solutions, and decide on an appropriate solution through a verification procedure. It is apparent that these are the general cognitive behaviors a learner must progress through to solve a problem—that is, to learn a skill—in order to produce a motor response.

It is important to identify the relationship between strategies and particular stages of processing (Trabasso, 1973). The relationship among mechanisms, cognitions, and strategies can be more elaborately depicted in a representation of the mental operations that are hypothesized to occur within any mechanism of the model. For example, corresponding to the perceptual mechanism, several strategies may become operational by a person to filter relevant stimuli from the incoming information. The learner may form strategies for anticipation, detection, and comparison of relevant stimuli to aid in the selective attention processes. By invoking strategies for recognition, feature matching, identification, coding, and classification, the learner is able to provide meaning to the input as a result of an elaboration of the information within the perceptual mechanism (Craik & Lockhart, 1972; Craik & Tulving, 1975). The learner uses the meaningful information to form clearer goal expectancies and more realistic performance expectancies.

Additional strategies may be available to be utilized by the learner so that information in short-term storage may be more elaborately analyzed (Craik & Tulving, 1975). Other strategies are also associated with the various control processes, and a learner may be capable of producing any of these strategies, although some learners are more capable than others of producing some strategies (Battig, 1975). When an individual chooses to move and makes the appropriate decisions based on previous or recently acquired knowledge of how to perform a movement, that movement will occur because sufficient information was available in memory to formulate response requirements. If permanent storage of the information is desired, it should be transmitted to the long-term store and stored in such a manner as to promote convenient retrieval.

Strategies may be developed by the trainee to facilitate the hypothesized functions of the short-term storage system on information prior to its generation to long-term storage. Organizational processes and rehearsal strategies may be applied by the learner to store selected information more permanently and effectively. See Figure 9.4 for the strategy–process–

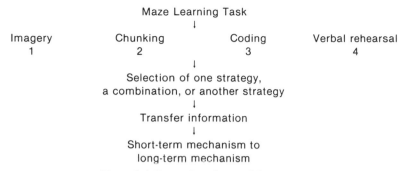

Figure 9.4 One task and potential strategies.

mechanism paradigm, showing the availability of alternative strategies from which to select. Other strategies are associated with the recall and recognition of information that results in the selection of a particular movement. Following that movement, strategies for adaptation and behavior regulation may be produced to aid in the processing of feedback to update response requirements of future movements.

In general, strategies are produced by an individual in conjunction with the information processing system to facilitate (*a*) storage and retrieval of information; (*b*) a comparison of incoming information with referents previously stored; (*c*) transformation of information; and (*d*) decision making as to the movement that will result in achieving the desired goal. The learner's appropriate use of strategies in these cases and many others is a significant determinant of motor learning and performance.

The manner in which a trainee develops and utilizes cognitions and strategies becomes evident in the acquisition rate and performance level of motor skills. An incorrect cognition, such as selecting the wrong motor program, or an inefficient strategy is sufficient to retard the learning process and lower the performance quality. Training procedures must be designed so that appropriate learning strategies can be identified, methods for enhancing the self-production of these strategies within a learner can be taught, and the content of these strategies may be made applicable to a wide range of motor behaviors. The conceptual orientation to motor learning discussed here so far is the logical first step in identifying several prerequisites related to skilled performance.

Following the identification of the physical capabilities a learner must possess and the control processes and the strategies a learner may employ to acquire a motor skill, it becomes necessary to determine those strategies that should be matched with particular categories of tasks. That is, what type of organizational structure does the learner impose on the task information through the use of cognitive strategies, and how is the learner able to use this structure to facilitate the storage and retrieval of information for different tasks? Tasks differ in the demands they place on a learner. As such, the differing task requirements must be determined in order for the learner to structure the movement information inherent in these skills. Then, strategies that would enhance the skill acquisition process could be accurately determined in accordance with the components of each activity or categories of activities. Ideally, a functional taxonomic classification scheme of both skills and associated learning strategies would be identified, and this information could be useful in constructing more effective training programs.

CATEGORIES OF TASKS

We are developing a psychomotor task classification system concurrently with our refinement of the motor behavior systems model and the clearer identification of control processes and strategies and the interactive relationships. Categories of motor tasks are being identified on the basis of commonalities with regard to situational demands and accommodating responses. The need for a classification system is paramount because there is no adequate present scheme of categories of psychomotor skills. Furthermore, the results of experimental investigations in motor learning often lack ecological validity (situational generalizability) because there is no unified conceptual framework within which researchers can work.

The problem is even more evident when one considers that the use of narrowly defined motor tasks, such as linear positioning or reaction time, has given rise to specialized domains of theory development (e.g., Gentile, Higgins, Miller, & Rosen, 1975; Schmidt, 1972). The minimal demands placed on the learner by these tasks do not allow researchers to identify the possible relationships among various motor tasks. For these reasons, the commonalities among psychomotor tasks must be determined, so that the findings derived from laboratory analyses of skill acquisition can be applied to practical situations in which the teaching and learning of motor skills is involved (Gentile *et al.,* 1975).

Several existing examples of classification schemes are those in which tasks have been categorized as open-loop or closed-loop (Adams, 1971; Keele, 1968; Kriefeldt, 1972; Schmidt, 1975), self-paced, externally paced, or mixed-paced (Kriefeldt, 1972; Singer, 1972, 1975), discrete or continuous (Kriefeldt, 1972; Schmidt, 1975), or open or closed (Gentile, 1972; Poulton, 1957). Each task type contains unique considerations that distinguish it from the other categories. Therefore, a description of each category along with an example of an associated motor task will be presented.

When a person performs a task in an *open-loop* manner, information about that performance comes at its termination. The movement, or a sequence of related movements, is programmed to occur too rapidly for the performer to utilize response-produced feedback during the movement itself, and consequently, any corrections must be made after the movement has been completed. The movement is preprogrammed to run off for a specific period of time (Keele, 1973; Schmidt, 1975) before feedback can be used to modify the program, if necessary. Then, another sequence of movements is programmed to occur. An example is the playing of a piano composition that requires rapid finger movements. The performer is not capable of using any feedback information until a sequence of movements (series of notes) has been completed.

In contrast to this type of task is the one in which the performer can utilize response-produced feedback during the movement itself to make error corrections, if necessary. When performing the *closed-loop* task, which occurs at a slower rate or over a longer period of time than an open-loop task, the person makes intermittent adjustments in the performance as a result of monitoring the match between referents and input cues (e.g., Adams, 1971). This requires the use of the peripheral nervous system by the performer (utilizing feedback from the sense receptors), whereas the performance of an open-loop task is under the control of the central nervous system (the storage of plans, programs, or schemata in the brain).[3] An example of tasks in the closed-loop category and a strategy pertinent to the execution of them is depicted in Figure 9.5.

The tasks in both of these categories may be performed under a variety of environmental conditions. When a learner initiates a movement at a subjectively determined time in a fixed or static environment, the task is described as *self-paced*. Self-paced tasks, or *closed* skills, are those in

Category: closed-loop tasks

Examples: archery pull
driving a car
basketball shooting
running
↓
Strategy: self-cueing to appropriate proprioceptive information
↓
Cognitive process: improve feedback monitoring
↓
Mechanism: effectors

Figure 9.5 A number of tasks and one strategy.

[3] We acknowledge that the coactivation of alpha and gamma motoneurons is necessary for the control of voluntary movements. However, our concern is with the behavioral, rather than the neurophysiological, aspects of movement control. The interested reader is referred to Smith (1976) for a review of the neurophysiological mechanisms of motor control.

which there is less concern for rapid perceptual adjustments and more concern for the acquisition of the appropriate sequence of responses. The individual has time to preview the situation, to respond when ready, and to progress at a chosen rate of speed because the environmental cues remain stable (e.g., hitting a golf ball). There are also cases when the optimal speed for performance is determined by the biomechanics of the situation, and the learner cannot actually perform at a preselected rate of speed. Thus, by being alerted to the conditions of the action prior to its occurrence, a learner can perform a predictable response while achieving a degree of response consistency in a stable environment.

When the environment is changing, as when unexpected situational demands arise, the performer is required to respond instantaneously. Tasks in which anticipation time and decision time for adapting responses to circumstances are very brief are categorized as *externally paced* tasks, or open skills (e.g., tennis). Because of situational uncertainties and the speed with which adjustments must be made, many alternative practice possibilities exist for the learning of these tasks. The emphasis in these practices must be on familiarizing the learner with a wide array of situations and cues, with response adaptability being the primary concern because of the unpredictable, and changing, environmental demands.

Response adaptability is also a concern when learning a *mixed-pace* task. This type of activity is one in which the situation is partially dynamic (e.g., hitting a baseball): (*a*) The learner is in motion but the object or situation is fixed (still); or (*b*) the learner is fixed and the object is in motion. Performing this task involves more uncertainties in the situation than performing the self-paced task; therefore, practice considerations should be similar to those designed for externally paced tasks. One could infer that these practice situations would involve more space needs, more gross bodily movement and involvement, and more instructional difficulties with large groups of learners than would practice sessions for self-paced tasks. The learner should experience a variety of ways that either the body or the object may be in motion, to be prepared better for future possible situations.

Any skill, regardless of the environment (dynamic or static) or the manner (open-loop or closed-loop) in which it is to be performed, can be classified further based on the time it takes to complete that task. Thus, tasks may be considered as *discrete* or *continuous*. A discrete task is one that has a predetermined beginning and end and is usually quite short in performance time (e.g., less than 5 seconds in duration) (Schmidt, 1975). An example of this type of task is a ballistic response, which usually has a movement time of less than 200 msec. Once initiated, the movement cannot be changed during this duration of time. A practical example of a ballistic activity is striking a ball with a bat or throwing a punch. Another example of a discrete task is a slow linear positioning response, which usually lasts more than 200 msec. In contrast, a continuous task has no recognizable breaks during performance, and there is usually some length of time that passes between the beginning and the end of the performance of the task. An example of a continuous task is any type of tracking skill, such as a pursuit rotor. When performing this task, a person is required to track a circular disc on a moving turntable for a certain period of time, usually about 30 seconds. Since there is no "break" during the 30-second performance, the task is usually considered to be continuous.

The development of a taxonomy of psychomotor tasks, similar to but more detailed than those presented earlier, would be based on the relationships and distinctions among motor skills. The determination of the commonalities in regard to situational demands and appropriate behaviors, and the subsequent categorization of skills according to these commonalities would lead to the identification of strategies for learning these classes of motor skills. The function of a strategy is to reduce the amount of information necessary to learn a task, so the rate of skill acquisition should increase if the strategy can be generalized across a range of tasks. Therefore, strategies may be categorized according to their facility in aiding the learning of a class of skills.

CATEGORIES OF STRATEGIES

The classification of strategies occurs first by grouping various strategies according to the way they can be applied to tasks with similar characteristics. In this way, a determination can be made as to how the learning of one skill can be facilitated by the use of several different strategies. A learning situation in which alternative solutions can all lead to the achievement of the final goal is quite desirable. Various solutions to a problem will not overload the learner's processing system because attention will not be directed to all the possible solutions at once. Rather, the provision of alternative solutions will allow the learner to choose a goal path that is in conjunction with personal capabilities. This will prevent an instructor from fostering a "correct" solution on a learner who is cognitively incapable of utilizing that particular information, whereas the use of other information may achieve the desired result.

The provision of alternative strategies for problem solving in an instructional sequence, generated first by the instructor and then by the learner who has achieved the necessary level of competence (Gagné, 1977), is a desirable feature of any instructional program. Of even greater service to a learner, however, would be identification of strategies that have been operationalized for the learning of several tasks. The generalizability of a strategy to the acquisition of a class of skills should facilitate the learning of those skills. This is due to the fact that, with increased skill level, information becomes more redundant (Marteniuk, 1976). Therefore, performance increases because less information about the task demands requires processing. Furthermore, additional processing capacity becomes available, so the learner may attend to information inherent in other tasks. Thus, not only is the rate of skill learning increased when strategies are generalizable, but the number of tasks that can be learned, as well as the rate of learning those tasks, increases.

This, then, should be the goal of any instructional designer: to identify strategies that, when learned, can be generalized to a variety of tasks. The relationship between strategies and tasks can be determined only by classifying tasks according to their situational and behavioral requirements and then determining which strategies will aid a learner in meeting those requirements. Categorizing tasks would facilitate identifying appropriate learning strategies. Therefore, the strategy taxonomy must be developed in conjunction with the task classification scheme. This strategy taxonomy is currently being formulated, but we have not completed a sufficient analysis to present a summary table, as was done with other material in previous sections of this chapter.

Our plan is to group motor skills according to their task demands in common. Then, the strategies that have been associated with particular tasks might be categorized according to their apparent facilitating qualities for the learning of a class of motor skills. Following this, a training program could be developed in which learners are taught strategies applicable to a variety of tasks, as well as the means with which they can acquire the competencies necessary to self-generate these strategies in future learning situations. Because the rate of learning will increase, the duration of the instructional program will decrease, thus placing more responsibility in the hands of the learner much sooner than expected.

By assuming responsibility for the outcomes of instruction, the learner engages in self-instruction. With the experience that is gained from continuing to pursue learning activities, the learner begins to acquire the characteristics of a "self-learner." That is, the learner is capable of managing the learning environment by employing personal skills and strategies to the task at hand (Gagné & Briggs, 1974). A training program that results in the learner's managing the learning environment is one in which the ultimate goal of instruction has been achieved: the development of the capabilities in a learner to make applications of previous experiences to apparently new situations in order to meet the demands of those situations without the need of an instructor to intervene.

FUTURE DIRECTIONS

The conceptual model of the human behaving system presented earlier will be continually refined as new research is reviewed. Literature in which investigations of motor memory, motor control, and verbal memory systems are analyzed will be of special interest in this regard. The mechanisms and processes we have currently identified will probably be elaborated upon as researchers become better able to describe the internal mechanisms of the brain and how they function. Profound changes in the model, however, are not foreseen. Rather, the revisions will be such that the behavioral processes that are hypothesized to occur will be clarified, and the mechanisms in association with these processes will be delineated more elaborately.

The conceptual model is the framework in which we are trying to identify learning strategies that are associated with particular cognitive processes and mechanisms in the system. At present several strategies have been identified, as well as their relationship with one or several of the mechanisms. As our work progresses, we will make a clearer identification of the learning strategies a person uses to acquire skill. They will, no doubt, reveal commonalities with verbal learning strategies, as well as unique considerations for motor learning.

The objective is to describe a minimal number of strategies unique to the learning of different categories of psychomotor skills. Presumably, when the learner deploys the best strategies, the functional capabilities of a given mechanism are enhanced, thereby increasing the rate of skill acquisition. However, the identification of strategies related to classes of psychomotor skills can occur only when the analysis of strategies and tasks is refined.

The present work is representative of our first attempt at categorization. With the further analysis of strategies and psychomotor tasks, both these classification schemes will be revised. We believe that the relationships identified within these taxonomies can be solidified by a more precise determination of the situational and behavioral requirements of motor tasks and a clearer understanding of the function of strategies a learner can use to acquire skill. These specific relationships will then be tested under laboratory experimental conditions.

Experiments

Based on the relationships between strategies and tasks identified within the classification schemes, a series of laboratory experiments will be designed. These investigations will be primarily computer-controlled, with the intent of determining which of alternative available strategies would be best suited to helping a student learn a particular class of motor skills.

For example, a student would be provided with alternative strategies for learning a ballistic, open-looped, self-paced response. An analysis of performance would help to determine which strategy resulted in the fastest rate of acquisition. Then, this strategy would be used in the learning of another task that would be in the same response class (e.g., Schmidt, 1975). If the strategy is appropriate, it should generalize effectively to the learning of the new skill, as well as to other skills in the same task category.

Another example of a psychomotor task in which the student is required to employ cognitive strategies involves serial learning. To acquire skill, a person must make a series of responses in appropriate sequential order. Various instructional techniques, such as prompting or problem solving, may be used to guide the acquisition of a serial skill. Several methods for the investigation of the acquisition of serial responses have been incorporated into a designated task and employed in our laboratory using a device called the Serial Manipulation Apparatus (SMA) (Singer & Gaines, 1975; Singer & Pease, 1976).

The SMA has been described in detail elsewhere (Singer, 1976). Briefly, it is a computer-controlled task in which the student must respond to auditory or visual stimuli by manipulating corresponding buttons, knobs, or switches. Additionally, the device may be programmed so that foot pedal responses are required, either separately or in conjunction with the hand manipulations. Students' responses can be measured as time to complete the sequence correctly or number of errors committed. It is believed that this particular task can be designed to simulate motor skill acquisition in real-world situations. Furthermore, the computer helps to provide desirable controls.

The programming capabilities that accompany a task of this type allow for many variations. The presentation rate of the sequence can be increased or decreased, the number of responses in the sequence can be changed from trial to trial, and the sequence itself can be randomly presented on each trial. The potential that these variations provide for examining psychomotor skill acquisition is enormous. Furthermore, as other variations are designed, more sophisticated experiments can be arranged in which the relationships between learner strategies, task type, and skill acquisition are investigated. The findings in these experiments will suggest instructional procedures, ultimately leading to self-management, or learner-initiated, strategies to undertake and to achieve in various situations.

Module Development

Learner strategy modules will be developed based on the results of the experimental investigations. Strategies will have been identified as applicable to a number of learning situations. Therefore, the generalizability of a strategy will be the primary determinant of its inclusion in a module. A module will contain a discussion of a series of strategies (e.g., selective attention, anticipation, rapid retrieval from memory) that will be appropriate for a given category of tasks. Consequently, it is intended that any module will hold implications for present-task mastery as well as accomplishments in other related tasks potentially confronted by the learner in the future. These modules will then have to be field-tested to confirm the results of the laboratory investigations and the effectiveness of the modules.

If the experimental tasks truly simulate real-world situations, the field research results should confirm the laboratory findings. The effectiveness of the modules will be observed following the development of specific evaluative procedures. Two levels of evaluation of each module are desirable. One is more immediate, the other more long-term. In answer to the question, "Are the modules teaching the learners the strategies they are supposed to?," evaluations will be made during the instructional program. To answer the question, "Are the learners better able to acquire psychomotor skills as a result of these experiences?," analyses must be made in a particular setting. Wherever possible, and if time permits, this long-term evaluation of field performance will occur. On the basis of feedback received from field data, the modules will be revised where necessary and made more functional.

The time required to complete a learner strategy module will vary, depending on the content material. The primary goal is to aid learners in achieving a high level of skill in a minimal amount of time, at a minimal expense, with minimal instructor–learner interactions (self-learning), and with materials that create an enjoyable and motivating atmosphere. The final objective is to leave the learners with the capabilities to employ these generalizable strategies in new, but related, learning situations.

Individual Differences

Although not directly addressed in this chapter, a major factor to be explored in the identification of learner strategies and the development of associated modules is individual differences in cognitive or learning style. Cognitive style is the manner in which an individual perceives the world and processes perceived information according to personal capabilities. The general topical area has been investigated in an aptitude-treatment interaction methodology (Cronbach & Snow, 1977).

The potential interaction between instructional methods and learner capabilities should receive primary emphasis in the design of any instructional system. If the method for providing the strategies associated with learning a task is not compatible with the learner's capabilities and personal learning style, the acquisition of skill will probably be impeded. Since the desire of an instructional systems designer is to develop the most efficient way for persons to learn skills, individual differences among learners must be taken into account when establishing an instructional program.

For these reasons, we will give careful consideration to differences in cognitive capabilities and learning styles among the learners with whom we will be working. Our major thrust into this area will occur during the experimental sessions and the subsequent development of modules. Although we will identify strategies that are generalizable across a range of tasks and trainees, it would be desirable to identify strategies that are unique to types of people—that is, strategies that can be used by learners to enhance skill acquisition even though their cognitive capabilities differ.

SUMMARY

We conducted an extensive review of the verbal and motor learning literature. The result was the development of a conceptual model of behavior with considerations unique to motor skills. We felt that the initial stage of our work required the identification of a sophisticated and comprehensive theoretical framework of motor behavior, from which the strategy-testing portion of our work would follow logically.

The primary reason for the development of a model of motor behavior was to facilitate the identification of learner strategies, as well as mechanisms and cognitive processes associated with these strategies. Particular strategies have been found to enhance certain cognitive processes that are necessary to acquire categories of motor skills. Therefore, a secondary result of our review of the literature was to develop and to organize preliminary task and strategy classification schemes. Tasks are categorized according to the environmental, information processing, and mechanical demands they place on the learner, whereas strategies are categorized according to the task or group of tasks that are learned more effectively when that strategy is employed. We have identified relationships between mechanisms (real or hypothesized), control processes and learner strategies, and tasks. Experiments are being designed to determine the existence of these hypothetical relationships. Extrapolations from the results of these studies can be useful in training programs. Learner strategies and their applications will be identified that can enhance the acquisition of strategies to learn training skills as well as anticipated on-the-job skills. A tangential result will be the identification of optimal instructional techniques related to categories of skills.

Our present efforts are somewhat preliminary and are geared to the design and administration of laboratory experiments to (a) identify the optimal learner strategies for the acquisition and retention of classes of motor skills; (b) develop methods to teach learners the importance of strategy usage, how to acquire strategies, and then how to invoke a particular strategy when it is appropriate; (c) determine the relationships between strategies and classes of motor skills so that the acquisition, retention, and transfer of these strategies and skills will be enhanced; (d) organize and field-test learner modules for skill acquisition; and (e) refine the current theoretical framework through our experiments and constant monitoring of current literature.

The primary intent of our efforts is **not** to improve the acquisition of specific motor skills. Rather, we are seeking to develop methods that will enable learners to **self-generate problem-solving strategies** and techniques in order that skills may be obtained more rapidly. The development of analytical and adaptation processes within a learner will lead to the creation of self-instructional environments. If the learner possesses the strategies and skills to produce a solution to a problem, then the amount of external guidance necessary for learning is reduced. Additionally, the acquired skill is probably retained to a greater degree, since the learner has been more involved in the learning experience.

We hope continually to bridge the motor and verbal learning areas, since there are many human mechanisms and processes that operate similarly for all behaviors. Thus, although we will be analyzing ways of improving performance in motor behaviors, many findings should be applicable to verbal behaviors. We have begun research into an area that contains many opportunities.

REFERENCES

Adams, J. A. A closed-loop theory of motor learning. *Journal of Motor Behavior,* 1971, *3,* 111–150.

Atkinson, R. C., & Shiffrin, R. M. Human memory: A proposed system and its control processes. In K. W. Spence & J. T. Spence (Eds.), *The psychology of learning and motivation* (Vol. 2). New York: Academic Press, 1968.

Baldwin, T. L., & Garvey, C. J. Components of accurate problem-solving communications. *American Educational Research Journal,* 1973, *10,* 39–48.

Battig, W. F. Within-individual differences in "cognitive" processes. In R. L. Solso (Ed.), *Information processing and cognition: The Loyola symposium.* Hillsdale, N.J.: Erlbaum, 1975.

Belmont, J. M., & Butterfield, E. C. The instructional approach to developmental cognitive research. In R. Kail & J. Hagen (Eds.), *Perspectives on the development of memory and cognition.* Hillsdale, N.J.: Erlbaum, 1977.

Bousfield, W. A. The occurrence of clustering in the recall of randomly arranged associates. *Journal of General Psychology,* 1953, *49,* 229–240.

Bower, G. H. Organizational factors in memory. *Cognitive Psychology,* 1970, *1,* 18–46.

Bruner, J. S. The act of discovery. *Harvard Educational Review,* 1961, *31,* 21–32.

Bruner, J. S., Goodnow, J. J., & Austin, G. A. *A study of thinking.* New York: John Wiley, 1956.

Butterfield, E. C., & Dickerson, D. J. Cognitive theory and mental development. In N. R. Ellis (Ed.), *International review of research in mental retardation.* New York: Academic Press, 1976.

Chi, M. T. H. Short-term memory limitations in children: Capacity or processing deficits. *Memory and Cognition,* 1976, *4,* 559–572.

Craik, F. I. M., & Lockhart, R. S. Levels of processing: A framework for memory research. *Journal of Verbal Learning and Verbal Behavior,* 1972, *11,* 671–684.

Craik, F. I. M., & Tulving, E. Depth of processing and the retention of words in episodic memory. *Journal of Experimental Psychology: General,* 1975, *104,* 268–294.

Cronbach, L. J., & Snow, R. E. *Aptitudes and instructional methods.* New York: Irvington Publishers, 1977.

Dansereau, D. F. The development of a learning strategies curriculum. In H. F. O'Neil, Jr. (Ed.), *Learning strategies.* New York: Academic Press, 1978.

Estes, W. K. *Learning theory and mental development.* New York: Academic Press, 1970.

Estes, W. K. *Handbook of learning and cognitive processes.* Hillsdale, N.J.: Erlbaum, 1975.

Gagné, R. M. *Learning and individual differences.* Columbus, Ohio: Charles E. Merrill Books, 1967.

Gagné, R. M. Educational technology and the learning process. *Educational Researcher,* 1974, *3,* 3–8.

Gagné, R. M. *Conditions of learning.* New York: Holt, Rinehart and Winston, 1977.

Gagné, R. M., & Briggs, L. J. *Principles of instructional design.* New York: Holt, Rinehart and Winston, 1974.

Gentile, A. M. Short-term retention of simple motor acts. (Doctoral dissertation, Indiana University, 1967). *Dissertation Abstracts International,* 1967–1968, *28,* 2986–A. (University Microfilms No. 68-49650)

Gentile, A. M. A working model of skill acquisition with application to teaching. *Quest,* 1972, *17,* 3–23.

Gentile, A. M., Higgins, J. R., Miller, E. A., & Rosen, B. M. The structure of motor tasks. *Mouvement,* 1975, *7,* 11–28.

Gentile, A. M., & Nacson, J. Organizational processes in motor control. In J. Keogh & R. S. Hutton (Eds.), *Exercise and sport sciences reviews* (Vol. 4). Santa Barbara, Calif.: Journal Publishing Affiliates, 1976.

Glanzer, M., & Koppenaal, L. The effect of encoding tasks on free recall: Stages and levels. *Journal of Verbal Learning and Verbal Behavior,* 1977, *16,* 21–28.

Hunt, E., & Lansman, M. Individual differences. In W. K. Estes (Ed.), *Handbook of learning and cognitive processes.* Hillsdale, N.J.: Erlbaum, 1975.

Johnson, J. H. Memory and personality: An information processing approach. *Journal of Research in Personality,* 1974, *8,* 1–32.

Jones, B. Outflow and inflow in movement duplication. *Perception and Psychophysics,* 1972, *12,* 95–96.

Jones, B. Role of central monitoring of efference in short-term memory for movements. *Journal of Experimental Psychology,* 1974, *102,* 37–43.

Kausler, D. H. *Psychology of verbal learning and memory.* New York: Academic Press, 1974.

Keele, S. W. Movement control in skilled motor performance. *Psychological Bulletin,* 1968, *70,* 387–403.

Keele, S. W. *Attention and human performance*. Pacific Palisades, Calif.: Goodyear, 1973.

Keele, S. W., & Summers, J. J. The structure of motor programs. In G. E. Stelmach (Ed.), *Motor control: Issues and trends*. New York: Academic Press, 1976.

Kelso, J. A. S. Planning and efferent components in the coding of movement. *Journal of Motor Behavior*, 1977, *9*, 33–48.

Kelso, J. A. S., & Stelmach, G. E. Central and peripheral mechanisms in motor control. In G. E. Stelmach (Ed.), *Motor control: Issues and trends*. New York: Academic Press, 1976.

Klapp, S. T. Short-term memory as a response preparation state. *Memory and Cognition*, 1976, *4*, 721–729.

Klapp, S. T. Response programming, as assessed by reaction time, does not establish commands for particular muscles. *Journal of Motor Behavior*, 1977, *9*, 301–312.

Kriefeldt, I. G. A dynamic model of behavior in a discrete open-loop self-paced motor skill. *IEEE Transactions on Systems, Man, and Cybernetics*, 1972, *2*, 262–273.

Laabs, G. E. Retention characteristics of different reproduction cues in motor short-term memory. *Journal of Experimental Psychology*, 1973, *100*, 168–177.

Lindsay, P. H., & Norman, D. A. *Human information processing*. New York: Academic Press, 1977.

Mandler, G. Organization and memory. In J. T. Spence & K. W. Spence (Eds.), *The psychology of learning and motivation* (Vol. 1). New York: Academic Press, 1967.

Marteniuk, R. G. Retention characteristics of motor short-term memory cues. *Journal of Motor Behavior*, 1973, *5*, 312–317.

Marteniuk, R. G. Individual differences in motor performance and learning. In J. H. Wilmore (Ed.), *Exercise and sport sciences reviews* (Vol. 2). New York: Academic Press, 1974.

Marteniuk, R. G. *Information processing in motor skills*. New York: Holt, Rinehart and Winston, 1976.

Massaro, D. *Experimental psychology and information processing*. Chicago: Rand McNally, 1975.

Miller, G. A. The magical number seven plus or minus two: Some limits on our capacity for processing information. *Psychological Review*, 1956, *63*, 81–96.

Nacson, J. *Effects of order presentation on arm positioning accuracy*. Unpublished doctoral dissertation, Teachers College, Columbia University, 1974.

Nacson, J., Jaeger, M., & Gentile, A. M. Organizational processes in short-term memory. In I. D. Williams & L. M. Wankel (Eds.), *Proceedings of the Fourth Canadian Psychomotor Learning and Sports Psychology Conference*. Ottawa, Canada: Department of National Health and Welfare, 1973.

Neisser, U. *Cognitive psychology*. New York: Appleton-Century-Crofts, 1967.

Newell, A., & Simon, H. A. *Human problem solving*. Englewood Cliffs, N.J.: Prentice Hall, 1972.

Norman, D. A. Toward a theory of memory and attention. *Psychological Review*, 1968, *75*, 522–536.

Norman, D. A. Memory, knowledge, and the answering of questions. In R. L. Solso (Ed.), *Contemporary issues in cognitive psychology: The Loyola symposium*. Washington, D.C.: Winston, 1973.

Norman, D. A. *Memory and attention*. New York: Wiley, 1976.

Norman, D. A., & Rumelhart, D. E. *Explorations in cognition*. San Francisco: W. H. Freeman, 1975.

Posner, M. I. *Cognition: An introduction*. Glenview, Ill.: Scott, Foresman, 1973.

Poulton, E. C. On prediction in skilled movements. *Psychological Bulletin*, 1957, *54*, 467–478.

Reitman, W. What does it take to remember? In D. A. Norman (Ed.), *Models of human memory*. New York: Academic Press, 1969.

Richardson, F. Behavior modification and learning strategies. In H. F. O'Neil, Jr. (Ed.), *Learning strategies.* New York: Academic Press, 1978.

Rigney, J. W. Learning strategies: A theoretical perspective. In H. F. O'Neil, Jr. (Ed.), *Learning strategies.* New York: Academic Press, 1978.

Roy, E. A., & Diewert, G. L. Encoding of kinesthetic extent information. *Perception and Psychophysics,* 1975, *17,* 559–564.

Scandura, J. M. Structural approach to instructional problems. *American Psychologist,* 1977, *32,* 33–53.

Schaeffer, B. Skill integration during cognitive development. In A. Kennedy & A. Wilkes (Eds.), *Studies in long term memory.* New York: Wiley, 1975.

Schmidt, R. A. Experimental psychology. In R. N. Singer (Ed.), *The psychomotor domain: Movement behavior.* Philadelphia: Lea & Febiger, 1972.

Schmidt, R. A. A schema theory of discrete motor skill learning. *Psychological Review,* 1975, *82,* 225–260.

Schneider, W. & Shiffrin, R. M. Controlled and automatic human information processing: I. Detection, search, and attention. *Psychological Review,* 1977, *84,* 1–66.

Shiffrin, R. M., & Schneider, W. Controlled and automatic human information processing: II. Perceptual learning, automatic attending, and a general theory. *Psychological Review,* 1977, *84,* 127–190.

Simon, H. A. The functional equivalence of problem solving skills. *Cognitive Psychology,* 1975, *7,* 268–288.

Singer, R. N. *The psychomotor domain: Movement behavior.* Philadelphia: Lea & Febiger, 1972.

Singer, R. N. *Motor learning and human performance* (2nd ed.). New York: Macmillan, 1975.

Singer, R. N. The serial manipulation apparatus. *Journal of Motor Behavior,* 1976, *8,* 69–73.

Singer, R. N. Motor skills and learner strategies. In H. F. O'Neil, Jr. (Ed.), *Learning strategies.* New York: Academic Press, 1978.

Singer, R. N., & Gaines, L. Effect of prompted and trial-and-error learning on transfer performance of a serial motor task. *American Educational Research Journal,* 1975, *12,* 295–403.

Singer, R. N., & Gerson, R. F. *Cognitive processes and learner strategies in the acquisition of motor skills* (TR-78-TH-10). Alexandria, Va.: U.S. Army Research Institute for the Behavioral and Social Sciences, December 1978.

Singer, R. N., & Pease, D. The effect of different instructional strategies on learning, retention and transfer of a serial motor task. *Research Quarterly,* 1976, *47,* 788–796.

Smith, J. L. Fusimotor loop properties and involvement during voluntary movement. In J. Keogh & R. S. Hutton (Eds.), *Exercise and sport sciences reviews* (Vol. 4). Santa Barbara, Calif.: Journal Publishing Affiliates, 1976.

Sperling, G. The information available in brief visual presentations. *Psychological Monographs,* 1960, *74.*

Stelmach, G. E., Kelso, J. A. S., & McCullagh, P. D. Preselection and response biasing in short-term motor memory. *Memory and Cognition,* 1976, *4,* 62–66.

Stelmach, G. E., Kelso, J. A. S., & Wallace, S. A. Preselection in short-term motor memory. *Journal of Experimental Psychology: Human Learning and Memory,* 1975, *1,* 745–755.

Sternberg, S. The discovery of processing stages: Extensions of Donders' method. In W. G. Koster (Ed.), *Attention and performance II.* Amsterdam: North-Holland, 1969.

Taub, E. Movement in nonhuman primates deprived of somatosensory feedback. In J. Keogh & R. S. Hutton (Eds.), *Exercise and sport sciences reviews* (Vol. 4). Santa Barbara, Calif.: Journal Publishing Affiliates, 1976.

Trabasso, T. Discussion of the papers by Bransford and Johnson; and Clark, Carpenter, and

Just: Language and cognition. In W. G. Chase (Ed.), *Visual information processing.* New York: Academic Press, 1973.

Tulving, E. Subjective organization in free recall of "unrelated words." *Psychological Review,* 1962, *69,* 344–354.

Tulving, E. Theoretical issues in free recall. In T. R. Dixon & D. L. Horton (Eds.), *Verbal behavior and general behavior theory.* Englewood Cliffs, N.J.: Prentice-Hall, 1968.

Tulving, E., & Donaldson, W. *Organization of memory.* New York: Academic Press, 1972.

Tulving, E., & Thomson, D. M. Encoding specificity and retrieval processes in episodic memory. *Psychological Review,* 1973, *80,* 352–373.

Decision Analysis as a Learning Strategy

ROY M. GULICK

LEARNING STRATEGIES AND DECISION STRATEGIES

> *We do ill to exalt the powers of the human mind, when we should seek out its proper helps.*
>
> —FRANCIS BACON

Effective learning strategies qualify as Bacon's proper helps for the human mind. Such strategies have been described as basic intellectual and affective skills that serve to improve subject mastery and thereby reduce the time and cost associated with training (O'Neil, 1978).

I view learning as a communication process. Information about a particular subject must be formatted, transmitted, and received, usually constrained by limited bandwidth (finite motivation) and the presence of noise (distraction). Ultimately, the receptor (the student) must process the received signal, perhaps distorted, into information and knowledge by establishing associations with previous information. Continuing in this vein, I consider a learning strategy a fundamental protocol, or organizing communications framework, that is used by students to improve their reception and facilitate their processing of incoming information about a subject. Davis (1974) elaborates on this model of human information processing.

Presumably, desirable learning situations are those in which well-formatted, high-quality instruction (transmission) is combined with a conducive learning environment (noise-free channel) and well-motivated students (reception). This combination, however, as necessary as it may be

COGNITIVE AND AFFECTIVE
LEARNING STRATEGIES

for learning, may be insufficient for quality learning to take place. Despite even the strongest motivation, a student's limited memory, attention span, or decision-making capabilities may cause serious stress and strain, degrade reception, and produce inefficient learning.

Because of their finite human information processing capabilities, all students, if they are to cope, are forced to apply, often subconsciously, various simple strain-reducing cognitive, affective, and motor learning strategies for receiving, organizing, and processing the incoming information. Obviously, some learning strategies are more effective than others in reducing stress and strain and promoting learning.

I presume that the most efficient learning situations are those in which well-motivated students are equipped with and actively employ effective learning strategies that help them better organize and process high-quality instructional information. That is, I assume that the use of effective learning strategies is a necessary condition for efficient learning to take place. This point of view, which is addressed quite thoroughly in the other chapters of this book, is represented graphically in Figure 10.1.

However, in contrast with the other chapters, which focus mainly on facilitating learning in schools, my chapter focuses on learning that follows one's academic preparation. Agreeing with Bruner (1963) that a basic structural framework is essential to subject comprehension, I extend the notion to the comprehension of information relevant to one of life's most com-

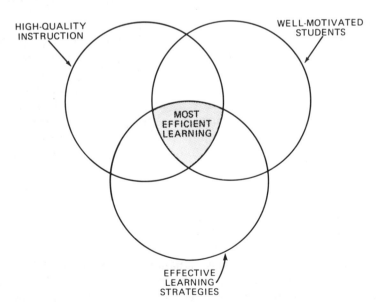

Figure 10.1 An efficient learning environment (shaded area).

mon learning situations: decision making. Thus my chapter's context is real-world.

In the normal course of business and life, there are many types of problematic learning situations that leaders, managers, and individuals face on a daily basis. Decision problems make up a significant portion of these, and they vary widely in their level of complexity and their degree of importance. Generally, decision problems can be divided into two broad classes: those that are important, and those that are not. The distinction is clarified by Townsend (1970), who, in advising executives on how to survive and run a successful business, defined the important decisions as those that are expensive to change. This chapter is about strategies for handling decisions of the first kind, the important ones that are expensive to change: those whose solution involves the irretrievable expenditure of valuable resources, such as money, time, or effort; those in which the process of deciding among alternatives poses a true dilemma.

To those who have dealt with such decisions in their own personal spheres (such as marrying or divorcing, purchasing a home, deciding which automobile to buy, and choosing among various career options and job opportunities), the enormous difficulties inherent in important decision making are apparent. Even at the relatively simple level of personal choice, one often encounters more relevant aspects of a decision than the intellect can cope with easily.

The difficulties become greatly magnified in business and government decision contexts; the problems are usually far more important and complex, the scope of uncertainties much greater, and the risks and stakes of enormous magnitude.

Faced with an important decision, a decision maker must elicit, collect, assimilate, sort, classify, evaluate, and structure sufficient information about the decision at hand to formulate rational alternatives and choose a logical and coherent course of action. The task is complicated, because the information bearing on the decision may consist not only of straightforward factual data but also of erroneous data and inherently soft data such as expert opinion, professional judgment, and pure conjecture. Furthermore, expert opinion and judgment, especially when they are elicited from different sources, are more often than not conflictive. To further complicate matters, most important decisions are also surrounded by future uncertainties that must somehow be taken into account. Finally, the criteria used by the decision maker to evaluate the alternative courses of action are usually conflictive and often poorly understood.

Deciding requires learning; thus an effective environment for decision making is not unlike an effective learning environment: It is one that combines high-quality information and advice with a well-motivated learner and decision maker. Presumably, as in the case for efficient learning, the most efficient decision making occurs when a well-motivated decision maker with sources of high-quality information is also equipped with, and employs, an effective decision strategy. Figure 10.2 illustrates an efficient decision environment.

There are several distinct behavioral phases of the serious decision-making process. As a problem solver, a decision maker must define and formulate the problem, generate an exhaustive list of viable and exclusive responses that deal with the problem, and finally decide on and implement one specific course of action. Presumably, the use of an effective decision strategy increases the likelihood that a decision maker will choose the most effective action from among the various alternatives. In this context, the most effective response is the one most likely to lead to a result that is consistent with the decision maker's preferences.

There are many well-known and well-tested systematic strategies for helping decision makers make well-informed, rational, and consistent choices. For example, one of the more classic descriptions of a personal decision strategy was provided by one of the Founding Fathers, Benjamin Franklin.

In 1772 Franklin, in a letter to the preeminent British scientist and discoverer of oxygen, Joseph Priestley, prescribed a decision strategy to assist Priestley in structuring an important personal decision. Priestley was then torn between remaining in England and enduring strong criticism for

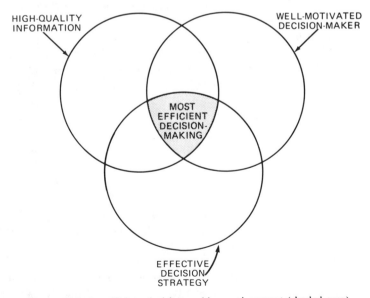

Figure 10.2 An efficient decision-making environment (shaded area).

his liberal views about the colonies, or leaving. Franklin's succinct advice, which appears in Janis and Mann (1977) and in many other treatises on decision making, was as follows:

London, Sept. 19, 1772

Dear Sir,

In the affair of so much importance to you, wherein you ask my advice, I cannot, for want of sufficient premises, advise you what to determine, but if you please I will tell you how.

When those difficult cases occur, they are difficult, chiefly because while we have them under consideration, all the reasons pro and con are not present to the mind at the same time; but sometimes one set present themselves, and at other times another, the first being out of sight. Hence the various purposes or inclinations that alternatively prevail, and the uncertainty that perplexes us.

To get over this, my way is to divide half a sheet of paper by a line into two columns; writing over the one Pro, and the other Con. Then, during three or four days consideration, I put down under the different heads short hints of the different motives, that at different times occur to me, for or against the measure. When I have thus got them all together in one view, I endeavor to estimate their respective weights; and where I find two, one on each side, that seem equal, I strike them both out. If I find a reason pro equal to some two reasons con, I strike out the three. If I judge some two reasons con, equal to some three reasons pro, I strike out the five; and thus proceeding I find at length where the balance lies; and if, after a day or two of further consideration, nothing new that is of importance occurs on either side, I come to a determination accordingly.

Though the weight of reasons cannot be taken with the precision of algebraic quantities, yet when each is thus considered, separately and comparatively, and the whole lies before me, I think I can judge better, and am less liable to make a rash step, and in fact I have found great advantage from this kind of equation, in what may be called moral or prudential algebra.

Wishing sincerely that you may determine for the best, I am ever, my dear friend, yours most affectionately.

B. Franklin

Although Priestley's decision was one involving personal choice, this same type of decision strategy was recently applied to an important administration decision involving U.S. national security. Hedrick Smith (1978), writing in the *New York Times,* described how President Carter used a checklist strategy to deal with the enormous complexities surrounding the B-1 bomber decision. According to Smith, the President resolved 47 pro and con arguments on the issue by assigning them relative importance weights and computing the totals, which went against the B-1, as did Carter.

During World War II, many statistical strategies for assisting decision makers were introduced under the name of operations research, and later under the name of management science. Most of those strategies, succinctly described in Bursk and Chapman (1963) and compared in some detail by

White (1975), are most applicable to highly specialized, clean-cut, and recurring problems, such as those involving systematic search, the allocation of fixed resources, and the analysis of queuing systems. Some of these strategies are candidates for providing a structural framework for learning. For example, Roberts (1978) reports success in teaching dynamic feedback systems theory and model building as a learning strategy for elementary school students. Similarly Argyris (1976) advocates using aspects of the same theory as a learning strategy for coping with life itself.

However, all of these strategies, such as linear programming, critical path analysis, and inventory control, are totally objective and deterministic; they ignore the human element: They omit any formal consideration of the subjective judgment and complex value structures that are an essential part of any important decision problem.

In the 1960s a more general technology began to emerge for imposing a logical problem structure that specifically includes the subjective reasoning that underlies an important decision situation. This decision strategy, called decision analysis, is a prescriptive, or normative, methodology that borrows from the two well-developed disciplines of systems analysis and classical decision theory. An accessory to the decision-making process, it specifically takes into account all of the data, both objective and subjective, that are relevant to any key decision problem. Furthermore, the strategy is theoretically sound and clinically tested. It has proven itself to be practical, useful, and usable.

Just as an effective learning strategy is a platform that helps a student organize the incoming information about a subject and so better learn, decision analysis is a platform that helps decision makers learn by enforcing discipline and coherence in important decision situations. Decision analysis is a sophisticated and effective learning strategy for coping with the complex decision problems of life, industry, and government.

DECISION ANALYSIS

> *A good problem statement often includes: (a) what is known,*
> *(b) what is unknown, and (c) what is sought.*
> —EDWARD HODNETT

I must reemphasize that in no sense does decision analysis replace decision makers with procedures devoid of human judgment. Rather, the purpose of the strategy is to provide an orderly, rigorous, easily understood, and intuitively appealing structural framework, or standard, to aid the decision maker. The framework integrates the objective data surrounding a decision with the wisdom of experts and the decision maker's own personal judgment on the many topics that may have to be addressed to support the choice and implementation of a particular decision option. Thus decision analysis is strictly an accessory to decision making: an organizing and clarifying framework that has proven to be especially useful for making sound decisions in the face of uncertainty, inconclusive evidence, conflicting opinion, and unclear personal judgments.

The name itself was derived by Howard (1966) from the related fields of statistical decision theory and systems analysis and design, and the discipline contains elements of both. Probability theory and utility theory form the cornerstones of the discipline, and, as Howard emphasizes, there are strong philosophical, psychological, and methodological foundations as well.

The discipline rests upon three tenets. As suggested by Lindley (1971), the fundamental one is that humans have faulty intuition, process diverse information very poorly, and are biased and inconsistent decision makers. This viewpoint is strongly supported in the behavioral research literature, excellent summaries and discussions of which appear in Edwards and Tversky (1967), Slovic (1972), and Slovic, Fischhoff, and Lichtenstein (1977).

The second tenet is that, despite human inconsistencies, the strong human element surrounding important decisions cannot be denied; that an effective and useful decision strategy must explicitly account for subjective judgment, however tenuous.

Finally, it is assumed that a formal, rigorous, and coherent decision strategy resting on sound theory is more effective than an intuitive strategy. Above all else, decision analysis emphasizes structure. By superimposing a logical organization on the analysis of decision problems, it forces the decision maker's thorough consideration of the multidimensional aspects, both objective and subjective, that are typical of complex decison problems. This, incidentally, invariably improves the quality of the internal communication and generates increased insight into the nature of the problem at hand.

The kinds of problems best suited for decision analysis are problems that are important in the sense previously mentioned: those in which the final decision involves the irretrievable expenditure of scarce resources and in which a severe penalty will be incurred by the decision maker should a suboptimal decision alternative be implemented. In addition to being important, the problems are usually unique, so that neither past experience nor historical data may be relevant to the situation.

Examples of personal problems that should be addressed by decision analysis include buying a home, choosing a new career, and changing marital status. Examples of organizational problems include strategic planning, plant relocation, policy formulation, marketing strategy, resource allocation, and negotiation. Those problems are difficult to deal with primarily because they lack structure; they appear to be virtually unbounded and difficult to contain. The decision objectives and criteria may be only loosely specified, and the desires and preferences of the individual or organization are usually phrased in purely qualitative and ambiguous terms. Most often, such problems are also compounded by the uncertain nature of future events that will impact on the eventual outcome.

A classical literary example of a personal decision problem of the type just described was that faced by Hamlet: to be, or not to be. Although the number of decision alternatives—two—is absolutely minimum, the problem is complicated by a future uncertainty of great magnitude (to suffer, to dream, or to sleep), and several complicated decision criteria ("the whips and scorns of time," "the pangs of disprized love," "the law's delay," and "the spurns that patient merit of the unworthy takes"). Graves and Lethbridge (1975) conducted a postmortem analysis of Hamlet's plight and concluded that he could well have benefited from the services of a qualified decision analyst.

Examples of more pressing organizational decision problems that have benefited from decision analysis include labor–management negotiations, procurement, international treaty negotiations, insurance underwriting, contingency planning, and resource allocations. Specific recent examples include Ulvila, Brown, and Packard's (1977) analysis of a capital investment problem involving new plant construction, and Hays and O'Connor's (1977) analysis of systems evaluation.

Typically, most problems like these are attacked in the manner shown in Figure 10.3. The decision maker's staff produces an analysis that usually takes the form of a checklist (like Franklin's) of qualitative considerations,

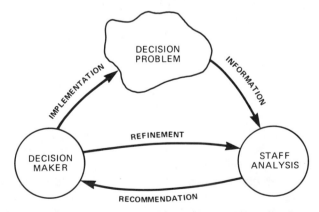

Figure 10.3 The fundamental decision-making process.

advantages and disadvantages, implications, and recommendations for action. The decision maker assesses the strength of the analysis and then either decides to implement the recommended decision alternative as a problem solution, or else rejects the recommendation and asks the staff to refine the analysis.

The decision-making cycle of Figure 10.3 is a fundamental and necessary part of all rational procedures for decision making. However, just as the recommended solution is subject to refinement and improvement, so is the analytic process itself. Argyris (1976) suggests that this point is often overlooked, that only rarely do we examine overriding frameworks themselves; we are usually too concerned with the product to examine the process. Decision analysis provides a highly effective means of examining and improving the analytic portion of the decision-making cycle.

Concise descriptions of the process of decision analysis are provided by Brown (1977) and Barclay, Brown, Kelly, Peterson, Phillips, and Selvidge (1977). Luce and Raiffa (1957) provide technical mathematical foundations, Lindley (1971) provides a nonmathematical description, and Brown, Kahr, and Peterson (1974) describe decision analysis for corporate managers.

I will describe, briefly, the three major steps. The first step in a decision analysis is to decompose the problem at hand and to construct a formal, logical, and relatively simple problem representation that effectively bounds the decision situation and displays its key features. The structure specifies an exhaustive and exclusive set of viable decision alternatives, a list of the key uncertainties and the future states that may obtain from those events, and a list of possible outcomes that result from the various combinations of the decision alternatives and the future states.

The second step is to obtain quantitative measures for the probabilities of the future states and the utilities to the decision maker of the various outcomes. With respect to these, I refer the skeptic to Lindley (1971), who argues very persuasively in layman's terms that valid measures of uncertainty and the desirability of the outcomes can be obtained. Mathematically sophisticated skeptics should also consult Edwards and Tversky (1967) and Phillips (1974).

The final step in the analysis is to invoke a decision rule: to select that alternative having the greatest expected utility to the decision maker.

In order to illustrate the decision-analytic process, let us consider a hypothetical personal decision problem wherein a freshman college student is seriously considering dropping a psychology elective because of poor course grades and a very pressing total course load. Though we might elaborate at length about the problem in qualitative terms, we can get right to the heart of it by examining the model shown in Figure 10.4. This

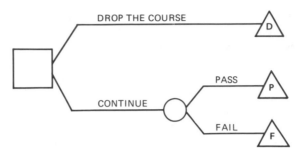

Figure 10.4 A prototypical decision tree.

representation, a decision tree, represents the essence of the student's problem. (Magee [1964] contains an excellent discussion of decision trees.)

As the flow proceeds from left to right, it reveals one fundamental decision (drop the course or continue it), one key uncertainty (pass or fail, given that the course is continued), and three possible decision outcomes (drop the course, pass, or fail, labeled D, P, and F, respectively). Outcome P, for example, corresponds to the case in which the student made the decision to continue the course and, after the fact, passed it.

The next step in the analysis is to identify and relatively weigh the various criteria by which the student would discriminate among the three final outcomes. The precise criteria depend, of course, on the student's overall objectives and value structures. Let us assume that the student has identified two key criteria: productive use of time and peace of mind. Further assume that the student has scored each of the three possible decision outcomes with respect to each criterion, as shown in Figure 10.5. For each criterion, the best outcome is given a score of 100 (100% utility), with supporting rationale, the worst outcome is scored 0, and the intermediate outcome is scored between 0 and 100. I must note that the assignment of intermediate scores is not a trivial task; Luce and Raiffa (1957), Lindley (1971), Brown, Kahr, and Peterson (1974), Pearl (1977), and Johnson and Huber (1977) all describe various techniques for eliciting such values.

Next the student establishes the relative weights of the two criteria on the basis of the relative importance assigned to the difference between the best and worst outcomes for each criterion. Assuming that the range of the outcomes with respect to peace of mind is judged only two-thirds as important as the range of the outcomes for productive use of time, the student would weigh the two criteria 40% and 60%, respectively, as indicated in the figure. This is a critical point: The relative weight of the multiple attributes is determined by the relative importance of their range of consequences with respect to the problem at hand, and not by some intuitive process based on the perceived global importance of the attributes. The student

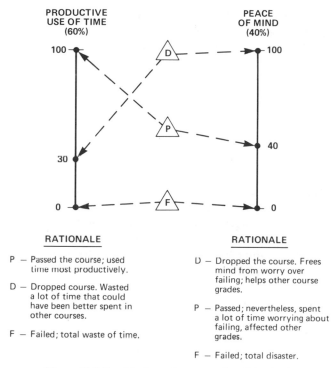

PRODUCTIVE
USE OF TIME
(60%)

PEACE
OF MIND
(40%)

RATIONALE

P — Passed the course; used
time most productively.

D — Dropped course. Wasted
a lot of time that could
have been better spent in
other courses.

F — Failed; total waste of time.

RATIONALE

D — Dropped the course. Frees
mind from worry over
failing; helps other course
grades.

P — Passed; nevertheless, spent
a lot of time worrying about
failing, affected other
grades.

F — Failed; total disaster.

Figure 10.5 Scoring the outcomes against the criteria.

must focus on the specific evaluation at hand in order to weigh the attributes.

At this point a single multidimensional value of utility can be computed for each outcome. Thus, Outcome P (continue the course and pass) receives a total utility value of 76: 60 from the first criterion (100 × 60%) and 16 from the second (40 × 40%). Similarly, Outcome D receives 58 and Outcome F receives 0.

The student is now faced with the difficult task of assessing the key uncertainty: determining the likelihood of passing the course if it is continued. What is required is a subjective probability that a unique future event will occur. A subjective probability should be viewed as no more than a concise expression of the relevant state of the student's knowledge regarding the future event, a notion of probability advanced as early as 1738 by Daniel Bernoulli. Furthermore, this notion contends that as the student's state of knowledge about the future event changes with additional evidence, so does the probability. Decision analysts accept this notion of probability, an excellent presentation of which is contained in Phillips (1974).

However, for those who view probability as an objective, inherent property of physical objects (such as dice) that is determined empirically by relative frequencies of occurrences, the notion of subjective probability holds little appeal. However, the notion of subjective probability actually includes the objectivist's notion of probability based on relative frequency, since the observed frequencies of events are evidence that can be used to revise initial subjective probability estimates. Lindley (1971) argues persuasively that the two separate notions of probability are in fact but one, that there exists but one form of uncertainty, and that its standard measure is probability.

Let us assume that, based on the student's best sources of information (and presumably that information will change with time), the probability of passing the course, given that it is continued, is assessed at 50%. The student feels that the likelihood of passing is the same as obtaining tails in a fair coin toss. The decision problem can now be represented as shown in Figure 10.6. The original tree has been modified to indicate the assessed value of each of the three outcomes and the probabilities of the uncertain future states.

If the student agrees that the structure shown in Figure 10.6 is a reasonable and coherent representation of the problem, then the student should choose that branch of the decision tree that maximizes the expected value of the final outcome. That is, consistent with the student's own value structure and state of knowledge concerning the future, the student should attempt to gain the maximum expected satisfaction across the two pertinent criteria: productive use of time and peace of mind.

Choosing the upper decision branch (drop the course) will result in a certain utility value of 58, since there is no intermediate uncertainty that complicates this path. The lower banch, however, is distinguished by the major uncertainty (pass or fail).

The path to the uncertain event has an expected value that is obtained by summing the outcome value of each of the uncertain branches multiplied

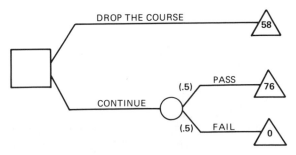

Figure 10.6 Decision tree with outcome values and event likelihoods.

by their respective probabilities of occurrence. Thus, the expected value of the decision path leading to the uncertain event (pass or fail) equals the utility value of the upper branch (pass) multiplied by its probability (76 × .5 = 38) plus the value of the lower branch (fail) multiplied by its probability (0 × .5 = 0). Thus, the uncertain event can be represented logically as a single outcome having an expected utility value of 38 (38 + 0), so that the original decision tree is equivalent to the representation shown in Figure 10.7.

The student, being rational, would now decide to drop the course, since based on the student's own value structure and state of knowledge, the utility of doing so (58) far exceeds the expected utility of continuing (38).

The analysis need not stop here, however. Additional insight into the decision can be gained by determining just how sensitive the ultimate decision (drop the course) is to the student's assessment of the subjective probability of the uncertain event, as well as to the relative weights assigned to the two criteria.

For example, further analysis reveals that the lower branch (continue the course) would become the preferred course of action only if, in the student's mind, the probability of passing the course should exceed 76%. Thus, the original estimate of the subjective probability of passing (50%) need not be precise; there is much room for error before the decision is changed. Furthermore, with respect to the criteria weights (holding the probability of passing at 50%), the lower branch (continue the course) becomes the preferred choice only when the weight of the first criterion (productive use of time) exceeds 80%.

The dual sensitivities of the probability of passing and the weight of the productive-use-of-time criterion are represented in Figure 10.8. The present state of affairs is indicated, showing graphically that, as things now stand, the student should drop the course.

This simple example was used only to illustrate the essential components of a decision analysis: the explicit structuring of the problem, the systematic decomposition of the problem into its crucial component parts (decision acts, uncertain events, eventual outcomes, and the preference

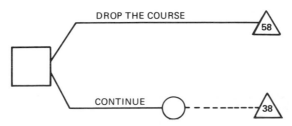

Figure 10.7 An equivalent decision tree.

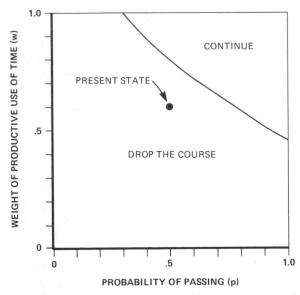

Figure 10.8 The combined sensitivity analysis. The higher valued alternative as a function of two variables: the weight of productive use of time (w), and the probability of passing (p). (The curve of indifference is $.4p + .7w + .6wp = 1$.)

criteria), eliciting quantitative specifications for the probability of the uncertain events and the relative desirability of the possible outcomes, and, finally, solving for the decision alternative that maximizes the expected value of the eventual outcome across all of the decision maker's criteria for success.

The example is relatively straightforward and belies the sophistication and power of the method. Serious decision problems require more complex structures and much more sophisticated treatment of the uncertainties, consequences, preferences, and risks. Nevertheless, the fundamental principle remains: The decision problem should be simply stated and well understood by decision-making participants on their own terms.

Although the example emphasizes the methodological aspects of a decision analysis, a great deal of art must be applied as well; structuring a decision problem is a dynamic and creative process of learning and discovery. For example, new options, new criteria, and new insights will present themselves as one proceeds through the analysis. Furthermore, there are always the fundamental judgmental questions of model creation and refinement: Are the alternatives, uncertain events, and criteria representative of the real problem, and just how detailed must a particular model be before it can be considered adequate? Surely a decision maker would do well to consider Einstein's advice that things should be made as simple as possible, but not simpler. Although a sensitivity analysis can help in this regard, the level of refinement and complexity is clearly a judgment call on the part of the decision maker. Whatever the degree of refinement, however, the decision structure must reflect, in a consistent and coherent manner, the true beliefs and preferences of the decision maker.

Hypothetical examples of applied decision analysis, such as the one just presented, have been used in courses taught by the leading business schools for several decades in order to illustrate the practical application of decision theory. However, in order to ascertain the full value of decision analysis, a practicing decision maker must turn from the otherwise credible and mature theoretical aspects to a more practical question: Can decision analysis contribute positively and significantly to real-world decision making?

To answer that question, the Defense Advanced Research Projects Agency (DARPA) in 1972 undertook a program of exploratory research dedicated not only to extending and enriching the theory, but also to applying the theoretical results to important real-world, time-constrained problems faced by various component organizations of the Department of Defense. As a staff member of DARPA, I managed that research program during its period of greatest application, 1976 to 1978, and selected most of the specific trial applications of the technology.

APPLIED RESEARCH

> *Innovations must go through the mill of objection, opposition, and contumely.*
> —WILL AND ARIEL DURANT

Since 1972, the Defense Advanced Research Projects Agency, through its Advanced Decision Technology Program, has addressed human decision-making processes in general, and the Defense decision-making environment in particular. Throughout the program, emphasis has been placed on the structural aspects of decision making. That is, the program has produced and prescribed several organizing frameworks and systematic procedures to assist decision makers in their handling of very complex operational decisions. These procedures form a set of generic decision strategies that may be superimposed on specific decision situations to guide and improve the decision-making process.

The resultant methodology could have been viewed by its intended users in the Department of Defense as speculation and promise, as no more than an assertion from an ivory tower of research that if only decision makers would use advanced decision methodology, then surely their decision-making procedures would become more efficient and more effective. Although such an assertion would have been based, of course, on considerable laboratory evidence gathered in rigorous controlled experiments, such evidence, even though it might have withstood the most careful scrutiny regarding scientific rigor, probably would not have withstood the scrutiny of practical relevance. The researcher's claim that an assertion has been validated by empirical evidence offers little assurance to those who are concerned only with the more fundamental and practical question: Does it work?

It is a very difficult question to answer. In order to answer it, DARPA diverted considerable resources from basic research in decision analysis to the exploratory development of applied decision analysis. Ten major (and 25 minor) experimental real-world applications of the methodology were sought, pursued, and implemented in order to gain first-hand clinical evidence as to the feasibility, acceptance, usefulness, and efficiency of decision-analytic methods in aiding real-world operational Defense decision makers. The 10 applications were very carefully selected to provide a broad variety of key decision problems spanning all four branches of the armed services. The applications were chosen for their importance, uniqueness, and complexity. All of them involved real, ongoing, and time-constrained problems that were heavily enmeshed in conflictive qualitative argument and subjective judgment. Many of the problems involved uncertainty. Significant Defense resources were at stake in all cases, and in all cases the problem was already undergoing analysis by the normal command and staff procedures (as illustrated in Figure 10.3) at the time that a decision-analytic strategy was introduced.

As one can imagine, social and cultural technological intervention of this type and on this scale is a most difficult, delicate, and risky process, one that rubs against ingrained intuition, personal experience, and organizational norms. Invariably it provoked lively discussion and skepticism and often outright dissent. Technological intervention of this kind is a complex process deeply mired in elements of philosophy, psychology, and organizational dynamics.

The pilot applications that were pursued can be grouped into two broad classes: those involving decision making under conditions of relative certainty, and those that involved decision making in the face of uncertain futures.

Examples of the applications in which decision making was performed in an environment of relative certainty include the prioritization and allocation of funds among diverse functionally oriented program elements competing in an austere environment (Buede & Peterson, 1977), the evaluation across multiple (in excess of 100) criteria of competing designs for new weapons systems (as reported by Hays & O'Connor, 1977), evaluation of the combat readiness of military units, and the evaluation and structuring of bilateral and multinational treaties (Barclay & Peterson, 1976). The relative lack of uncertainty does not rid these problems of the confusion that attends evaluating the possible outcomes across multiple attributes.

Examples of the applications that involved decision making under uncertainty include the basing and posturing of military forces (Kelly & Stewart, 1977), evaluation of the indications and warnings attending potential crisis situations (Daly & Davies, 1978), contingency planning, and selection of policy options.

In order to illustrate the real-world use of decision analysis, I will use a problem involving decision making in an uncertain future. The decision analysis actually took place in an ongoing military crisis situation. The problem involved the posturing of naval forces in the face of possible evacuations of U.S. citizens from Lebanon in 1976. The decision analysis was conducted by Headquarters, U.S. European Command, in conjunction with several decision analysts provided by DARPA contract. A more detailed description of the analysis appears in Kelly and Stewart (1977).

Four alternative alert postures for the naval evacuation force were generated, ranging from its normal posture to a very advanced posture in which the fleet was positioned just offshore near the potential evacuation area. The fundamental decision was that of choosing and implementing one of the four postures.

The staff identified several key uncertainties that influenced the choice of posture: whether or not an evacuation would eventually be required; whether the evacuation, if it proved necessary, would be permitted (noncombatant) or opposed (hostile) by the Lebanon authorities; and, finally, the number of U.S. nationals who would require evacuation, should it become necessary.

The decision tree that applied to this problem is shown in abbreviated form in Figure 10.9. Note that the uncertain events branches that appear for the normal posture alternative also apply to each of the other three decision alternatives. Thus the complete tree has 20 possible outcomes. Outcome N4, for example, is the state of affairs in which the fleet was in a normal day-to-day posture and it became necessary to evacuate in a hostile combat situation some 2000 U.S. nationals.

The staff identified four criteria for discriminating among the 20 outcomes: the risk to U.S. citizens, political ramifications, loss of fleet flexibility in the Mediterranean, and changes in the level of force readiness. Relative weights were established for each of these four criteria.

In order to facilitate the scoring of the 20 possible outcomes against each criterion, the outcomes were represented in a matrix form, as shown in

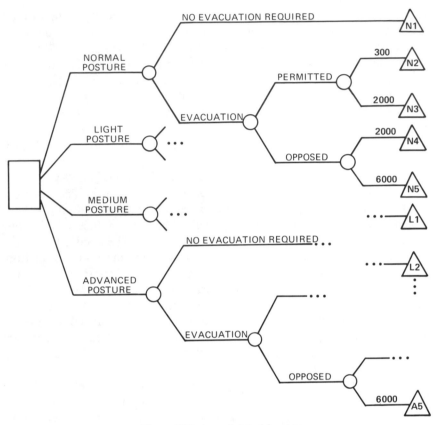

Figure 10.9 A partial decision tree.

Figure 10.10. The matrix represents the 20 outcomes scored against only one of the four criteria: exposure risk. Four such matrices were developed, one for each criterion.

Each matrix was scored by assigning values representing the loss of opportunity, or operational regret, associated with each possible outcome. That is, the decision maker was asked to imagine that, having chosen a certain alternative posture, a particular outcome actually resulted. With respect to each outcome, the decision maker was asked how much regret the decision maker experienced for having chosen that posture. In this manner, scores were assigned to each block in the matrix, ranging from 0 for no regret, to 100 for the maximum regret. Most importantly, supporting written rationale was captured for the assignment of the regrets.

Expressions of regret, a negative quality, were found to be easier to elicit than were expressions of utility opportunity, a positive quality.

Criterion: Exposure Risk

	NO EVACUATION REQUIRED	PERMITTED, 300 PEOPLE	PERMITTED 2,000 PEOPLE	OPPOSED 2,000 PEOPLE	OPPOSED 6,000 PEOPLE
NORMAL POSTURE	0	60	80	100	100
LIGHT POSTURE	0	20	30	80	90
MEDIUM POSTURE	5	0	0	25	30
ADVANCED POSTURE	10	5	0	0	0

Figure 10.10 A regret matrix: prior posture versus the eventual outcome for the criterion: exposure risk.

Since each one of the 20 outcomes received four separate scores (one from each of the four criteria), each outcome has a unique combined value of regret that is computed by properly weighting its score from each criterion and then adding the four scores.

At the same time that regrets were elicited, intelligence experts assigned subjective probabilities to the five uncertain states of the future: no evacuation, permissive evacuation of 300 people, etc. Once this was done, then an expected value of regret was computed for each of the four posturing alternatives. Furthermore, since the crisis situation was dynamic, with new evidence appearing daily, there were corresponding changes in the perceived likelihood that an evacuation would be required. A sensitivity analysis was used to produce an explicit relationship between the probability of an evacuation and the posturing alternatives, as shown in Figure 10.11. The analysis showed that one of the decision alternatives, the light posture, was never a preferred course of action, regardless of the estimated probability of evacuation, and was eliminated from consideration. For a given probability of evacuation, the decision alternative having the least value of regret should be selected (the lowest line on the figure).

Perhaps the greatest advantage in the use of decision analysis in the posturing decision was that the explicit decision model facilitated communication among the various headquarters staff elements. Staff resources were allocated to producing and validating the consistency of both the values of regret and the subjective probabilities of the uncertain events. The decision tree model served as the organizing framework for staff integration and action, thus focusing the efforts of the various levels of staff expertise, producing additional insight into the nature of the problem, and forcing the systematic inclusion of all the key factors. In this particular ex-

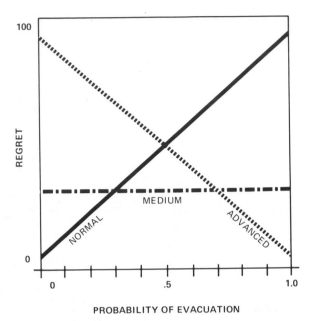

Figure 10.11 A sensitivity analysis: the least regretful decision alternative versus the probability that an evacuation will occur.

ample the medium pastime alternative was recommended and in fact implemented. The evacuation itself was carried out in a nonhostile environment. Security was provided by both the U.S. Navy and the PLO.

Similar decision-analytic techniques were used by the same staff in subsequent planning actions. Close liaison with the planners revealed that, in the planner's opinions, considerable learning took place during the analyses; the strategy had become almost second nature to them. This was also found to be true in several of the other applications throughout the services.

CONCLUSIONS

> *I like a person who knows his own mind and sticks to it; who sees at once what, in given circumstances, is to be done, and does it.*
>
> —WILLIAM HAZLITT

There are few people who would disagree with Hazlitt's criteria for decision making. Foresight, decisiveness, and resolution are individual qualities essential to personal success and to the successful leadership and management of others. Business organizations, as well as military ones, prize the gifted decision maker: the one who takes command, who can size up a difficult situation, initiate direct, firm, and conclusive action, and transform an impending crisis into opportunity and resounding success. Intuitive decision-making skill of that kind is indeed an invaluable and rare talent.

The fact is that it is too rare a talent; today's organizations, public and private, require much more systematic procedures for analyzing their important decision problems. Common sense, experience, intuition, and the very best of intentions are no longer sufficient to produce optimal decisions consistently. As I have pointed out, there is a compelling need for accountability in decision making, for systematic procedures designed to improve both content and structure.

Only recently have the traditionally unstructured intuitive approaches to decision making started to give way to the more systematic procedures of operations research, management science, and decision analysis. Thirty years after the introduction of structured decision strategies into the military and business worlds, we still find that they are used on a very modest scale. There is still a pronounced reluctance at the senior levels of management to deal objectively with subjective issues. Managers know that there is a definite cost (and risk) involved in implementing such procedures, and the benefits to be gained by implementing systematic decision strategies are sometimes very difficult to perceive. (Watson and Brown [1978] have proposed an innovative methodological framework for handling the cost–benefit analysis of conducting a decision analysis.)

It was not long ago that White (1975) found that "even the most formally developed and rigorous" of all the decision strategies, decision analysis, has seen very little application in the real world. Certainly in my experience, White's observation holds true for the use of decision analysis in the Department of Defense, although some significant progress has been made during the past 3 years, as discussed in the previous section.

There remain, however, many formidable obstacles to the widespread acceptance and application of the discipline, most of which are described in an excellent monograph by Fischhoff (1977) on the art and/or science of decision analysis. My own experience leads me to conclude that, of many obstacles, the following four are the most significant ones with regard to the introduction of decision analysis and, by implication, a formal learning strategies program.

First of all, I found that almost all the prospective users of decision analysis were, from the outset, uncomfortable with its quantitative nature. Many senior officials, military and civilian alike, were quite defensive and raised serious objections to the idea of quantifying subjective judgment. In fact, no less than a half-dozen immediately made a negative association with some of the more unpopular systems analysis quantification procedures introduced under the McNamara administration of the Department of Defense. This initial association was a formidable, if unjustified, hurdle to overcome.

Furthermore, the quantitative, content-specific nature of decision analysis invoked personal defensive mechanisms. Many officials quite obviously did not like the idea that their own subjective value structures would be not only made explicit but also put on display. Even worse, they did not like the idea that their reasoning in the form of written rationale would be revealed as well.

The very difficult problem of overcoming objections to quantification has no easy solution; it requires both philosophical and psychological methods of attack. There is simply a need for more senior officials who are comfortable with quantitative procedures and accept them as efficient and effective tools for clarification, communication, and progress.

The second obstacle has to do with organizational inertia. I found several gross examples of it, although it was not as widespread as I had expected it to be. Without exception, the more pressing the problem, the less the inertia. Decision makers and their staffs involved in serious and time-constrained problems such as the Lebanon evacuation problem and the allocation of scarce funds in an impending budget submission readily accepted the intrusion of quantitative decision analysis, used it to good effect, and then sought other applications for its use. On the other hand, 2 of the 10 problems still remain unsolved. One problem became much less time-critical, and interest in its solution faded; correspondingly, so did interest in the use of decision analysis. The other problem still remains an extremely important one, and its analysis is still proceeding—not decision analysis, however. The organization, one of an academic nature whose senior executive requested that the organization not be identified, participated in and completed a decision analysis of the problem, but was pressured by strong inertial forces into reverting to a more traditional qualitative analysis to supplement the decision analysis.

Organizational inertia is hard to defeat; a successful attack requires the unflagging support of both the top executive and those at the working level who must grind out recommended solutions to problems. Convincing the former requires a strong philosophical argument with practical examples; the latter require technical arguments and specific examples of how the technology would be used on the problem at hand.

The third obstacle has to do with the overall objective of applied research: actually to transfer the technology, in this case to institutionalize decision analysis. There are two smaller hurdles in this area. First, decision analysis is not so much a technique or tool that is being transferred as it is a new way of thinking about decision making. There are strong individual philosophical overtones, and those are extraordinarily difficult to transfer to an individual, much less an organization. Second, conducting an effective decision analysis requires a formally educated, skilled, and well-experienced decision analyst. That skill cannot be transferred; it is up to the organization to either develop or procure an accomplished practitioner. It must be willing to pay the price.

The final obstacle has to do with computer technology. I have not even mentioned computer technology up to this point, even though all of the applications that I have discussed used a minicomputer and model–building computer software to assist in the analysis. The reason I have not mentioned this fact is that I wanted the reader to focus on the strategy of decision analysis and not be sidetracked by the tool used to conduct it. Computers, especially when used in conjunction with decision making, still receive undue attention and arouse quite emotional reactions. This was certainly true in my experience: I had to downplay deliberately the use of computers when introducing decision analysis to prospective users. That should not be the case, yet senior people who should know better still want to impart exceptional powers (or errors) to computers.

We used minicomputers to perform the laborious computational, accounting, and documentation procedures that are associated with decision analysis. The monumental manual task of sensitivity analysis, for example, is performed easily, rapidly, and accurately by the computer. A description of the model-building software used in the posturing example appears in Selvidge (1976). We provided user-oriented model-building computer software that enabled users who were not sophisticated in computer technology to construct and manipulate their own decision models.

Nevertheless, despite the widespread infusion of computer technology throughout the public and private sectors (and into our own lives), the mere mention of the word *computer* in conjunction with decision making still generates emotional feelings of suspicion and distrust. I am confident that this problem will be overcome with time, but today it still remains a serious impediment to technology transfer.

To close on a positive note, let me add that I was fortunate to find that the large majority of senior Defense decision makers, military and civilian, were quite objective in their reaction to the intrusion of decision analysis into their world. Despite initial reservations, sometimes strongly expressed, they not only permitted but encouraged the impartial trial applications of the technology. In most cases, the technology has been successfully transferred to the organization.

REFERENCES

Argyris, C., *Increasing leadership effectiveness*. New York: John Wiley, 1976.

Barclay, S., Brown, R., Kelly, C., Peterson, C., Phillips, L., & Selvidge, J. *Handbook for decision analysis* (Technical Report TR 77-6-30). McLean, Va.: Decisions and Designs, Inc., 1977.

Barclay, S., & Peterson, C. *Multi-attribute utility models for negotiations* (Technical Rep. DT/TR 76-1). McLean, Va.: Decisions and Designs, Inc., 1976.

Brown, R. How to analyze decisions. *Management Today*, 1977, *14*, 80-82.

Brown, R., Kahr, A., & Peterson, C. *Decision analysis for the manager*. New York: Holt, Rinehart and Winston, 1974.

Bruner, J. S. *The process of education*. New York: Vintage, 1963.

Buede, D., & Peterson, C. *An application of cost-benefit analysis to the USMC program objectives memorandum (POM)* (Technical Rep. TR 77-8-72). McLean, Va.: Decisions and Designs, Inc., 1977.

Bursk, E., & Chapman, J. *New decision making tools for managers*. Cambridge, Mass.: Harvard University Press, 1963.

Daly, J., & Davies, T. *The early warning and monitoring system: A progress report* (Interim Technical Rep. PR 78-17-39). McLean, Va.: Decisions and Designs, Inc., 1978.

Davis, G. *Management information systems*. New York: McGraw-Hill, 1974.

Edwards, W., & Tversky, A. (Eds.). *Decision making*. Baltimore: Penguin, 1967.

Fischhoff, B. *Decision analysis: Clinical art or clinical science?* Eugene, Ore.: Decision Research, 1977.

Graves, D., & Lethbridge, D. Could decision analysis have saved Hamlet? *Journal of Management Studies*, 1975, *12* 216-224.

Hays, M., & O'Connor, M. Relating promised performance to military worth: An evaluating mechanism. *Defense Management Journal*, 1977, *13* (4), 36-46.

Howard, R. Decision analysis: Applied decision theory. In *Proceedings of the Fourth International Conference on Operational Research*. New York: John Wiley, 1966.

Janis, I., & Mann, L. *Decision making*. New York: Free Press, 1977.

Johnson, E., & Huber, G. The technology of utility assessment. *IEEE Transactions on Systems, Man, and Cybernetics*, 1977, *7*, 311-325.

Kelly, C., & Stewart, R. *The decision template concept* (Technical Rep.). McLean, Va.: Decisions and Designs, Inc., 1977.

Lindley, D. *Making decisions*. London: John Wiley, 1971.

Luce, D., & Raiffa, H. *Games and decisions*. New York: John Wiley, 1957.

Magee, J. Decision trees for decision making. *Harvard Business Review*, 1964, *42* (4), 126-138.

O'Neil, H. F., Jr. (Ed.). *Learning strategies*. New York: Academic Press, 1978.

Pearl, J. A framework for processing value judgments. *IEEE Transactions on Systems, Man, and Cybernetics*, 1977, *7*, 349-354.

Phillips, L. *Bayesian statistics for social scientists*. New York: Thomas Y. Crowell, 1974.

Roberts, N. Teaching dynamic feedback systems thinking: An elementary view. *Management Science*, 1978, *24*, 836-843.

Selvidge, J. *Rapid screening of decision options* (Technical Rep.). McLean, Va.: Decisions and Designs, Inc., 1976.

Slovic, P. From Shakespeare to Simon: Speculations—and some evidence—about man's ability to process information. *Oregon Research Institute Monographs*, 1972, *12* (12).

Slovic, P., Fischhoff, B., & Lichtenstein, S. Behavioral decision theory. *Annual Review of Psychology*, 1977, *28*, 1-39.

Smith, H. Problems of a problem solver. *New York Times* (Sunday magazine), January 8, 1978, pp. 30–31.

Townsend, R. *Up the organization*. Greenwich, Ct.: Fawcett, 1970.

Ulvila, J., Brown, R., & Packard, K. A case in on-line decision analysis for product planning. *Decision Sciences,* 1977, *8,* 598–615.

Watson, S., & Brown, R. The valuation of decision analysis. *The Journal of the Royal Statistical Society, Series A,* 1978, *141,* 69–78.

White, D. *Decision methodology*. London: Wiley, 1975.

11

Developing Literacy and Learning Strategies in Organizational Settings[1]

THOMAS G. STICHT

The acquisition of literacy includes the development of processes for recognizing and producing written language, the learning of vocabulary and conceptual knowledge, techniques for comprehending sentences and larger segments of discourse, and various strategies for learning using written materials. Though much of the current research on learning strategies is concerned with the latter aspect of literacy (O'Neil, 1978; and elsewhere in this volume), the present chapter discusses research aimed at the development of all aspects of literacy.

This research has been conducted within the context of organizational development, the goal of which is to increase the overall health and effectiveness of organizations (Schein, 1970). Because most research on learning strategies has focused on improving **individual** effectiveness rather than **organizational** effectiveness, approaches for improving organizational effectiveness that involve improved selection and classification of individuals into positions that suit their skill levels, or the redesign of jobs and job training programs to reduce demands on literacy and other learning skills have not been considered. Attention has been given neither to the cost-effectiveness of organizational programs to improve learning, through literacy or other learning strategies training, nor to the consideration or organizational structures and functions that must be developed to implement and sustain support for literacy or other programs for improving learning skills.

[1] The findings and opinions expressed in this report do not necessarily reflect the position or policy of the National Institute of Education or the U.S. Department of Health, Education and Welfare. The research reported herein was conducted while the author was a staff member of the Human Resources Research Organization, Western Division, Monterey, California.

The present research has as its general goal the improvement of organizational effectiveness through a better understanding of the nature of literacy, how literacy skills are involved in organizational effectiveness, and how organizations may develop cost-effective methods for accommodating people whose literacy skills are lower than the minimal standards the organization generally sets for itself.

The concern for literacy development in organizational settings arises from a variety of circumstances. For one thing, it is now clear that, although more and more people are completing high school in our nation, many high school graduates are not highly skilled in literacy. Standardized test results from national norming studies indicate that some 15 to 30% of twelfth-grade students read below the ninth-grade level (Fisher, 1978). In a sample of over 5000 non-high school graduates who applied for Navy duty, Duffy (1976) found that 14% read below the eighth-grade level, whereas 10% of some 12,000 high school graduates scored below the eighth-grade level in reading. It seems clear, then, that for the foreseeable future substantial numbers of high school graduates and dropouts will reach adulthood in need of further literacy development at fairly basic levels.

It seems equally certain that various organizations will have to accommodate these less capable members of the young adult population. For instance, open admission policies at 2- and 4-year colleges rule out the option of screening out persons who do not have the minimum literacy skills traditionally thought necessary for accomplishing college-level study. Hence research to find effective means for developing fundamental literacy skills within the organizational setting of institutions of higher learning is needed (Rouche & Snow, 1977).

Demographic data, too, indicate the need for research to understand how organizations can effectively utilize and develop less literate persons. Population figures predict a reduction in the population of people aged 18 to 24 from 13% in 1975 to 8% in 1995 (Canter, 1978). Thus organizations that draw on this age group for their student or work force will have to compete for recruits from a shrinking pool. A successful approach to literacy development within the organizational setting would add to organizational effectiveness in the recruitment function by reducing entry-level literacy requirements, hence increasing the number of people in the population pool qualified for recruitment into the organization.

DEVELOPING LITERACY IN ORGANIZATIONAL SETTINGS: A CASE STUDY IN THE DEPARTMENT OF DEFENSE

One major organization that is concerned with literacy is the Department of Defense. A United States General Accounting Office report cites

Army data showing that about 20% of some 38,000 recruits tested between January 1 and March 31 of 1976 read below the seventh-grade level (General Accounting Office, 1977).

This same report goes on to say:

> Military services data indicate some enlisted personnel have reading abilities below the written material they are expected to use during their careers. This problem is not new to the services, and a continued flow of recruits with low reading ability is predicted. When compared to the normal recruit population, poor readers tend to
> —have higher discharge rates,
> —experience more difficulty in training,
> —perform less satisfactorily on the the job, and
> —lack the potential for career development.
> The Secretary of Defense needs to develop a policy to effectively address the illiteracy problem.

The General Accounting Office's recommendation that the Secretary of Defense develop a policy with regard to literacy and illiteracy is based upon considerable research conducted by the various branches of the armed services. Much of this research is reviewed in Sticht and Zapf (1976). That review indicates that the policy of the Department of Defense with respect to problems of illiteracy has been (a) to avoid them when possible by raising entry level aptitude scores so that the less able applicants for service are screened out, and (b) when it has not been possible to avoid the problem, to implement brief, 6–12-week long courses of remedial literacy. The latter response has been and is still the typical approach to literacy problems of personnel in the military. This is so despite the repeated demonstration that such training generally has little effect either on literacy skill improvement or on any of several indicators of job proficiency. In this regard, the armed services are in the same situation as civilian organizations that typically attempt to resolve long-lived literacy problems with short-lived literacy programs (Ryan & Furlong, 1975).

Taking cognizance of the repeated failure of brief, one-shot, "general" literacy programs in improving either literacy or job performance, the present research on organizational development was undertaken to better understand the Department of Defense as a setting in which literacy skills are used, to understand the types of literacy tasks personnel perform, and to determine the feasibility of developing a literacy development **system,** rather than a brief, temporary program, that would make possible the development of literacy skills **and** job technical skills in a cost-effective manner. The latter requires that attention be given to the three major subsystems that comprise the armed services' human resources development capability: the job technical training system, the general education (including remedial literacy) system, and the counseling system. These three components must interact in such a way that sustained attention can be given to the development of literacy skills at various stages of a person's career progression.

The research described below begins with an overview of a career development system that, though not exactly the same in the three services studied (i.e., the Army, Air Force, and Navy), nonetheless provides a generalized framework for understanding the setting for literacy development in the armed services. Within the context of the discussion of this career development system, research conducted within the Navy setting will be discussed that indicates the extent to which literacy tasks are performed at various career progression stages.

Following the overview of the military career development system, with information regarding general literacy demands of the system, research to identify literacy tasks in greater detail will be discussed. This research is concerned with the problem of developing a job analysis tool, in the form of a job reading task inventory, that can be used to identify the literacy tasks performed in various jobs and indicate the general level of literacy skill needed to perform the various tasks in a job. Such an instrument would be useful for more accurately setting selection criteria and for developing literacy training objectives that match the literacy requirements of jobs. The present chapter discusses only the analyses that went into the development of the inventory, not the inventory itself. Exploratory research on the inventory is reported in Sticht, Fox, Hauke, and Zapf (1977a).

Next, research for the Army and Air Force is discussed that aims to develop literacy training that incorporates job technical training concepts and vocabulary and tasks performed while reading on the job. This research represents an attempt to demonstrate that job literacy and technical skills training can be integrated into a single training program. This research shows that brief, separate literacy programs that identify their students as "remedial" can be replaced with a continuous job technical skills training program that permits less literate students to spend time developing literacy skills within the job technical skills training context. This research is conducted in two parts. First, research to develop literacy programs for the Army and Air Force that are job-related, but separate, 6-week programs, like traditional literacy programs, is discussed. This research demonstrates the feasibility of incorporating job reading requirements into literacy training. The second part of the literacy program development research shows how literacy and job technical skills training can be accomplished at the same site and within the same training day with no exta training costs. This demonstrates, in an admittedly small-scale project, how technical skills training can incorporate literacy and learning strategies training in a more cost-effective program of human resources development than is currently in place in the services.

In summary, this chapter presents an overview of the career development system of the Department of Defense, an indication of the general and specific literacy tasks encountered in military jobs in the Navy, and the development of literacy and learning strategies training programs that are integral parts of the career development, job technical training system, rather than separate "add-ons" to the training system that stigmatize participants and add unnecessarily to the training time and costs of the organization.

THE CAREER DEVELOPMENT SYSTEM
IN THE DEPARTMENT OF DEFENSE

Figure 11.1 presents a general conceptualizaton of the components of the career development systems of the armed services. Three major subsystems are involved: the general education system, the job skills training system, and the career counseling system. Within the general education system, the various programs of remedial literacy training are of special interest for this report. To develop a more effective literacy development system, it is necessary to understand these three major subsystems and to identify any existing formal or informal linkages between these subsystems that might be used to facilitate the integration of job skills and literacy skills training.

Research to understand these three subsystems within the U.S. Navy was conducted in 1976–1977 (Sticht *et al.,* 1977a, 1977b) and will be summarizd here. Although the specific findings are limited to the Navy context, the general approach and some findings are also applicable to the Air Force

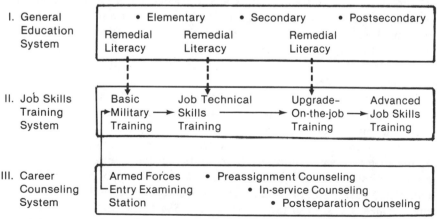

Figure 11.1 A generalized overview of the career development system of the Department of Defense.

and Army. Information concerning these career development subsystems was obtained via site visits to Navy training centers, interviews with cognizant Navy and civilian training personnel, and review of relevant Navy and civilian documents.

Job Skills Training System

The Navy's job skills training system closely follows that illustrated in Figure 11.1. Briefly, Navy enlisted personnel are selected into the Navy based on the results of mental and physical examinations administered at the Armed Forces Entrance and Examination Stations. Upon induction, these personnel proceed through a series of training programs—basic military training and job technical skills training—before being assigned to their first tour of duty. During their initial duty assignment, new personnel receive on-the-job training under the direction of their work supervisor, as part of their regular work assignment. After mastering an entry-level job, a person is eligible for advanced job training, generally provided as a reenlistment incentive by the Navy. Upon completion of that training, the person returns to the regular work force and continues in the training–work cycle until career termination.

A major reason for studying the job skills training system is to identify where reading requirements, as imposed by some career activity, might act as a barrier to career advancement. Review of appropriate Navy policy and training documents indicated that, with the exception of promotion from the first pay level to the second, all further advancement stages have substantial reading requirements. In fact, as soon as a person applies to enter the Navy, a formidable literacy skill requirement is faced in the form of the aptitude testing that occurs at the Armed Forces Entrance and Examination Station. Since most aptitude tests are paper-and-pencil tests, the person's literacy skills have a direct effect on ability to demonstrate "true" aptitude. Performance on these tests has a lasting importance, in that the scores obtained are used to determine initial and future career and job training assignments.

In the first formal Navy assignment, basic military training, the new recruit again faces a formidable literacy-skills requirement in the form of taking lecture notes, studying them, and studying the *Basic Military Requirements Manual* and *Bluejacket's Manual* in preparation for taking the four paper-and-pencil multiple-choice tests that must be passed in order to complete basic military training. Interviews with Navy personnel who had completed basic military training and with students currently in basic training revealed that 35% of the graduates and 5% of the students reported experiencing some reading problems. Students reported spending a medium of 1.1 hours reading and .5 hours writing per day. This is considerably less time spent in literacy activities than is typical of job technical skills training, and a little less than the time spent in performing literacy tasks on the job in permanent duty status (see Table 11.1).

Upon successful completion of basic military training, the recruit is assigned to job technical skills training, where again extensive use is made of literacy skills. Observation of 10 technical training schools indicated that these schools rely heavily on the lecture–note-taking–text-reading–written-test-taking procedures of training. This is indicated in Table 11.1, where it is seen that 4.5 hours were reported to have been spent reading and writing in job technical training, though this figure may be inflated somewhat because it was not possible to determine clearly whether the time spent reading included reading what one has written (as, for example, on a form). In some schools, estimates of time spent in reading only, not writing, were as high as 5 or more hours. These schools make heavy use of programmed texts. Clearly, the training at this stage of a person's career relies heavily upon the person's ability to obtain and demonstrate attainment of knowledge through the use of literacy skills. In this regard, some 56% of students interviewed reported having some problems understanding (reading) the materials used in job technical skills training.

Once an enlisted person is permanently assigned to a duty station, the next series of major literacy skill requirements, in reference to formal career advancement, occurs either when one prepares for advancement to the next pay level or when one is sent for advanced training in a job skills area. The Navy makes extensive use of correspondence courses that personnel must complete to be promoted from one pay–skill level to the next. Altogether, five correspondence courses may be required after job technical skills school. Over a third of personnel interviewed reported having some difficulty understanding the correspondence course materials. In fact, 73% of technical school instructors indicated they had difficulty with their correspondence courses. Table 11.1 indicates that, when job in-

TABLE 11.1
Average Number of Hours Spent Reading and Writing in Navy Job Training and Performance Activities

	Basic military training	Job skills technical training	Duty station	
			Doing a job	Correspondence courses
Reading	1.1	2.0	1.8	1.6
Writing	.5	2.5	.5	—
Total	1.6	4.5	2.3	1.6

cumbents were studying their correspondence courses, they spent, as a rough approximation, about 1.6 hours in study per day. This typically extended for 4.5 weeks.

This general survey indicates that the Navy's job training system raises numerous barriers that require literacy skills if they are to be hurdled. I will take a closer, more detailed look at the types of reading and learning tasks performed in this system later on. Next, however, I will discuss the Navy's general educational development system and indicate relations (or lack thereof) with the job skills training system.

General Education Development System

Paralleling the job skills training system is the general educational development system, which is supposed to provide military personnel with opportunities for personal growth and development in general education. For present purposes we may consider this system to be composed of two major components: (*a*) remedial literacy training, which is offered during duty hours, and (*b*) off-duty general education programs.

As Figure 11.1 indicates, all services offer remedial literacy training prior to basic military training. Formal policy linkages exist between the job skills training system and the education system at this point. Regulations require that personnel having trouble in job skills training because of poor literacy skills must attend remedial reading training. The aim of the literacy training in the Army and Navy is to raise recruit reading levels to the fifth grade; the Air Force attempts to increase reading levels to the sixth grade.

Presently, only the Army offers remedial literacy training after basic military training and before job technical skills training, though the Navy is currently developing such a program. Unlike the Army program, which is linked only by policy to job skills training, the Navy's program will be both policy- and content-linked to the job technical skills training program and will aim to provide job-related literacy skills to prepare personnel for job technical skills training.

Both the Army and the Air Force have a formal policy requirement for remedial literacy training to be given to permanent duty personnel. Air Force regulations require that all personnel who score below 50 on the Airman Qualifying Examination and below the 9 reading grade level on a standardized test be enrolled in a reading improvement course concurrent with job skills upgrade training. (The latter is a correspondence course designed to prepare personnel for the next higher level of job skills and duties.) The regulations also permit other personnel identified as having reading problems on the job or in the upgrade training to be assigned to the reading training program. The objective of the reading training is the achievement of a 9 reading grade level. The Army policy permits development of reading programs for personnel reading below the twelfth-grade level, but this is not a required activity. Thus, the Air Force is the only service that has a formal policy requirement for literacy assessment and training beyond the entry stages of a person's military career. Presently, the Air Force is attempting to establish content linkages between the duty station literacy training and the job skills training system by providing job-related reading for duty station personnel. The Air Force program will be discussed in greater detail below.

Outside the remedial literacy training programs, there is very little relation between the off-duty education program and job technical training. In the Navy, policy requires that personnel receive educational counseling within 30 days of their arrival at a new duty station. However, discussion with education staff indicated that there is not close adherence to this policy. Other than this limited policy, there seem to be no other formal Navy policy-imposed linkages between the job skills training and the education system. This lack of linkage was confirmed in interviews with Navy job performers, where it was found that over 90% had never participated in off-duty education.

Survey of Army and Air Force regulations and cognizant persons revealed the same lack of linkage between the general education and job skills training systems. In general, the education system provides opportunities for post secondary and some secondary education, leaning toward obtainment of academic degrees, and is not viewed as of direct importance to the improvement of job skills, though presumably it is expected to contribute to career development broadly construed. Whether and in what ways it might do so is yet to be determined.

Career Counseling System

Information about career counseling within the Navy system was obtained from a study by Meshi, Holoter, Dow, and Grace (1972) and by interviews with counseling personnel at one Navy training center. As indicated in Figure 11.1, Navy career counselors operate within the context of three career phases: (*a*) preassignment contacts; (*b*) in-service counseling; and (*c*) postseparation counseling. In the preassignment contacts at the Armed Forces Examination Stations and during basic military training counseling personnel (*a*) acquaint civilians with careers in the Navy, as part of the recruitment function; (*b*) administer and interpret selection and classification tests; and (*c*) initiate the recruit's Navy career by assignment to an entry-level job skills training program. It was learned in interviews that, typically, recruits receive only about 10 minutes of career counseling in basic military training, during which test scores are explained and job assignments are offered and accepted.

In in-service counseling, personnel are supposed to be kept informed of occupational and educational opportunities. However, as noted above, the fact that some 90% of the Navy personnel we interviewed do not get involved in off-duty education suggests that education counseling could be improved. We obtained no information regarding the efficacy of the occupational in-service counseling or of the effectiveness of the postseparation counseling.

Summary of the Career Development System Survey

The following conclusions can be drawn from this survey:

1. There are many occasions in the job technical skills training program where heavy demands are made on literacy skills, and hence undereducated persons may encounter formidable barriers to career advancement.

2. The general education system seems to be poorly linked, in either policy or content, to the job skills technical training component, and is only loosely related to the career counseling system. Remedial literacy training available through the education system has offered general literacy training rather than literacy training focused directly upon the types of literacy tasks people will encounter in job training and on the job. This situation is being modified somewhat, with the Navy currently developing a job-related literacy program to be offered between basic military training and job skills training, and the Air Force has field-tested the job-related reading program for duty station personnel, to be discussed later in this chapter.

3. The career counseling system of the Navy has formal policy linkages to the job skills training system and acts in an interacting manner with that system early in a recruit's career by conducting screening and classification testing and career assignment activities. However, education counseling, which links the education and counseling systems, is apparently not too effective, as witnessed by the fact that fewer than 10% of the Navy personnel interviewed utilize the off-duty education programs.

IDENTIFICATION OF JOB READING TASKS

The research reviewed above clearly shows the importance of reading in job training programs and in job performance in the Department of Defense. However, a more precise determination of reading demands of jobs is required if we are actually to design and develop a job-related literacy training system as an integral part of a comprehensive program of human resources development within the military setting. For the latter purpose, we would like to know what the reading tasks people have to perform in various jobs are, and what level of skill is needed to perform those tasks.

In research of an exploratory nature for the Navy, we attempted to develop an inventory for job analysts that they could use to (a) identify the reading tasks people perform in various jobs, and (b) determine the percentage of people reading at various skill levels (expressed in reading grade levels) who could be expected to perform the job reading task accurately (Sticht *et al.*, 1977a). This research involved the study of two major classes of reading tasks. One category of tasks involves reading to look up information that can be applied and then forgotten. This we call a *reading-to-do* task. The second category of reading task is one in which the information read must be learned for later use, such as passing an examination. This type of task we call a *reading-to-learn* task.

Information about reading-to-do and reading-to-learn tasks was obtained in structured interviews of 1.5–2 hours' duration with 178 Navy personnel drawn from three phases of the Navy's training system: students in job skill training schools ($N = 68$), active job incumbents ($N = 78$), and instructors in training schools ($N = 32$). In the interviews, respondents were asked to report two instances in which they had been doing some job task or school assignment in which they had to perform a reading subtask. One instance was to be of a reading-to-do subtask and one of a reading-to-learn subtask. When respondents said they had performed one or the other reading task, they were asked to obain the material they had read, to indicate the exact portion they had read, and to tell the interviewer exactly what kind of information was being sought. The interviewer obtained copies of all materials the personnel reported reading and noted the types of information needs the personnel had in mind when they used the reading materials. The latter formed the basis for developing job reading task tests in which the test questions were made up of the types of questions the personnel sought to answer by reading their job materials.

Reading-to-Do

Analysis of reading-to-do tasks identified in the structured interviews included first noting what type of search strategy personnel used when they showed the interviewer the exact section of material they read in a manual. Interest here was on the respondents' use of either the table of contents, the index, or a "flipping through" strategy for locating information. Efficient use of such strategies is important in job performance tasks in which reading of reference manuals to locate specific information is necessary. In addition to noting which strategy personnel used, the interviewers also rated the skill with which the strategy was applied, using a simple high, medium, or low judgment, with a bias toward leniency.

Results showed that tables of contents and indexes were used for only about 25% of the tasks for which they were applicable (some tasks involved single sheets for which no search strategy was necessary). Leafing or flipping through was used more than 90% of the time, occasionally in conjunction with the use of the table of contents or index. Overall, skill ratings were high, though some 10% were judged to have been performed with a low level of skill.

The reading-to-do tasks were analyzed to determine the specific types of information personnel sought in the materials and to identify the types of materials used. Altogether 186 reading-to-do tasks were identified. Interviewers obtained photocopies or originals of the exact materials people reported reading and reports of the type of information people were looking for. To identify what kinds of skills these reading tasks called for, the analysis procedures given in Figure 11.2 were followed. First, the reading tasks were sorted into three job clusters made up of the 10 jobs that were included in the survey. In general, the *Service maintenance* cluster contains electronics and other higher-skilled jobs; the *Technical maintenance* cluster contains lower-skill-level maintenance jobs; and the *Data-oriented* cluster contains administrative and supply jobs.

Having sorted materials by job clusters, the next step was to identify (*a*) the type of information sought in performing each task, and (*b*) the type of display in the reading materials, classified as either *text,* which would be written language; *figures,* including line drawings, photographs, schematic

---

1. The jobs were grouped into three job clusters:

Service maintenance	Technical maintenance	Data-oriented

2. The reading tasks within each job cluster were classified by the type of information sought:

Fact finding	Following directions

3. Within the above classification, the reading tasks were further classified by the type of reading materials:

Text	Figures	Tables
Text plus figures	Text plus tables	Figures plus tables

Figure 11.2 Procedures for analyzing Navy reading tasks.

diagrams, etc.; *tables,* including both numerical and verbal tabulations; *texts plus figures; texts plus tables;* and *tables plus figures.*

This analysis revealed that the type of information sought was usually some type of factual data, or the person was trying to find out how to do something. Thus, categories of skills called *fact finding* and *following directions* were identified. Using these definitions, three raters sorted the 186 reading-to-do tasks into one or the other of these two skill classifications. Initial interrater agreement was 70–80%, and was raised to 100% agreement in group discussions.

Table 11.2 shows the results of the classification analysis for instructors, students, and job incumbents in each of the job clusters. Most tasks were classified as fact-finding. Instructors and job performers used fact-finding skills two to four times more than following-directions skills, whereas students used following-directions skills much more than fact-finding skills, except in the data cluster.

The final analysis sorted the reading-to-do task materials into the six display categories of Figure 11.2. Initial agreement among raters ranged from 80 to 100% across job clusters, with the average agreement being 90%. Discussion among raters resulted in the classifications shown in Table 11.3. As indicated, reading tasks requiring either fact-finding or following-directions skills applied to the six display types were found in all of the jobs studied. Clearly, literacy tasks are not restricted to the use of text only. In many cases, both text and figures are used together. In fact, for all 325 reading tasks identified as reading-to-do and reading-to-learn in the Navy research, only 32% of the tasks involved reading textual materials only; 25% involved only the use of figures; and 37% involved reading and using both text and figures. This would suggest that research on reading comprehension and learning strategies ought to include more studies of texts and figures in combination.

It should also be noted in Table 11.3 that personnel reportedly used tables as well as figures at times for following directions. They did this even though the displays were not designed to provide directions. Rather, the

TABLE 11.2
Number of Fact-Finding (FF) and Following-Directions (FD) Tasks in Three Navy Job Clusters Reported by Instructors, Students, and Job Incumbents

Job clusters	Instructors		Students		Job incumbents		Total	
	FF	FD	FF	FD	FF	FD	FF	FD
Service maintenance	5	2	4	11	26	13	35	26
Technical maintenance	14	2	2	16	18	20	34	38
Data-oriented	4	2	10	6	27	4	41	12
Total	23	6	16	33	71	37	110	76

reader knew some of the steps to be taken in some tasks and figured out what to do next by examining tables or figures. Thus, it is not possible from analysis of materials alone to know what reading task that material may serve. This means that approaches to determining the reading difficulty of materials such as traditional readability formulas, which use only one type of comprehension criterion in scaling the reading level of materials, do not give a complete accounting of the types of tasks that the material may be involved in. Hence, the readability approach is not completely valid as an indicator of the reading requirements of materials.

It should also be noted in Table 11.3 that the combination of table plus figure did not occur very often. Apparently, tables and figures are used more to complement text than each other. Further research along this line might reveal interesting information about the use of representations (textual, figural, tabular) for various functions, including the complementary or coordinated use of display types for various problem-solving purposes. For instance, it might be useful to designers of textbooks to understand why figures and tables are used in a complementary fashion with textual materials in certain situations, but alone or (rarely) as complementary to one another in other situations. Presumably the designer uses these different forms of representing information in different combinations to permit the reader to solve some problem in an effective manner. I have not seen a detailed analysis of the use of such representations for well-defined purposes.

The foregoing analyses answer the question, What are the reading tasks personnel have to perform in various Navy jobs? They look up facts in texts; they look up directions in texts; they look up facts in figures; they follow directions using figures, etc. In the design of the job-related reading

TABLE 11.3
Number of Different Types of Job Reading Materials and Tasks in Three Navy Job Clusters

| Reading material | Job clusters | | | | | | | |
| | Service maintenance | | Technical maintenance | | Data-oriented | | Total | |
	FF[a]	FD	FF	FD	FF	FD	FF	FD
Text	16	25	24	33	25	11	65	69
Figures–forms	26	12	31	25	15	6	72	43
Tables	7	10	12	6	20	2	39	18
Text plus figures	5	9	14	9	6	3	25	21
Text plus tables	0	7	1	1	7	1	8	9
Tables plus figures	1	0	0	0	3	0	4	0
Total	55	63	82	74	76	23	213	160

[a] FF = fact finding; FD = following directions.

programs to be discussed, practice in performing these types of tasks was required so that skill in reading-to-do might be developed.

Reading-to-Learn

In the interviews with Navy personnel, students in job skills training programs reported performing reading-to-do and reading-to-learn tasks to about the same extent, whereas job performers reported three times as many reading-to-do tasks as reading-to-learn tasks. Thus, as might be expected, reading-to-learn is a more characteristic task for students than for job incumbents. Since reading-to-learn requires very complex learning strategies and reading-to-do does not, it appears that job training programs may require a greater degree of literacy skill than actual job performance requires. Literacy training that aims to prepare students to perform the reading-to-learn tasks involved in job technical skills training must involve the teaching of strategies for learning from textual, figural, and tabular materials.

To understand better the ways in which personnel go about learning when performing a reading-to-learn task, respondents in the Navy study were asked if they could recall any particular activity that had helped them learn the information in a reading-to-learn task. Table 11.4 shows the

TABLE 11.4
Learning Strategies Reported for Reading-to-learn Tasks

Learning strategy	Study technique	Number
Reread–Rehearse	Reread–repeat	34
(R–R)	Memorize by repetition	7
	Preview, then read	4
	Copy verbatim in writing	2
	Record on tape, listen to tape	1
	Teach to someone	1
		49 (34%)
Problem-solve–	Practice problems	21
Question (P–Q)	Check problems against book	8
	Take test–answer questions	7
	Review questions–answers in text	6
	Use study guides	1
		43 (30%)
Relate–Associate	Use pictures–diagrams and relate to text	15
(R–A)	Discuss with someone	4
	Associate to other information	3
	Listen to lecture	3
	Use mnemonic device	2

(continued)

TABLE 11.4 (Cont.)

Learning strategy	Study technique	Number
	Make drawings	2
	Use other reference materials	1
	Watch demonstration	1
	Relate notes and book	1
	Relate to previous work	1
		33 (23%)
Focus attention	Take notes–study notes	12
(FA)	Pick out key points	3
	Use outline	1
	Underline	1
	Use study schedule	1
		18 (13%)
Grand total		143 (100%)

various learning activities reported for 143 reading-to-learn tasks. The various activities are grouped within four general learning strategies:

1. *Reread–Rehearse (R–R):* Involves repeating the processing of information taken from text, with minimal elaborations or transformations
2. *Problem-solve–Questions (P–O):* Involves answering text questions, solving problems in texts, and performing tasks that stimulate a search through materials to obtain specific answers
3. *Relate–Associate (R–A):* Involves use of mnemonics, discussion of materials, associations of new information with other information, and elaborations.
4. *Focus attention (FA):* Involves activities that reduce the amount of information in some manner: underlining key points, outlining, taking notes

As shown in Table 11.4, the reread–rehearse strategy was reported most frequently, accounting for 34% of the total responses. The focus-attention strategy was reported least frequently, accounting for only 13% of responses.

Those outcomes were obtained by asking personnel to recall how they had learned a specific reading-to-learn task. In another approach to understanding learning strategies used by Navy personnel, they were asked to complete a checklist indicating the frequency with which they used various study methods. Table 11.5 lists those techniques, categorized under the four learning strategies defined above. As shown, the "read material over" strategy was rated as being used frequently by 60% of the personnel.

TABLE 11.5
Frequency of Use of Learning Strategies by Navy Personnel (*N* = 144)

Strategy-technique	Frequency (in percentage)		
	Almost never	Occasionally	Frequently
Reread–Rehearse (R–R)			
Scan material before studying	15	42	43
Try to memorize	28	26	46
Read material over	7	33	60
Problem-solve–Question (P–Q)			
Ask self questions	20	34	46
Relate–Associate (R–A)			
Draw pictures	38	36	26
Use dictionary	37	37	26
Focus attention (FA)			
Make outline	50	32	18
Underline important parts	18	25	57
Take notes	23	31	46

However, contrary to the earlier findings, the "underline important parts" strategy was highly rated, being used frequently 57% of the time.

It is not clear why the underline activity was rated high when personnel were asked to tell how frequently they used study strategies and very low when people told how they learned in a specific reading-to-learn task. But regardless of these differences, which are of importance only in cases where normative data are being sought about the frequencies with which various learning strategies are used, a major point of interest with regard to Tables 11.4 and 11.5 is that Table 11.4 contains a wide range of activities that people said helped them learn, whereas Table 11.5 contains only nine such activities. Many studies on learning strategies have used relatively restricted categories of activities, like those of Table 11.5, to identify the types of learning strategies people use (Dansereau, Actkinson, Long & McDonald, 1974). The data of Table 11.4 suggest that people use a wide range of activities to help them learn what they have read, including non-text-related activities like talking with someone, listening to a related lecture, or watching a demonstration. It seems that there is a fruitful field of investigation in understanding the "ecology" of naturally occurring strategies that people develop for coping with learning tasks.

An indication of the types of learning strategies that people may develop for coping with system-imposed learning tasks was obtained in research to develop a job-related reading program for the Air Force (Huff, Sticht, Joyner, Groff, & Burkett, 1977). In this research an attempt was made to determine whether there were certain learning strategies that distinguished personnel who were successful in completing their career development courses from those who were unsuccessful. Career development courses are self-study correspondence courses given to permanent duty personnel as part of their upgrade training. Typically, a course consists of three or four volumes. Each volume contains a series of chapters composed of specific objectives, followed by narrative text and then a series of questions, chapter review exercises, to guide the student's study. At the completion of each volume, the student completes a volume review exercise, which is an open-book multiple-choice exercise on the information in the volume.

Eighteen Air Force personnel who had successfully completed their correspondence courses and nineteen who had failed their courses at least once and had not completed a career development course at the time of the study were interviewed to find out their learning strategy by their responses to a question designed to identify the sequence of study activities engaged in. Table 11.6 lists the alternative responses available to the students, ranked in terms of decreasing study time likely to be required by the use of that study sequence.

As indicated, both the successful and unsuccessful group frequencies are nearly identical for the first four study sequences. The last two sequences show some interesting results. Seven of the successful but only two of the unsuccessful students concentrated on the parts of the volume necessary to answer the volume review exercises. This is the most efficient method simply to get by the hurdle of course requirements. It appears that the successful students were able to perceive this fact and adjust their study habits

TABLE 11.6
Study Sequences Used by Air Force Students Who Were Either Successful or Unsuccessful in Completing Correspondence Courses

	Students	
Study sequence	Successful	Unsuccessful
Preview volume, then read word for word, complete CREs[a] and VREs[b] (ECI prescribed approach)	6	6
Preview volume, read word for word, complete VREs	2	2
Read only parts of volumes necessary to answer CRE and VREs	2	3
Skim through volume, then read only parts necessary to answer VREs	1	2
Read only parts of volume necessary to answer VREs	7	2
Do not study or do not read	0	4
Total students	18	19

[a] CRE = Chapter review exercises.
[b] VRE = Volume review exercises.

to achieve this goal. This interpretation is supported by research in which students estimated the number of final course examination questions that came from the volume review exercise questions. About two-thirds of the successful students, compared with only one-third of unsuccessful students, estimated that 90% of course examination questions were taken from volume review exercise questions. In actuality, in the administration career field, 100% of final course examination questions are taken from the volume review exercises, whereas in the aircraft maintenance career field this percentage ranges from 70 to 90%.

This limited study suggests that learning strategies can and will be developed to expedite the passing of a perceived barrier to career advancement. Many personnel perceive much of the correspondence course work as a contrived barrier and not a useful source of job information. This was indicated by the fact that only 2 of the 37 Air Force personnel interviewed said that they got most of their job knowledge from career development courses (these were two unsuccessful students!) A large majority reported acquiring most of their job knowledge through job experience. Navy job performers also spoke disparagingly about job training correspondence courses, saying that some 70% of what was studied was needed to pass the tests, whereas only 50% needed to be learned to perform specific job activities. Whether or not these Air Force and Navy personnel are reacting to the fact that training programs must frequently teach more than what is required to perform at any one job site, since exact duties may differ from locale to locale, is not known. However, the fact that personnel perceive the training requirements to be relatively unimportant to their job performance suggests the need for careful review of course requirements to ensure that there are not artificial requirements for career progression. The fact that 4 of 19 Air Force personnel who did not successfully complete career development courses had not read the materials (Table 11.6) suggests a need for a more adequate counseling system to explain the importance of upgrade skill training in the person's career development. A necessary condition for the application of strategies for learning from text materials is that the text materials be picked up, opened, and examined. If these activities do not occur, there is not much need to worry about whether or not the person uses elaborative encoding, mnemonics, preview–review, or other learning strategies. The first goal must be to bring the person into contact with the materials to be learned.

On the other hand, data from Table 11.6 also indicate that successful and unsuccessful students **did** use the same study strategies to a large extent, but not with the same successful outcomes. Why this is so is not certain, though seven of the unsuccessful students stated they had reading (vocabulary, comprehension, difficulty with questions) problems with the materials, whereas none of the successful students reported such problems. It is with such personnel that deliberate literacy and learning strategies training might prove useful. Data reported later on indicate that these students can benefit from such training and that it gives them greater confidence in their ability to read and understand job reading materials.

Discussion and Summary

The research on literacy tasks for job skills training and job performance reported herein has occurred over a long period of time, in separate, unrelated projects for different military sponsors having somewhat different goals for the projects. Hence, our understanding of job reading tasks is still fragmented and limited. A major conceptual problem lies in defining the basic unit of a reading task: Is it the word, the sentence, a paragraph, a paragraph and figure combined, or a subsection of a manual? Is it all of these? Are they used for different purposes? A major methodological problem lies in obtaining a representative sample of reading tasks. This is compounded by the fact that a given material may be used to perform various tasks (learning, doing). This means that materials per se do not define "tasks." But if people's use of materials must be taken into account, then we can never be certain that a new person will not find a new use for an old material—or that a new material may not be given an old but perhaps unexpected use. These problems make it difficult, if not impossible, to establish **the** literacy demands of jobs, as desired by the General Accounting Office (1977) and others (Miller, 1974). Perhaps the best we can do is to come up with various conceptualizations of reading tasks and methodologies for estimating the skill demands of **some** of the possible reading tasks. We can then say that jobs at least have these demands, even if we cannot say what the definitive literacy demands are.

With all its many limits, the research discussed here has provided, I think, certain useful insights about job-related reading tasks:

1. Tasks may be usefully characterized as reading-to-do and reading-to-learn tasks. Inteview results indicate that personnel in training and on the job report these tasks differently, with students reporting reading-to-learn tasks at twice the rate of that of job incumbents.

2. Reading tasks may involve texts, figures, tables, and combinations of these display types. Thus, our understanding of literacy and learning strategies must include combinations of text and figures and text and tables. The combination of figures and tables was found to occur very infrequently, suggesting the need for studies of the use of combinations of display types for various problem-solving purposes.

3. Learning strategies used by personnel in reading-to-learn tasks show a wide variety of activities that enhance learning. These activities can be roughly grouped as rereading or rehearsing, answering questions or solving problems, relating or associating the information with other information, and using techniques for focusing attention, to limit what might have to be reread, perhaps. A better understanding of "ecologically valid" learning strategies might lead to improved methods for facilitating "natural" learning.

4. Interviews with Navy and Air Force personnel indicated that anywhere from 5% to 30% report some difficulty with the reading of and learning from training and job performance materials. This suggests the need for literacy and learning strategies training that could improve personnel skills in the use of job reading materials (see Sticht *et al.,* 1977b, for results of interviews with Navy personnel in which they indicated an interest in and need for job-related literacy training).

DEVELOPMENT OF COST–EFFECTIVE JOB–RELATED LITERACY AND LEARNING STRATEGIES TRAINING PROGRAMS

The study of the career development system of Figure 11.1 indicated that all three military services offer some form of remedial literacy training. In all cases, such training is offered as an add-on to the training sequence. For instance, the Air Force literacy training at entry into the service, which aims to prepare the new recruit for basic military training, is a separate training program of up to 12 weeks' duration. The job-related reading program being developed by the Navy is planned to be presented as a 6-week program between basic military training and job technical skills training. As such, it will add 6 weeks of training time to the training "pipeline" for literacy students.

For any organization, time spent in training counts against productivity, since the trainee is not actively performing a job. It is therefore desirable to keep training time to a minimum. A program of literacy training that adds 6–12 weeks to training costs is in a precarious position, because there is a tendency for management to view the program as an additional cost that should be abolished just as quickly as possible. To avoid the cost of such training, management may choose to screen low literates out of the organization if there is a sufficiently large work force of more highly qualified persons that can be recruited. Although this may solve the organization's problems, the person whose literacy skills are too low for admission into gainful employment within the organization still has a problem, and so does our society at large. It is in the best interest of the individual, the society, and the organization if successful, cost-effective methods for developing literacy skills can be developed.

To develop cost-effective methods for teaching literacy, research was conducted that integrated literacy and job technical skills training such that both types of training were given at the same site during the same training day with no increase in the overall training time. This research is discussed in two phases. The first phase deals with research demonstrating that job-related literacy training can be developed that integrates the teaching of job knowledge and literacy. This research involved the development of two literacy programs, one of which, like traditional literacy programs, was conducted as an add-on to the regular training sequence. The second phase of research to be discussed demonstrated that the job reading training could be integrated into the job technical skills training program without adding to the overall training time.

Development of Two Job-Related Literacy Programs

Two projects attempted to relate job and literacy skills training. One project, conducted for the Army (Sticht, 1975), produced a 6-week, job-oriented literacy training program to be given after basic military training but prior to job technical skills training.

A second project, conducted for the Air Force, produced a job-oriented program for personnel at their duty station. (Huff *et al.,* 1977). This program was attended for 2 hours a day by job incumbents to prepare them for performing job reading tasks and correspondence course training more effectively.

Both the Army and the Air Force programs use materials and content taken directly from job skills training programs and from job manuals and other job performance aids. Instruction in reading and learning of these materials is presented in both programs by means of two curriculum strands.

Strand 1: Reading-to-Do

This strand provides extensive drill and practice in locating and extracting information from job reading materials. The Army program provides practice in six modules: the use of tables of content, indexes, and tables and graphs; looking up information in the body of a manual; following procedural directions; and filling out job forms. The Air Force program, being aimed at a somewhat higher-level reader, deletes the practice in using tables of contents and indexes. Otherwise, it provides training similar to the remaining four modules in the Army program. Again, however, it should be recalled that the actual materials and content differ, and are taken from job reading materials.

Each job reading module is accompanied by a Pre-Proficiency Test (Pre-PT) and a Post-Proficiency Test (Post-PT), which determine eligibility for the module training and mastery in terms of both accuracy and time scores.

Each module consists of source materials and numerous worksheets requiring that the person perform the tasks indicated by the module name. The worksheets were designed to emphasize three factors: structure, content, and difficulty.

A structural worksheet causes the person to notice how an information source–display is put together (e.g., a table may have rows, columns, headings). Specific questions were developed to require the processing of information about structural features.

A content worksheet causes the person to attend to the content of an information display (e.g., a procedural direction worksheet might ask for a person to locate a specific step in a given display).

The difficulty dimension is incorporated into both structural and content worksheets. Essentially, the worksheets start with easy questions and gradually become more difficult, in terms of the information to be presented, or the amount of paraphrasing, which calls for a wider range of vocabulary use by the student.

In essence then, the reading-to-do strand provides extensive practice in applying whatever reading skills a person has to the performance of fact-finding and following-directions tasks involving the types of materials the person will encounter in job skills training or on the job.

Strand II: Reading-for-Learning

The reading-for-learning strand contrasts with the reading-for-doing strand in being concerned with the processing of information for future use, and hence emphasizes the development of learning strategies for learning from written texts. To process information for learning, people must be prepared in at least two ways: They must have the knowledge base that can be brought to bear in comprehending the material to be learned, and they must possess knowledge of skills for studying materials and relating what they read to what they already know.

To promote the acquisition of a relevant knowledge base that would help literacy students learn better from their job training materials, the reading-for-learning curriculum includes specially developed materials written at a lower difficulty level than those encountered in job training and that incorporate the basic concepts and topics within a given job career field.

For the Army program, the basic concepts in six job career clusters were identified through study of job skills training program curriculum guides and consultation with instructors. In each job cluster, 12 major concepts were identified, and specific knowledge objectives were developed for each concept area. Figure 11.3 shows the knowledge objectives for two concept areas in the cook's career field.

For each of the 12 job concepts, a 300–400-word passage was written that included the knowledge objectives for the concept. These passages were written at the seventh- to ninth-grade levels of difficulty, as contrasted to the actual job materials, which are written at the eleventh-grade and above levels.

Similar concept passages and knowledge objectives were developed for two career clusters in the Air Force program. In this case, since higher-ability students were enrolled in the Air Force program, passages were written to be around 1000 words in length and of ninth- and tenth-grade difficulty.

The concept passages were written without the redundancy and elaboration usually needed to explicate concepts in written materials, because in the reading-for-learning activities each student performs repeated readings of the materials and constructs various representations of the messages in

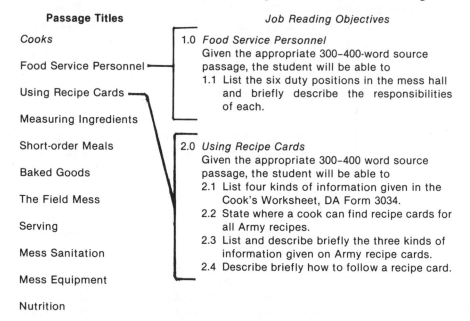

Passage Titles   *Job Reading Objectives*

Cooks

Food Service Personnel

Using Recipe Cards

Measuring Ingredients

Short-order Meals

Baked Goods

The Field Mess

Serving

Mess Sanitation

Mess Equipment

Nutrition

Storing Food Items

1.0 *Food Service Personnel*
Given the appropriate 300–400-word source passage, the student will be able to
1.1 List the six duty positions in the mess hall and briefly describe the responsibilities of each.

2.0 *Using Recipe Cards*
Given the appropriate 300–400 word source passage, the student will be able to
2.1 List four kinds of information given in the Cook's Worksheet, DA Form 3034.
2.2 State where a cook can find recipe cards for all Army recipes.
2.3 List and describe briefly the three kinds of information given on Army recipe cards.
2.4 Describe briefly how to follow a recipe card.

Figure 11.3 An example of the knowledge objectives for the Strand II: Reading-to-learn curriculum in the Army's job-related reading program.

the passages. For instance, in some cases students read the concept passages and then draw pictures of what they have read. In other cases students read the concept passages and produce classification tables or flow charts representing the major concepts presented in the passage. Having transformed concept passages into pictures, classification matrixes, or flow charts, students then discuss their newly developed representations orally, thus producing another representation transformation.

By means of this *representation transformation* process, cognitive elaboration of job concepts is produced, which helps students to gain the job knowledge that can then be used in comprehending job reading materials. At the same time, analytical tools are learned for dissecting written passages and reorganizing them by superordinate and subordinate categories, in the case of classification tables, and by sequential steps and decision branching points in the case of flow charts. These learning strategies help to clarify what written passages are all about and in the process engage the reader in the cognitive elaboration required to acquire the job knowledge.

The instructional method for the reading-for-learning curriculum strand consists of small group work, in contrast to the individual work of the reading-to-do strand as one proceeds through each module. In the reading-to-learn strand, students may work alone or together to produce a representation transformation. In a full day program, such as the Army program, this adds needed variety to the day's activities.

In addition to the representation transformation activities, the reading-to-learn program for the Army includes special instruction in how to analyze sentences into the *main idea* and *more about the main idea*. This instruction was developed for the lower-level Army readers when it was discovered that many of these students had difficulty in figuring out who was doing what to whom or what in many sentences. This type of training was not provided for the more advanced Air Force students.

Evaluation of the Job-Related Reading Programs

Several approaches for evaluating the effectiveness of the job-related reading programs were used. For both the Army and Air Force programs *summative* evaluation data were obtained by pre- and postprogram tests of general reading and job-related reading. *Formative* evaluation data were obtained from the pre- and postmodule proficiency tests of the Strand I: Reading-to-do program. Formative data for the reading-to-learn strand were obtained for Army personnel in a small-scale study in which specially constructed representation transformation tests were administered before and after training in the reading-to-learn activities.

In addition to the direct evaluation of the training effectiveness of the job-related literacy programs described above, the Army program was further evaluated by comparing the summative pre-and posttraining general and job-related reading test data with such data obtained by a group of Army personnel in technical training who had received no literacy training, and with such data obtained by Army and Air Force literacy students in programs teaching only general literacy, not job-related literacy.

Finally, in addition to the test-score data, information from questionnaires was obtained from Army and Air Force students regarding their perceived value of the job-related literacy training in improving their literacy skills, and from Air Force supervisors regarding their perceptions of the effects of literacy training on Air Force students.

In the following discussion, the reading-for-doing module formative evaluation data are discussed first, followed by the reading-for-learning formative data. Next the summative evaluation data for the Army and Air Force programs will be discussed, followed by a brief consideration of the studies comparing the summative data for the Army job-literacy program to the no-literacy training and general literacy training groups. The questionnaire data are summarized last, just before we turn to a discussion of the fully integrated job literacy and technical training program.

Formative Data for Reading-to-Do

Table 11.7 presents the pre- and postproficiency test scores for the reading-to-do modules of the two programs. No data are presented for the

TABLE 11.7

Performance on Strand 1: Reading-to-Do Modules in Job-Related Reading Programs for the Army and Air Force

(1) Module	(2) N	(3) Passed pretest[a]	(4) Passed posttest	(5) Did not complete	(6) Training effectiveness[b]
		Army program			
Table of contents	710	19	67	14	83
Index	710	16	56	28	67
Tables and graphs	710	20	53	27	66
Body of manual	710	3	49	48	48
Procedural directions	710	9	30	61	33
		Air Force program			
Tables and graphs	92	12	28	60	32
Body of manual	92	10	21	68	23
Procedural directions	92	17	32	51	39

[a] Figures in columns 3, 4, 5, and 6 are in percentages.
[b] Column 4 divided by columns 4 + 5 equals the training effectiveness.

A
Types of Bars

Crowbars are used for moving timbers and rocks. They are available in 4- and 5-foot lengths with a diameter of 1 or 1 1/4 inches. Pinch bars are from 12 to 36 inches long and are used for prying out spikes and nails. Pinch bar diameters range from 1/2 to 1 inch depending on their length. Wrecking bars have diameters of 1/2 to 1 1/8 inches and are available in lengths from 12 to 60 inches. They are used for the same things as crowbars. Pry bars are used for prying out gears and bushings. They are 16 inches long and have a diameter of 1 1/16 inches.

B

Type	Use	Length	Diameter
Crowbar	Moving timbers and rocks	4–5 feet	1 or 1 1/4 inches
Pinch bar	Prying out spikes and nails	12–36 inches	1/2 to 1 inch
Wrecking bar	Moving timbers and rocks	12–60 inches	1/2 to 1 1/8 inch
Pry bar	Prying out gears and bushings	16 inches	1 1/16 inches

C
When You Are Lost—EAT PLANTS

If you are lost and out of food there are many types of plants that you can eat. Marsh marigolds are best during early spring. They are found in swamps and in streams. The leaves and stems are the only parts that you should eat. The leaves, stems, and flowers of the rock rose are all good to eat. You can find them along streams and lakes in early spring. Fireweed is also good to eat. It is usually found in burned-over areas during spring and summer. You can eat the leaves and flowers of the fireweed but not the stem. The roots of the mountain willow are also good to eat. Mountain willow is found in high mountains in early summer.

D

TABLE ?

Figure 11.4 The classification table representation transformation test from the Army job-related reading program.

Forms modules because in these modules each form served as its own pre- and posttest, and training consisted simply of practicing filling out the form.

In many cases students were not able to progress at the rate needed to master the criteria for each proficiency test, which were to obtain 90% accuracy within a 20-minute time period (see Sticht, 1975, for the development of these criteria). In these cases, students were moved into the next module anyway so that they could obtain practice in those job-related reading tasks before the 6-week training period ended. Since the modules do not represent a hierarchy, no cumulative learning problem results from this practice.

As Table 11.7 indicates, the training effectiveness, which is the percentage of those reaching criterion divided by the percentage attempting the module, was better for the Army than for the Air Force program. Most likely this reflects the differences in the number of hours of training time. Army personnel attended class for 6 hours a day for 6 weeks, whereas Air Force personnel attended class for only 2.5 hours per day for 6 weeks. This difference in time on task seems to have been reflected in the training effectiveness data (see Koehler, 1978, for a discussion of the effects of time on task on learning). Despite these differences in effectiveness, both the Army and the Air Force reading-to-do modules appear to bring about considerable improvement by the students who worked through the modules.

Formative Data for Reading-to-Learn

A small-scale study evaluated the effectiveness of the reading-to-learn strand of activities. Thirty-six students in the Army literacy program were administered representation transformation tests that involved the student in transforming a prose passage into either a classification table or a flow chart. Figure 11.4 presents an example of the test for the classification table. At the top of each test is an example of a text, and below that is a representation of the text transformed into a table. Then there is another piece of text. Using the latter, the student is supposed to transform information in the passage into the type of classification table shown in the top half of the page. In other words, this is an analogies problem such that Text A is to Classification Table B as Text C is to a table, D, to be constructed by the student. A similar test was constructed for the flow chart transformation task.

Mean pre- and posttest scores changed from 65 to 95% correct on the classification test, and from 37 to 61% correct on the flow chart test, with the pre- and posttest administration separated by not less than 4 weeks to reduce the likelihood that a simple practice effect might have produced these gains. The latter was a possibility since the pre- and posttests were exactly alike. Given the difficulty that the literacy students had in learning most tasks, even with extensive practice, simple practice effects or recall from the pretest seems a most unlikely occurrence. Thus, these data are taken to suggest that the representation transformation (learning strategy) training did improve students' skills in making such transformations.

Summative Evaluation of the Two Programs

Table 11.8 presents pre- and posttraining test data for entry into and exit from the two programs. Scores are given in reading grade levels for both the general and job reading task tests, with the latter reading grade levels established through small-scale norming studies relating job and general reading test performance.

The results indicate that, in both programs, job reading gain was much larger than general reading. This is important because it indicates that people are learning **what they are being taught.** In many evaluation studies, standardized reading tests are used to evaluate programs with no good rationale as to why it is believed the test scores should change. Usually, there is no demonstration that the standardized tests reflect what is being taught. Clearly the present results show that "reading" is not altogether a generic skill assessable by any test of "general" reading. There is no reason why vocabulary components of general reading tests should improve unless the word meanings are taught. General decoding skills do not teach word meanings. The job reading task test results show that specific literacy skills can be developed and assessed for generalizability **in the domain area that corresponds to what was taught.** The latter point is demonstrated by the fact that performance on the job reading task tests improved even though the specific content and questions asked were not included in any training module.

Additional Evaluation Data

Additional evaluation data were obtained that compared the job literacy training achievements of Army literacy students with reading improvement by a group of Army personnel who received job technical skills training,

TABLE 11.8
Summative Reading Improvement Data for Students in Army and Air Force Job-Related Reading Programs[a]

Test score	General reading		Job-related reading	
	Army (N = 714)	Air Force (N = 93)	Army (N = 714)	Air Force (N = 93)
Entry	5.3	9.2	5.2	10.2
Exit	6.0	9.7	7.3	11.3
Gain	.7	.5	2.1	1.1

[a] Scores are expressed in reading grade levels.

and hence exposure to Army reading, but no job literacy training per se. Results showed superior gains for the job-related reading trained group, with the latter improving 2.6 years compared with the former's 1.1 years in job-related reading test performance. Similarly, comparisons of the job-related-literacy-trained group with students in Air Force and Army general literacy programs indicated that the job literacy training produced 2 to 4 times as much improvement in job reading skills as the general literacy programs did, whereas the job reading programs equaled the general literacy programs in the amount of general reading test score improvement accomplished.

Further indication of the effectiveness of the programs was obtained in the Army research by obtaining feedback from graduates who had gone on to job skills training. Of 353 follow-up questionnaires, 74 (20%) were returned completed. Eight out of 10 felt that the job literacy training helped them in their job training. Several suggested additional activities to be included in the literacy training.

In the Air Force program, 60% of personnel who completed an end-of-course questionnaire reported that they felt more confident in their ability to read and understand their job reading materials since taking the literacy training. Two-thirds of the supervisors of the students reported that the job-oriented reading program had made some or very much improvement in the person's job performance.

Thus, the results of module tests, pre- and postsummative tests, and end-of-course and follow-up questionnaires indicate that improvements in job reading skills resulted from participation in the functional literacy programs. This indicates that it is feasible to integrate literacy and job skills technical training, at least in terms of content.

Integrating Job Technical and Literacy Skills Training

Though the foregoing projects demonstrate that job technical skills knowledge and reading tasks can be incorporated into a literacy training program, those programs still require that a separate training program be established and that people be specially assigned to the program for an extended period of time. Though the above data also show that such job-related literacy training is more effective in improving job reading skills than the programs the services currently offer, and hence is more cost-effective because it is no more costly than the general literacy programs, it remains to be demonstrated that the literacy and job technical skills programs can be fully integrated into the same training day and at the training site. Such a demonstration was accomplished in further work for the Army (Sticht, 1975).

To integrate job technical skills training and job-related literacy training, a two-step process was followed in an exploratory study involving one

Army job: the supply clerk's job. In this research, the supply clerk's training program was first converted to a self-paced instructional program by Hungerland and Taylor (1975). They found that in the lock-step course students were held in the program for 35 training days, whereas the average time in the self-paced course was 25 days, with a range from 13 to 44 days. Only 7% of the self-paced trainees required additional time to complete course requirements. All graduates of the self-paced course met the same end-of-course test criteria used in the regular, lock-step course.

Having demonstrated that the supply clerk's training program time could be significantly reduced, in numbers of personhours, the second step was to incorporate job reading training into the supply course for those who had difficulty in performing job reading tasks. To incorporate reading training into the supply clerk's course, the clerical material from the Army job reading program was modified to focus exclusively on the supply clerk's materials. Reading training was provided for 2 hours per day. Results showed that performance on the job reading tests rose from an average reading grade level of 5.5 before training to 7.2 after training, suggesting that it is feasible to introduce job skills training and job reading training within the same training day without adding to the overall training time of traditional lock-step job skills training programs. And it is possible to make significant improvements in job reading skills **and** job technical skills during this integrated training program. Since this also deletes the need for a 6-week add-on to the regular training pipeline, it is a more cost-effective way to provide literacy training.

SUMMARY

This chapter has discussed research concerned with the improvement of adult literacy and learning strategies within an organizational setting. The goal of this organizational development research is to improve organizational effectiveness in the recruitment function by making it possible for organizations to lower the entry requirements they have established for literacy and other learning skills, sometimes stated as "aptitude" requirements, while maintaining high levels of effectiveness in other functions, such as training and job performance.

In a case study, research was reviewed that is concerned with the development of a more effective human resources development system within the Department of Defense. This research included (a) an examination of the current human resources development system in the Department of Defense, including the general education system, the job technical skills training system, and the career counseling system; (b) study of the literacy and learning requirements of jobs and job training programs; and (c) the design, development, and evaluation of job-related literacy training that was more effective than general literacy programs in improving job reading skills and that could be incorporated into the job technical skills training system with an overall savings in training costs.

Though limited in scope, this work suggests that it is feasible to design organizational programs of human resources development that make it possible for organizations to lower their literacy requirements, to provide access to employment for a larger number of people, and at the same time to conduct a cost-effective program of job technical and literacy skills development to open up opportunities for the less skilled employee.

This research also indicates that for organizations to make very large improvements in the literacy and learning skills of their employees, there must be a commitment to a long-term institutionalized program that is construed as "developmental" rather than as "remedial." The literature is replete with the failures of brief remedial programs (Ryan & Furlong, 1975). The present research indicates that, even with literacy training focused directly on job-related reading, many students achieved only modest gains in skill, whereas others did not improve at all, at least to any measurable extent. Thus, it seems likely that the achievement of genuine, long-lasting improvements in literacy skills will require a long-lasting development effort. This requires a greater degree of cooperation and interrelatedness among organizational elements such as the counseling, educational, and job technical skills components investigated in the present research. Recognizing this, the General Accounting Office (1977) has recommended to the Department of Defense that, if remedial programs are to be continued, the services should

> make certain that they are integrated with (job technical) skill training, career counseling, and general education development [pp. ii–iii].
>
> This approach could not only improve the operational effectiveness of the services, but in the longer view, better prepare personnel for productive roles in society after completing their military careers [pp. 21–22].

Intensive research and development efforts are needed, in a variety of organizational settings, if we are to learn how organizations can **develop** as well as **utilize** the literacy and learning skills that people need to be productive in all walks of life.

ACKNOWLEDGMENTS

I am indebted to Lynn Fox, Diana Welty Zapf, Robert Hauke, John Caylor, Richard Kern, Kent Huff, and John Joyner for their outstanding work as members of the research team who conducted the research projects summarized here.

REFERENCES

Canter, R. R. *Organization management and the volunteer force: Policy and research issues.* Paper presented at the Security Issues Symposium: Army Strategic Environment 1985-2000, Strategic Studies Institute, U.S. Army War College,Carlisle Barracks, Pennsylvania, April 1978.

Dansereau, D. F., Actkinson, T. R., Long, G. L., & McDonald, B. *Learning strategies: A review and synthesis of the current literature* (AFHRL-TR-74-70). Lowry Air Force Base, Colo.: Air Force Human Resources Laboratory, Technical Training Division, December 1974.

Duffy, T. M. Literacy research in the Navy. In T. Sticht & D. Zapf (Eds.), *Reading and readability research in the armed services* (HumRRO Tech. Rep. FR-WD-CA-76-4). Alexandria, Va.: Human Resources Research Organization, September 1976.

Fisher, D. L. *Functional literacy and the schools.* Washington, D.C.: National Institute of Education, January 1978.

General Accounting Office. *A need to address illiteracy problems in the military service* (Report Number FPCD-77-13). Washington, D.C.: Author, March 1977.

Huff, K. H., Sticht, T. G., Joyner, J., Groff, S. D., & Burkett, J. R. *A jop-oriented reading program for the Air Force: Development and field evaluation* (AFHRL-TR-77-34). Lowry Air Force Base, Colo.: Air Force Human Resources Laboratory, Technical Training Division, May 1977.

Hungerland, J., & Taylor, J. *Self-paced instruction in a cognitively oriented skills course: Supplyman, MOS 76y10.* Alexandria, Va.: Human Resources Research Organization, June 1975.

Koehler, V. Classroom process research: Present and future. *Journal of Classroom Interaction,* 1978, *13,* 3-11.

Meshi, J., Holoter, H. A., Dow, D. S., & Grace, G. L. *Preliminary description of the Navy career counseling process* (ISDC TR No. 1). Santa Monica, Calif.: Systems Development Corporation, November 1972.

Miller, G. A. (Ed.). *Linguistic communication: Perspectives for research.* Newark, Del.: International Reading Association, 1974.

O'Neil, H. F., Jr. (Ed.). *Learning strategies.* New York: Academic Press, 1978.

Rouche, J. E., & Snow, J. J. *Overcoming learning problems.* San Francisco: Jossey-Bass, 1977.

Ryan, T. A., & Furlong, W. Literacy programs in industry, the armed forces, penal institutions. In J. Carroll & J. Chall (Eds.), *Toward a literate society.* New York: McGraw-Hill, 1975.

Schein, E. H. *Organizational psychology.* Englewood Cliffs, N.J.: Prentice-Hall, 1970.

Sticht, T. G. *A program of Army functional job reading training: Development, implementation, and delivery systems* (HumRRO Tech. Rep. FR-WD-CA-75-7). Alexandria, Va.: Human Resources Research Organization, June 1975.

Sticht, T. G., Fox, L. C., Hauke, R. N., & Zapf, D. W. *Integrated job skills and reading skills training system* (NPRDC TR 77-41). San Diego, Calif.: Navy Personnel Research and Development Center, September 1977.(a)

Sticht, T. G., Fox, L. C., Hauke, R. N., & Zapf, D. W. *The role of reading in the Navy* (NPRDC TR 77-40). San Diego: Calif.: Navy Personnel Research and Training Center, September 1977.(b)

Sticht, T. G., & Zapf, D. W. *Reading and readability research in the armed services* (HumRRO Tech. Rep. FR-WD-CA-76-4). Alexandria, Va.: Human Resources Research Organization, September 1976.

12

Applications of Cognitive Psychology to Education and Training

M. C. WITTROCK

INTRODUCTION

The preceding three chapters have emphasized applications of research and theory in cognitive psychology to instruction in the military services. These three chapters raise the question, "What does cognitive psychology have to offer instruction?" I will try to answer this question by indicating some of the relationships that exist between recent research in cognitive psychology and learning from instruction, as they occur in the three chapters.

I am thankful for the opportunity to discuss these chapters because I have often wanted but never before had an occasion to relate my 2 years of experience with instruction in the armed forces to my career as an educational psychologist researching cognitive processes in instruction. As a student in an excellent 6-months-long, electronics course for officers, and later as an education officer, I learned to respect the high quality and extensive nature of the instruction and general education provided by the military services. Later I learned about some of the research and development projects sponsored by Department of Defense that contributed to the design of these military training programs. It is gratifying and not surprising to learn now that the armed services are in the forefront of application of principles of cognitve psychology to instruction.

TWO PRINCIPLES OF COGNITIVE PSYCHOLOGY

Recent research in cognitive psychology emphasizes several important principles for instruction. I will discuss two of them. They reflect cognitive psychologists' preference for studying the effects of internal processes or activities upon learning.

Individual Responsibility

The first principle, individual responsibility for success and failure to learn, comes primarily from research on motivation. Attribution theory (Kelley, 1971; Rotter, 1966; Weiner, 1976) and research on locus of control (deCharms, 1972) exemplify this principle. In research on locus of control, achievement in class has been increased by teaching students to believe that they can influence their destiny in school by their efforts. deCharms (1972) taught teachers and children to believe that they were origins—people who cause their behavior—rather than pawns—people largely under control of their environment or of other people. With many students the belief that one is largely helpless or externally controlled is often a problem that interferes with learning. Without necessarily changing curricula, instructional materials, or situational characteristics but by developing the attitude that each person can be influential in determining his future, deCharms (1972) increased learning from instruction.

Attribution theory leads to a closely related point (Weiner, 1976). Some people attribute successes and failures in their lives largely to luck or task difficulty, which respectively are variable or stable external causes, rather than to effort or ability, which respectively are variable or stable internal causes. Locus of control, internal or external, influences affectivity. Internal ascriptions increase emotional reactions. Stability of causal processes influences expectancy of success or failure. Failure attributed to stable causes leads to increased expectancy of failure, but failure attributed to lack of effort or bad luck is less likely to lead to increased expectancy of failure.

For instruction, one implication from research on locus of control and attribution theory is clear. Attribution of success or failure to an unstable internal cause, i.e., to effort, can lead to increased perseverance, to success, to positive emotional reactions, and to increased self-esteem. Especially with students with little history of success in schools or in training programs, including some students of marginal literacy or of lower socioeconomic status, enhancing their cognitive attributional processes and those of their instructors promises in some situations to facilitate learning.

Constructed Meaning

The second principle from cognitive psychology is that we mentally construct the reality in which we live. The human brain constructs a representation or model of reality (Jerison, 1977). Rather than reacting automatically to our environments, we use the information it supplies along with our schemata and our history of previous learning to construct meaning out of nearly any ambiguous or well-structured situation. Ambiguous pictures, for example, where we can see either a vase or two heads, or either the young woman or the old woman, exemplify this ability actively to construct different meanings by processing spatial information in different ways.

The study of the cognitive processes of the brain, including arousal, attention, encoding, storage, and retrieval, involved in these constructions of meaning is a major area of research in cognitive psychology. Chapter 5 of this volume presents an excellent discussion of arousal and anxiety in relation to instruction. In the study of attention, cognitive research with value for instruction includes recent studies of the effects of inserting questions between the paragraphs of a text or of inserting objectives into the lessons. These questions or objectives given to learners influence learning, apparently by directing the learner's attention to relevant information and away from less relevant information (Wittrock & Lumsdaine, 1977).

In studies of encoding, storage, and retrieval, it has often been shown that memory and understanding are enhanced when the learner elaborates the information he is reading or is trying to learn (see Chapter 2 of this volume). Since the days of ancient Greece, it has been known that the development of vivid images involving interactions between unfamiliar information and familiar information facilitates their association and their retrieval (Yates, 1966). Today imagery is frequently found to facilitate memory (Levin, 1976).

With text and prose, verbal elaborations, such as the underlining of learner-chosen important words in a text (Rickards & August, 1975), generation of paragraph headings and summary sentences (Wittrock, 1974), and the generation of hierarchical relationships among words (Bower, Clark, Lesgold, & Winzenz, 1969; Wittrock & Carter, 1975) facilitate memory. Construction of sentences from serially ordered words (Bower & Clark, 1969) also enhances memory. Children's elaborations involving familiar story contexts (Wittrock, Marks, & Doctorow, 1975) facilitate reading comprehension. The processing people perform upon information they receive, as well as the information itself, influences learning, probably by allowing the learners to construct relations among their distinctive memories, previous experiences, schemata, and the incoming information. Although the data are far from being conclusive, from recent research on the human brain (Wittrock, Beatty, Bogen, Gazzaniga, Jerison, Krashen, Nebes, & Teyler, 1977) and on verbal processes and imagery, it seems that the brain uses at least two strategies to construct these relationships: (*a*) a verbal–analytic strategy and (*b*) a gestalt–holistic strategy.

For instruction, the implications of the second principle of cognitive psychology, which is that we generate our own reality, are many. One of these implications is that learners should be induced to construct mental elaborations of the materials they are trying to learn. Analogies, similes, and metaphors may sometimes help them to construct verbal elaborations; and pictures, graphic models, concrete examples, and concrete words may sometimes help them to construct imaginal elaborations.

A second implication of the principle of constructed or generated reality is that learners differ in the mental processes best for each of them to use to learn different kinds of information. Instruction will sometimes need to compensate for the learners' lack of generative elaborations and sometimes need to capitalize upon the individual aptitudes of different learners. In either case the facilitation of understanding and memory involves active cognitive processing of information, especially the active generation of relationships between different segments of new information and between past learning and new information. The learning strategies used to process information include analytic and holistic organizational processes and verbal and imaginal encoding processes.

MILITARY TRAINING PROGRAMS AND COGNITIVE PSYCHOLOGY

Now we will discuss relationships between the two principles of cognitive psychology I have introduced and the training programs and teaching processes presented in the chapters by Sticht, Gulick, and Singer and Gerson.

A Career Development System

Sticht reports that the Department of Defense has a responsibility for the growth and development of its personnel that is broader than, but still closely related to, the efficient development of technical work skills. Much of his thoughtful chapter explores a career development system, recommended by the General Accounting Office, designed to integrate literacy training, job skills training, general educational development, and career counseling. From a cognitive psychological perspective, an integrated career development system is promising because it provides a meaningful context for training the generic skills of newly recruited personnel, such as the cognitive skills involved in reading, comprehension, literacy, decision making, problem solving, self-concept, and morale. Especially with marginally literate people, some of these generic skills may not be well developed.

By closely coordinating general education programs with technical skill training, one should often be able to enhance the learner's positive affectivity by increasing the perceived ability to influence one's future in the military services and in private life. An integrated program also provides an opportunity through general education to measure and to change attribution processes. When one learns to read job-related materials, the reasons for learning are apparent and the results of student efforts are likely to be meaningful. A program that combines development of generic cognitive skills with training of specific job-related skills has advantages for the enhancement of motivation and self-esteem, and for inducing changes in attribution processes.

Sticht also applies the principle of constructed meaning to the instructional procedures used within the training programs. In Strands I and II of the reading programs, learners are taught to construct holistic transformations by drawing pictures and flow charts, and analytic transformations by locating superordinate and subordinate verbal categories in the reading material. In the reading-for-learning program, his Strand II, learners are trained to relate their knowledge base to the new information provided in the text. In sum, Sticht's suggestions and teaching procedures are consistent with recent research in cognitive psychology.

For the future, I would suggest incorporating into the integrated career development program additional generative tasks for learners to perform, such as the underlining of learner-chosen important phrases and the construction of summary sentences and topic sentences for paragraphs or at least for sections of the text. To induce constructive activities that involve the learner's knowledge store in interaction with new information in the manuals and other texts, I would also include analogies, metaphors, similes, high-imagery words, and instantiations of general principles.

Another prospect for the future that I would suggest involves construction of new kinds of tests. The Department of Defense has a well-earned reputation for pioneering the development of useful selection and classification instruments based upon models of intelligence and empirical research in differential psychology. The emerging need to train literacy skills and generic cognitive skills of some people in the service provides an excellent opportunity to develop new types of placement and classification tests based upon recently developed process models of aptitudes, abilities, and individual differences. The long-term results of such a developmental program could again be of fundamental importance to improving training programs in the military services, to fundamental growth in the field of differential psychology, and to bettering general education in schools. When service needs for training and testing are juxtaposed with implications of recent research in cognitive psychology regarding process models of aptitudes, some interesting and far-reaching possibilities result for future research and development projects to explore.

Decision Making

In a different way and within a different context, Gulick also discusses applications of a cognitive model to an important military problem. Using Raiffa's decision analysis theory as a base, Gulick describes a systems analysis approach to problem solving in the military. The decision theory–systems analysis approach involves the teaching of a logical sequence of activities for analysis of so-called fuzzy problems of military strategy. The sequence includes, in order, (a) abstraction of relationships, alternatives, and criteria; (b) integration and weighing of facts and data; (c) focusing of a discussion around pertinent information criteria and realistic alternative reactions to the problem; and (d) generation of a tree structure of options and their probable effects. Gulick briefly mentions an advanced decision technology training program designed to teach his decision analysis strategy to military commanders.

The decision analysis strategy is best characterized, as Gulick describes it, as an **analytic** processing strategy, which is related to a type of information processing strategy described in several studies of neuropsychology and sociology. Warren TenHouten (1971) suggests a correlation between socioeconomic status and use of an analytic information processing strategy, as opposed to a global or holistic strategy, in modern industrial societies. His approach to information processing predicts that executives, managers, and many others high in socioeconomic status in industrial societies will make greater use of an analytic information processing strategy and less use of a global appositional strategy than will people lower in socioeconomic status. Cohen (1969) presents a closely related conception of information processing strategy and socioeconomic status. Zelnicker and Jeffrey (1976) found that children lower in socioeconomic status often tend to use a global information processing strategy, while middle-class children often tend to use an analytic information processing strategy.

The teaching of logical, sequential, and analytic information processing strategies, such as the one Gulick employs, is clearly defensible in terms of recent research in neuropsychology on cognitive processes. From Gulick's preliminary findings, it seems that complex military problems involve teachable generic, analytic cognitive skills and strategies. It would be interesting to follow further implications of recent research in neuropsychology on processes of the brain (Wittrock et al., 1977) and to try to teach additional generic strategies, such as an integrative gestalt–holistic strategy, to complement the analytic strategy Gulick has developed. For different problems and with different officers, a repertoire of strategies offers advantages over a single strategy.

In sum, considering the important consequences of command decisions in the military services, the teaching of decision-making strategies is an area well worth study. Principles emerging from cognitive psychology are relevant to the understanding, construction, and teaching of useful decision-making strategies, such as the analytic strategy studied by Gulick. Although it would be easy to criticize the study of strategies of decision making as an area too complex for scientific research to investigate, it is more prudent to support studies in this area that involve the application of cognitive models and statistical models to important societal problems. It is important to keep the horse before the cart and to study significant problems, which inappropriate models and methods might reject as unfit for study, and to choose state-of-the-art statistical methods and cognitive models appropriate for the nature and complexity of the problem. The alternative is to let the methodology determine the problems that we study.

Motor Behavior

Singer and Gerson provide yet another approach toward applying models and principles of cognitive psychology to education and training in the military services. After years of research on motor behavior, much of which is summarized in a book by Singer (1975), they have recently developed a cognitive model of motor behavior. The model combines elements of information processing models, cybernetic models, and so-called adaptive or hierarchical models of movement. From information processing models, they derive the concepts of arousal, sensory register, selective attention, short-term store, encoding, (including verbal rehearsal and imagery), long-term store, and recall. These parts of their model are largely comparable to other stage models of information processing and encoding, with the notable exception of having sensory data enter, or more properly, be modulated by long-term memory **prior to** entry into short-term memory.

From cybernetic models, they introduce the concepts of open-loop, or externally paced, tasks and close-loop, or internally paced, tasks. The latter task involves a feedback for self-regulation of motor behavior. The adaptive or hierarchical component of the model pertains mostly to the movement generator and the effectors of motor behavior, the last stages of the model.

One interesting application of the model follows from their focus upon the conscious control processes of rehearsal, recall, and imagery. These conscious processes lead to active control of the environment by abstraction of its common elements and association of skilled motor movements to these abstracted elements. The import of this part of the model is that motor behavior is an important part of cognitive psychology, closely related in cognitive processes to other kinds of human behavior. Motor behavior involves the application of strategies, which Singer and Gerson call principles and rules, generated to enhance the operation of control processes and to solve problems. Movements reflect cognitive strategies and thought processes. The movements become attempts to solve problems. The teaching of movements involves identifying and training the cognitive strategies used to solve different psychomotor tasks.

To view the learning of complex motor tasks, such as landing an airplane, dancing, or hitting a golf ball, as examples of verbal and imaginal encoding problems is refreshing. Within this model analogies, metaphors, and similes are relevant to the teaching of motor behavior because it involves the transfer of previously learned strategies and movement patterns to new and different tasks and situations. To teach movements one might start with an assessment of individual differences in cognitive strategies.

Clearly, Singer and Gerson's model emphasizes relations between cognitive psychology and applied problems of teaching and training. These authors bring motor behavior into the field of cognitive psychology and emphasize its close relationship to other forms of cognitively mediated human behavior. I believe the implications of the model, rather than the separate hypothetical stages presented in the flow charts, are its most salient and important features.

In three different ways, the three chapters reviewed here present important relations between cognitive psychology and applied problems of teaching and training, a newly developing field of study with much promise for both the military services and the field of psychology.

REFERENCES

Bower, G. H., & Clark, M. C. Narrative stories as mediators for serial learning. *Psychonomic Science*, 1969, *14*, 181–182.

Bower, G. H., Clark, M. C., Lesgold, A. M., & Winzenz, D. Hierarchical retrieval schemes in recall of categorized word lists. *Journal of Verbal Learning and Verbal Behavior*, 1969, *8*, 323–343.

Cohen, R. Conceptual styles, culture conflict, and nonverbal tests of intelligence. *American Anthropologist*, 1968, *71*, 828–856.

deCharms, R. Personal causation training in the schools. *Journal of Applied Psychology*, 1972, *2*, 95–113.

Kelley, H. H. *Attribution in social interaction.* Morristown, N.J.: General Learning Press, 1971.

Jerison, H. J. Evolution of the brain. In M. C. Wittrock, J. Beatty, J. E. Bogen, M. S. Gazzaniga, H. J. Jerison, S. D. Krashen, R. D. Nebes, & T. J. Teyler (Eds.), *The human brain.* Englewood Cliffs, N.J.: Prentice-Hall, 1977.

Levin, J. R. What have we learned about maximizing what children learn? In J. R. Levin & V. C. Allen (Eds.), *Cognitive learning in children: Theories and strategies.* New York: Academic Press, 1976.

Rickards, J. P., & August, G. J. Generative underlining strategies in prose recall. *Journal of Educational Psychology,* 1975, *67,* 860–865.

Rotter, J. B. Generalized expectancies for internal versus external control of reinforcement. *Psychological Monographs,* 1966, *80* (1, Whole No. 609).

Singer, R. N. *Motor learning and human performance* (2nd ed.) New York: Macmillan, 1975.

TenHouten, W. D. *Cognitive styles and the social order* (Final Report, Part II, OEO Study B 00-5135). Los Angeles: University of California, Los Angeles, 1971.

Weiner, B. J. An attributional approach for educational psychology. In L. S. Shulman (Ed.), *Review of research in education* (Vol. 4). Itasca, Ill.: Peacock, 1976.

Wittrock, M. C. Learning as a generative process. *Educational Psychologist,* 1974, *11,* 87–95.

Wittrock, M. C., Beatty, J., Bogen, J. E., Gazzaniga, M. S., Jerison, H. J., Krashen, S. D., Nebes, R. D., & Teyler, T. J. (Eds.). *The human brain.* Englewood Cliffs, N.J.: Prentice-Hall, 1977.

Wittrock, M. C., & Carter, J. Generative processing of hierarchically organized words. *American Journal of Psychology,* 1975, *88,* 489–501.

Wittrock, M. C., & Lumsdaine, A. A. Instructional psychology. In M. R. Rosenzweig & L. W. Porter (Eds.), *Annual review of psychology* (Vol. 28). Palo Alto, Calif.: Annual Reviews, 1977.

Wittrock, M. C., Mark, C. B., & Doctorow, M. J. Reading as a generative process. *Journal of Educational Psychology,* 1975, 484–489.

Yates, F. *The art of memory.* London: Routledge & Kegan Paul, 1966.

Zelnicker, T., & Jeffrey, W. E. Reflective and impulsive children: Strategies of information processing underlying differences in problem solving. *Monographs of the Society for Research in Child Development,* 1976, *41* (5, Serial No. 168).

Author Index

Numbers in italics refer to the pages on which the complete references are listed.

Subject Index